THE EXPANDED SOCIAL
SCIENTIST'S BESTIARY

THE EXPANDED SOCIAL SCIENTIST'S BESTIARY

A Guide to Fabled Threats to, and Defenses of, Naturalistic Social Science

D. C. PHILLIPS

ROWMAN & LITTLEFIELD PUBLISHERS, INC.
Lanham • Boulder • New York • Oxford

ROWMAN & LITTLEFIELD PUBLISHERS, INC.

Published in the United States of America
by Rowman & Littlefield Publishers. Inc.
4501 Forbes Boulevard, Suite 200, Lanham, Maryland 20706
http://www.rowmanlittlefield.com

12 Hid's Copse Road
Cumnor Hill, Oxford OX2 9JJ, England

British Library Cataloguing in Publication Information Available

Library of Congress Cataloging-in-Publication Data

Phillips, D. C. (Denis Charles), 1938–
    The expanded social scientist's bestiary : a guide to fabled threats to, and
defenses of, naturalistic social science / D. C. Phillips.
        p. cm.
    Rev. ed. of: Social scientist's bestiary. 1st ed. 1992.
    Includes bibliographical references and index.
    ISBN 0-8476-9890-4 (cloth : alk. paper) — ISBN 0-8476-9891-2 (pbk. : alk. paper)
    1. Social sciences—Philosophy. I. Phillips, D. C. (Denis Charles), 1938– Social
scientist's bestiary. II. Title.

H61 .P5418 2000
300'.1—dc21   00-028412

Printed in the United States of America

♾™ The paper used in this publication meets the minimum requirements of American
National Standard for Information Sciences—Permanence of Paper for Printed
Library Materials, ANSI/NISO Z39.48–1992.

BESTIARY: . . . work in verse or prose describing with an allegorical moralizing commentary the appearance and habits of real and fabled animals.

—Webster's Dictionary

The Microbe

The microbe is so very small
You cannot make him out at all,
But many sanguine people hope
To see him through a microscope.
His jointed tongue that lies beneath
A hundred curious rows of teeth;
His seven tufted tails with lots
Of lovely pink and purple spots,
On each of which a pattern stands
Composed of forty separate bands;
His eyebrows of a tender green;
All these have never yet been seen—
But scientists, who ought to know,
Assure us that they must be so. . . .
Oh! Let us never, never doubt
What nobody is sure about!

—Hilaire Belloc

CONTENTS

PREFACE: ON GOOD AND BAD BEASTS

Not every change that takes place with the passing of the years can be regarded as an improvement. One case in point concerns the availability of literary genres: Folk in earlier ages had at their command genres that now have faded from use or that linger on only to be sources of amusement. A prime example, of course, is the bestiary. The poet Hilaire Belloc is one of the few writers in the twentieth century to have used this medieval form in any extended manner, and his wonderful "cautionary verses" manage to preserve the moralizing tone of the genre; but the facts that he wrote in simple verse and with humor have given the impression to many that the bestiary is fit only for the entertainment of children.

But the truth is otherwise—there is still a great need for bestiaries addressed to adults, for on the cusp of the new millennium life is fraught with dangers. The momentous political events of the first few years of the 1990s may have made the physical existence of the human species a little more secure (although this is not entirely clear), but the intellectual sphere is not unlike a swamp populated with a variety of exotic beasts—"isms" and "post-isms" abound; ideologies or paradigms are multiplying beyond necessity, and at the same time doctrinal fundamentalism is on the increase; too many people who should know better try to sway others by rhetoric or by appeals to crass self-interest rather than by reasoned argument; clarity and logical soundness of argument seem to be prized by diminishing numbers; and the intellectual ideals of the search for truth and of objective inquiry are held in some quarters to be outmoded inheritances from the past, or worse, they are seen as part of the technology of dominance of some groups, and some viewpoints, over others. The humanities are home to many of these beasts, but the social sciences also offer hospitable environmental niches.

Now, ecologists of the late twentieth century argued that all species of living things, whether beastly or not, have a right to exist; they ought not to face the threat of extinction. And it is probably a counsel of wisdom to adopt a similar policy in the intellectual realm. John Dewey (inspired in this, as in many other matters, by Hegel) would argue that if an intellectual position exists, there must be some problem-situation that inspired it and to which it proffers a solution; moreover, the fact that the position exists and has vocal adherents indicates that at least it has *some* "truth value." (See Dewey 1956, for a simple discussion of the origin of "schools of thought.") It is hoped that the Deweyan spirit pervades the discussions in this present book; a number of positions are analyzed, and their beastly nature is exposed, but on the whole it has been remembered that beasts are complex and have both good and bad features. Very few of them are condemned outright, and some pains have been taken to indicate the genuine problems or influences that have served as stimulus to their evolution. It should be noted that while some chapters bear the name of an important beast in the title, others do not, and instead refer to some positive influence that the beast-hunter can use with profit. (Of course, beastliness resides to some degree in the eye of the beholder, so the chapters that do not—in the author's opinion—refer to beasts ["Popperian Rules," for example] might be regarded as so doing by those readers with a different orientation. Added to which it must be said that not all beasts are *bad;* the elephant is nowadays highly regarded, although the Roman soldiers who first met the species when Hannibal used it against them in battle were not so positive in their evaluations.)

As in many bestiaries, the chapters of the present volume are—as far as possible—self-contained; they do not have to be read in any particular order. Without lapsing into self-delusion, it can be said that in this respect the book is like a mini-encyclopedia, for the beast of interest can be investigated without the effort, or drudgery, of reading a host of preliminary material. (Given this organizational feature, there is a small degree of overlap between the chapters; a nice quotation, for example, might be used in more than one chapter, rather than giving it once and then later referring to it, which would necessitate the interested reader flipping back through the perhaps unread pages to track it down.) As there seemed no better arrangement, the chapters appear in alphabetical order. It is hoped that these various features will make the book useful to the harried or task-oriented social scientist.

It is worth pointing to one other aspect of this volume. Again, as in most classic bestiaries, beneath the diversity of subject matter, there is an underlying philosophical orientation that should impose some coherence upon the whole. The remainder of the preface will be given over to highlighting this.

A good place to start is a story told (in a different context, of course) by the philosopher and anthropologist Ernest Gellner:

> A quarter of a century or so ago there was a well-known eccentric in Edinburgh who used to accost passers-by on Prince's Street and ask them—are you sane? If any replied Yes, he would retort—ah, but can you *prove* it?
>
> And, as they could not, he proceeded triumphantly to show them that *he* at any rate could prove his sanity, by producing his own certificate of discharge from a mental hospital. (Gellner 1979, 41)

In much the same way, one can imagine a skeptical (and eccentric) intellectual accosting a social scientist and asking—Is social science possible? Rising to the bait, the scientist would most likely reply by saying— "Yes"; and when asked for proof would point to the work that he or she is doing—"Look, I am *doing* social science, ergo it *is* possible!" To which the quick-witted eccentric would be liable to respond by pointing to the case of alchemy. For the point is, if we could travel back in time and ask the alchemist if he thought alchemy was possible, the reply would be the same: the alchemist would point to the fact that he was *doing* alchemy, hence it must be possible. But—armed with twentieth-century hindsight—we would not find this answer acceptable. We would argue that the alchemist was *deluded*. The alchemist genuinely believed his craft to be possible, but it was not, for it rested upon mistaken theories and erroneous philosophical foundations. And the twentieth-century skeptic would take a similar stance with respect to the answer given by the social scientist—the fact that social scientists *think* they are doing social science clearly is not sufficient proof that the enterprise is not chimerical. There are numerous skeptics like this in the late nineteenth and twentieth centuries; to cite merely one example, the philosopher A. R. Louch (building to some extent on the work of Peter Winch in his *The Idea of a Social Science*) has written that "my main intent has been to show that the idea of a science of man or society is untenable" (Louch, quoted in Gellner 1979, 66).

Is there no better answer available to the social scientist? What would satisfy the skeptic? The trouble here is that it is always difficult to argue that something *is* possible; but there is solace in the fact that it is even more difficult to establish that something is *im*possible. So, one strategy that is available—although clearly it is not quite as convincing as producing a direct proof—is to examine the arguments put forward by the skeptics and to show that, although they are often motivated by genuine and important concerns, their own arguments do *not* establish what they think they do! In short, the attempt can be made to defuse the arguments that have led skeptics to the conclusion that the pursuit of social science is a delusion.

This, then, is the program that underlies this bestiary: In the contemporary world there are many who are skeptical about the possibility of producing a naturalistic social science, that is, a social science that is in important respects structurally or methodologically similar to the natural sciences. Some of these skeptical concerns run deeper than others, and some of the social sciences are more "at risk" from this attack than are others. It will be argued that these skeptical arguments—these beasts— fail to achieve their goal, although the social scientist would be wise to take seriously many of the issues that are raised. The bestiary, in short, is an indirect defense of the possibility of producing naturalistic social science.

It is clear that it is a matter of more than passing concern to clarify precisely in what sense of the term *social science* can or cannot aspire to be *naturalistic*. While it can be said, with some justice, that it is up to the skeptics to make clear what they have in mind and what it is to which they have objections (obligations that they often fail to fulfill satisfactorily), nevertheless the defender of naturalistic social science cannot rest entirely content with trying to pass the buck. Thus, the fifth chapter—"Naturalistic Ideals in Social Science"—is of some importance in at least giving a preliminary map of the territory. It could have served as the introductory chapter to the whole work.

ACKNOWLEDGMENTS

The plan for this book was first conceived in the mid-'80s, when I was asked by a social scientist colleague to address her research group. Members of the group had felt that theories in their field were deficient, especially in light of the data they had collected, and they hoped to produce something better. But they had started to argue about the *nature* of a theory, and, in their desperation, had turned to a philosopher for help. My talk to them was inadequate but served to outline the relevant positions and controversies in philosophy of science, and the members of the group found it surprisingly helpful—they urged me to publish my remarks. And this led to the bestiary.

It is difficult for a busy member of the academic community to work single-mindedly on one project over an extended time period; for one thing, there is the expectation that one will make appearances at conferences and symposia. So it was not possible to avoid the temptation to deliver earlier versions of most of the chapters as talks at conferences and symposia at universities in the United States, Australia, New Zealand, Israel, and a number of countries in Europe, in all of which venues I received vigorous feedback! Inevitably some of the chapters—in their earlier form—found their way into print. Thus, thanks are due to the editors and publishers of a number of journals or books for their cooperation in allowing reuse of material already published; they are acknowledged in detail at the end of the relevant chapters.

Finally, friends and colleagues on several continents have provided critical input on one or more of the chapters. I am especially indebted to Eric Bredo, Debby Kerdeman, Ray McDermott, Nel Noddings, Rich Shavelson, and Harvey Siegel. Valerie Phillips not only helped with the preparation of the original manuscript but loaned a critical eye when I wanted to submit particularly tricky draft passages to careful scrutiny.

Michele Norton and Barbara Barrett of Pergamon Press gave encouragement during the production of the 1992 edition; Jill Rothenberg and then Dean Birkenkamp were sources of support during the production of the expanded edition by Rowman & Littlefield.

NOTE CONCERNING THE EXPANDED EDITION

For the new edition, four new chapters have been added. One of these, on a Popperian approach to issues of research design in the social sciences and educational research, replaces a previous chapter comparing Popper and Dewey—a chapter whose thesis I still maintain, but which I always regarded as sitting a little uncomfortably with the rest of the volume. The other new chapters reflect preoccupations I have had since the original bestiary appeared—narrative research (on which I have written three papers) and various forms of constructivism (on which I have written four, as well as having edited a National Society for the Study of Education Yearbook). To my mind these were major beasts that needed to be addressed if the volume is to have contemporary relevance. I also took advantage of the new edition to make a few small changes to all of the other chapters.

One beast, at first sight, seems to be absent from the volume—postmodernism—although the discerning hunter will detect its footprints in a number of places throughout the volume. I have had an intellectual struggle with this remarkable beast for some years and have learned much from interactions with colleagues such as Debby Kerdeman, Nick Burbules, Harvey Siegel, Jim Marshall and Michael Peters (from New Zealand), and Roland Reichenbach (from Switzerland). While I have not reached the stage where I could undertake a major, sustained piece of writing on this complex topic, some of my thoughts have infiltrated various chapters of the expanded bestiary, especially the chapters on constructivism and the social construction of knowledge, but also appear in other chapters that touch on truth and objectivity.

1

CONSTRUCTIVISM AND ITS MANY FACES: THE GOOD, THE BAD, AND THE UGLY

CONSTRUCTIVISM: AN INITIAL CHARACTERIZATION

Across the broad fields of social science and educational research, constructivism has become something akin to a secular religion. In her book *Evolution as a Religion* (1985), Mary Midgley wrote that the theory of evolution "is not just an inert piece of theoretical science. It is, and cannot help being, also a powerful folktale about human origins. Any such narrative must have symbolic force" (1985, 1). She might well have written the same about constructivism, which is, whatever else it may be, a "powerful folktale" about the origins of human knowledge. As in all living religions, constructivism has many sects—each of which harbors some distrust of its rivals. This descent into sectarianism, and the accompanying growth in distrust of nonbelievers, is probably the fate of all large-scale movements inspired by interesting ideas; and it is the ideological or ugly side of the present scene, which is reflected in the chapter's title.

The educational literature on constructivism is enormous and growing rapidly. A significant indicator is that one scholar who has been documenting this literature estimated in the early 1990s that there were more than 2,500 journal articles or anthology chapters (Duit 1993), and a host of bewildering "flavors" or varieties of constructivism were referenced in the recent 99th Yearbook of the National Society for the Study of Education (NSSE) that was devoted to the topic (Phillips 2000). Part of my purpose in this essay is to complexify matters even more by pointing to relevant discussions in other literatures that are rarely, if ever, mentioned by those embroiled in the educational debates (some of the contributors to the NSSE Yearbook are an exception). In particular, I will try to show that in the fields of epistemology and philosophy of science, in the relatively young discipline of science studies (an interdisciplinary philosophical,

1

sociological, and historical field), and in the rapidly burgeoning feminist literature, there is much of relevance and interest to be found. The term *constructivism* does not occur with great frequency in these other bodies of literature—for example, the recent encyclopedic volume edited by Dancy and Sosa (1992), *A Companion to Epistemology,* gives it only three passing references—but, nevertheless, closely related ideas are the subject of vigorous debate.

In order to compensate for introducing these new complexities, however, I also will offer a way of viewing the various forms of constructivism that, I claim, will produce some order and clarity. Much of my discussion, then, will be descriptive and clarificatory in orientation, although I will try not to leave the reader guessing about what I regard as the good and bad features of constructivism; my more extended reflections on one major branch of constructivism—social constructivism—will be found in chapter 11.

The rampant sectarianism, coupled with the array of other literatures that contain pertinent material, makes it difficult to give even a cursory introductory account of constructivism, for members of the various sects will object that their own views are nothing like this! But to get the discussion underway, this oversimple gloss should convey the general idea (a more precise account of the issues at stake shall emerge as the discussion progresses): These days we do not believe that individuals come into the world with their "cognitive data banks" already prestocked with empirical knowledge or with preembedded epistemological criteria or methodological rules. Nor do we believe that most of our knowledge is acquired, ready-formed, by some sort of direct perception or absorption. Undoubtedly, humans are born with *some* cognitive or epistemological equipment or potentialities (the nature and degree of which the experts in developmental psychology still dispute—witness, for example, the well-known argument between Piaget and Chomsky about innateness and genetic programming), but, by and large, human knowledge and the criteria and methods we use in our inquiries are all *acquired.* Furthermore, the bodies of knowledge available to the growing learner are themselves human constructs—physics, biology, sociology, and even philosophy are not disciplines the content of which was handed down, ready formed, from on high; scholars have labored mightily over the generations to construct the content of these fields, and no doubt "internal politics" has played some role. Thus, in sum, human knowledge—whether it be the bodies of public knowledge known as the various disciplines or the cognitive structures of individual knowers or learners—is *constructed*. Some constructivist sects focus their attention on the cognitive contents of learners, others focus on the growth of the "public" domains, while a few brave groups tackle both—thus doubling the amount of quicksand that has to be negotiated.

THE RANGE OF CONSTRUCTIVIST AUTHORS

Even on the basis of so preliminary and sketchy an account, it should be clear that, potentially, an enormous number of authors can be considered as being in some sense constructivist. The following nonexhaustive list is indicative of the range, complexity, and "symbolic force" of constructivist ideas:

1. Ernst von Glasersfeld, who has had very great influence in the contemporary international science and mathematics education communities, quotes with some approval the words of Ludwig Fleck (1929), a precursor of Thomas Kuhn—"The content of our knowledge must be considered the free creation of our culture. It resembles a traditional myth" (von Glasersfeld 1991a, 118). Elsewhere he writes that from

> the naive commonsense perspective, the elements that form this complex environment belong to a *real* world of unquestionable objects, as *real* as the student, and these objects have an existence of their own, independent not only of the student but also of the teacher. Radical Constructivism is a theory of *knowing* which, for reasons that had nothing to do with teaching mathematics or education, does not accept this commonsense perspective. . . . Superficial or emotionally distracted readers of the constructivist literature have frequently interpreted this stance as a denial of "reality." (von Glasersfeld 1991b, xv)

2. The complex epistemology of Immanuel Kant was quintessentially constructivist. The human cognitive apparatus (in particular, our "category-governed modes of synthesis" in the case of natural science, as one commentator put it) was responsible for shaping our experience and giving it causal, temporal, and spatial features. As Kant wrote at the beginning of his *Critique of Pure Reason*,

> But though all our knowledge *begins* with experience, it does not follow that it all arises *out of* experience. For it may well be that even our empirical knowledge is made up of what we receive through impressions *and of what our own faculty of knowledge* . . . supplies from itself. If our

faculty of knowledge makes any such addition, it may be that we are not in a position to distinguish it from the raw material. (Kant 1959, 25)

3. Earlier in the eighteenth century, Giambattista Vico formulated the so-called *verum factum* principle, which is sometimes taken as an early paradigm case of constructivism: "the criterion and rule of the true is to have made it" or "the true is what is made" (Vico 1982, 55, 51).

4. Steve Fuller, in his book *Social Epistemology* (1988), writes that "Without knowing anything else about the nature of social epistemology, you can already tell that it has a *normative* interest. . . . the social episte- mologist would like to be able to show how the *products* of our cognitive pursuits are affected by changing the social relations in which the knowl- edge *producers* stand to one another" (Fuller 1988, 3). Or, again, "it would not be farfetched to say that, when done properly . . . , the philosophy of science is nothing other than the application of political philosophy to a segment of society, the class of scientists" (Fuller, 3).

5. In the introductory section of their edited *Feminist Epistemologies* (1993), Linda Alcoff and Elizabeth Potter also focus upon the sociopolitical processes by which our public bodies of knowledge are constructed. They write that the

> philosophical myth, like the myth of natural science, is that politics may motivate a philosopher to undertake philosophical work and that work may be put to better or worse political uses, but that a philosopher's work is good to the extent that its substantive, technical content is free of political influence. . . . The work presented here supports the hypoth- esis that politics intersect traditional epistemology. . . . [these essays] raise a question about the adequacy of any account of knowledge that ignores the politics involved in knowledge. These essays show . . . that to be *adequate*, an epistemology must attend to the complex ways in which social values influence knowledge." (Alcoff and Potter 1993, 13)

6. The work of Thomas S. Kuhn on scientific revolutions and para- digms has been a major influence on several of the constructivist sects, for he stressed the active role of scientific communities in knowledge- construction. He wrote near the end of his book:

> The very existence of science depends upon vesting the power to choose between paradigms in the members of a special kind of community. Just how special that community must be if science is to survive and grow may be indicated by the very tenuousness of humanity's hold on the

scientific enterprise. . . . The bulk of scientific knowledge is a product of Europe in the last four centuries. No other place and time has supported the very special communities from which scientific productivity comes. (Kuhn 1962, 166–167)

7. Jean Piaget is also generally regarded as a foundational figure by many constructivists. The following is clear enough:

> Fifty years of experience have taught us that knowledge does not result from a mere recording of observations without a structuring activity on the part of the subject. Nor do any a priori or innate cognitive structures exist in man; the functioning of intelligence alone is hereditary and creates structures only through an organization of successive actions performed on objects. Consequently, an epistemology conforming to the data of psychogenesis could be neither empiricist nor preformationist, but could consist only of a constructivism. (Piaget 1980, 23)

8. The cognitive psychologist Donald Norman writes: "What goes on in the mind of the learner? A lot: people who are learning are active, probing, constructing. People appear to have a strong desire to understand . . . [and] will go to great lengths to understand, constructing frameworks, constructing explanations, constructing huge edifices to account for what they have experienced" (Norman 1980, 42).

9. John Dewey, influenced here by William James, wrote that all the difficulties connected with the problem of knowledge spring

> from a single root. They spring from the assumption that the true and valid object of knowledge is that which has being prior to and independent of the operations of knowing. They spring from the doctrine that knowledge is a grasp or beholding of reality without anything being done to modify its antecedent state—the doctrine which is the source of the separation of knowledge from practical activity. If we see that knowing is not the act of an outside spectator but of a participator inside the natural and social scene, then the true object of knowledge resides in the consequences of directed action. (Dewey 1960, 196)

10. Jürgen Habermas, in his *Knowledge and Human Interests*, suggests that in the empirical-analytic sciences, the hermeneutic sciences, and the critical sciences, different "knowledge-constitutive human interests" have been at work—these different types of knowledge have been built up from, in order, an "orientation toward technical control, toward mutual

understanding in the conduct of life, and toward emancipation" (Habermas 1971, 311).

As can be seen from these ten views from across the spectrum, constructivism can be developed in interesting psychological, epistemological, sociological, and historical directions. But because there are so many versions of constructivism (these ten being merely the tip of an immense iceberg), with important overlaps but also with major differences, it is difficult to see the forest for the trees—it is a matter of pressing concern to find some way of categorizing them so that the overall picture does not get lost.

A FRAMEWORK FOR COMPARING CONSTRUCTIVISMS

Each of the various forms of constructivism is complex; they are not "single issue" positions, but they take a stand on a number of deep matters. To take merely one example from the ten figures cited earlier, von Glasersfeld is not simply putting forward a view about the teaching of mathematics and science; it is clear that he is advancing also an epistemology, a psychology, and his own interpretation of the history of science and philosophy. But Piaget, Dewey, Kuhn, and the feminist epistemologists are no less complicated. As a result of their complexity, then, the various forms or sects of constructivism can be spread out along a number of different dimensions or continua or axes (each of which represents one key issue); forms that are close along one axis (i.e., are close on one issue) may be far apart on another.

1. The first axis or dimension requires relatively little discussion, as it was pretty obvious in the examples cited earlier. For convenience it can be given the label *"individual learning versus public discipline."* Some constructivists—Piaget, von Glasersfeld, Dewey (in at least some of his writings), and Vygotsky would be quintessential figures here—they have been concerned with how the individual goes about the construction of knowledge in his or her own "cognitive apparatus"; in short, their focus is *how individuals learn*, and they can be labeled *psychological constructivists* (although one does not have to be a psychologist to believe that individuals construct their own understandings). For other constructivists, however, the individual learner is of little interest, and the focus of concern is the construction of the public bodies of knowledge or the disciplines; these are usually called *social constructivists* or sometimes social constructionists.

Many of those engaged on one side of the so-called "science wars" that have been a feature of intellectual life during the last decade of the millennium are social constructivists; some recent feminist epistemologists belong to this second group, as do neo-Marxists and sociologists of knowledge who have supported the radical "strong program" of the Edinburgh School (on all of which much more will be said in chapter 11). In the middle of this first continuum, however, are a number of constructivists who have an interest in *both* poles and who believe that their theories throw light on both the question of how individuals build up bodies of knowledge and how human communities have constructed the public bodies of knowledge known as the various disciplines (it seems that Karl Popper is to be located here).

It needs to be stressed that constructivists who have the same general interest—for example, in how individuals learn or construct knowledge—may differ markedly with respect to the *mechanisms* they see at work. Piaget and Vygotsky, for example, gave quite different accounts of this matter; one stressed the biological/psychological mechanisms to be found in the individual learner, while the other focused on the social factors that influenced learning. (The moral here is that labels are extremely misleading; psychological constructivists focusing on individual learning can be nonpsychologists and can stress the vital role played in individual learning by parents, teachers, peers, language, the media, and other cultural artifacts and resources—social factors all!)

2. The second dimension or axis along which the various versions of constructivism can be spread is, arguably, the most crucial one—for it is the dimension that, in essence, allows us to define a thinker as being *constructivist*. This dimension or continuum can be characterized crudely in terms of the label *"mankind the creator versus nature the instructor."* The

Diagram 1.1 The First Constructivist Dimension

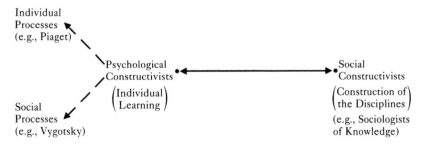

issue is as follows: When knowledge is constructed (whether it is in the mind or cognitive apparatus of the individual learner, or whether it is a public discipline), is the process one that is influenced chiefly by the minds or creative intelligence of the knower or knowers, together perhaps with the "sociopolitical" factors that are present when knowers interact in a community? Or, at the other extreme, is the knowledge "imposed" from the outside; does nature serve as an "instructor" or as a sort of template that the knowing subject or subjects (or community of knowledge builders) merely copy or absorb in a relatively passive fashion? In short, is new knowledge—whether it be individual knowledge or public discipline—*made* or *discovered?*

It is arguable that theorists who occupy the "outer" or "external nature" or "discovery" end of the axis—like, for example, the late-seventeenth-century British empiricist philosopher John Locke—are at best only minimally constructivist in orientation or are not constructivist at all, for in their theories the contribution of human activity to knowledge construction is relatively insignificant. But "true-blue" constructivists are spread out along the continuum, with some of them being nearer than others to the "outer" or "nature as instructor" pole of the continuum.

It will be instructive to pursue the case of the empiricist John Locke a little further. In his work, and that of his associationist descendants, nature external to the knower is the source of the sensations that produce "simple ideas" fairly mechanically or automatically (although it is important to remember that for Locke other types of simple ideas come from reflection or inner experience); and from these simple units the more complex armamentarium of ideas is built up by various inborn combinatorial processes (or faculties). The mind (or "the understanding") is described in Locke's writings in very passive terms—the mind is a receptacle (an empty cabinet, a wax tablet, a piece of blotting paper) for storing whatever ideas come from experience. The mind is not able to produce simple ideas of its own, so that, for example, if the knower has not had experience of a particular color, he or she—no matter how clever—cannot invent the simple idea of that color. Thus Locke writes, using the example of a snowball:

> the power to produce any idea in our mind, I call "quality" of the subject wherein that power is. Thus a snowball having the power to produce in us the ideas of white, cold and round, the powers to produce those ideas in us as they are in the snowball, I call "qualities." (Locke 1947, 45)

In short, it is the object in the external realm of nature—the snow-ball—that is causally responsible (via experience) for producing our knowl-edge; the snowball's qualities have "the power to produce in us" the ideas of whiteness and so on.

The position just described hardly warrants the label "constructivist" at all. What makes Locke's case more complex to assess is his insistence that once the "understanding" is "furnished" with a number of (externally produced) simple ideas, the mind *can* operate on these to construct some-thing new:

> In this faculty of repeating and joining together its ideas, the mind has greater power in varying and multiplying the objects of its thoughts . . . it can, by its own power, put together those ideas it has, and make new complex ones. (Locke 1947, 65)

Our simple ideas may be mere reflections of nature, but complex ideas are produced (constructed) by the human mind.

Unfortunately, there is another complexity: While statements like this seem to place Locke over the border and into the constructivist camp, the picture is muddied again by the fact that these combinatorial powers or faculties (that produce the complex ideas) are "wired in" before birth and function virtually automatically. (This is certainly the way the faculties are depicted in the "mental chemistry" of Locke's nineteenth-century associationist followers; and it should be noticed that there is a parallel issue here for our contemporaries who are enamored of computational theories of the mind—such theories sometimes are forced to assume the existence of an inner "homunculus," in order to leave some room for hu-man creativity. See Searle 1992, chap. 9.) The only thing that seems safe to say, then, is that Locke is close to the "outside/instruction by nature/ discovery" end of the dimension under discussion here, and he also is close to the outer perimeter of constructivism—which side of the border he actually is on is a difficult judgment call.

We do not have to look far for examples of theorists at the other, "man-kind the creator" pole of this second constructivist continuum or dimen-sion. Most varieties of late-twentieth-century constructivism have as a major tenet the claim that knowledge is produced by humans, in processes that are unconstrained—or minimally constrained—by inputs or instruc-tion from nature. But at this end of the continuum there is a great deal of confusion, for (as we saw earlier) some constructivists are focusing upon how developing individuals learn, while others are looking at how the "public" disciplines originate. There is further bifurcation even than this, for some hold that knowledge production comes about solely from "inner" processes in the knower, while for others the processes are held to be sociopolitical and not simply or solely "inner," mental, or intellectual in nature. These various views are combined in several different ways, as will become evident later.

A couple of examples will illustrate some of the possibilities here.

a. Members of the "strong program" in the sociology of knowledge (such as Barnes 1974 and Collins 1985)—who are working on the origin of the public bodies of knowledge known as the disciplines, especially the sciences—can be read as being far from the "nature as template" view, but also as being far from the "creative activity of individual human intelligence" view; at their strongest, they hold the view that sociopolitical processes can account fully for the form taken by the bodies of knowledge codified as the various disciplines.

b. Perhaps the clearest example of a theorist who is in the "individual creative activity" camp, and also far from the "nature as instructor" end of the continuum, is Ernst von Glasersfeld. He provides the following striking rejection of the "nature as template" view and affirms that it is the cognitive effort of the individual that results in the construction of knowledge:

> The notion that knowledge is the result of a learner's activity rather than that of the passive reception of information or instruction, goes back to Socrates and is today embraced by all who call themselves "constructivists." However, the authors whose work is collected here, constitute the radical wing of the constructivist front. . . . This attitude is characterized by the deliberate redefinition of the concept of knowledge as an *adaptive function*. In simple words, this means that the results of our cognitive efforts have the purpose of helping us cope in the world of experience, rather than the traditional goal of furnishing an "objective" representation of a world as it might "exist" apart from us and our experience. (von Glasersfeld 1991b, xiv–xv)

c. Karl Popper is a philosopher who is situated at about the middle of the "mankind the creator versus nature the instructor" continuum. For his theory of the development of knowledge can be summarized as "man proposes, nature disposes"—a view that nicely involves both poles of the continuum. Popper's view offers an account of the growth of public bodies of knowledge (especially the sciences), but it can also be interpreted in such a way as to throw light on the psychology and epistemology of

Diagram 1.2 Complexities of the Second Constructivist Dimension

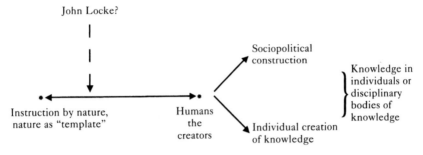

individual learning (Berkson and Wettersten 1984). Popper was fond of expounding his view in terms of a crude flow diagram:

"problem → tentative theory → error elimination → new problem"

The tentative theory is a creation of the human intellect; the error elimination (via testing) is done by nature.

3. The third dimension for comparing types of constructivism was touched on earlier: The construction of knowledge is an *active* process, but the activity can be described in terms of individual cognition or else in terms of social and political processes (or, of course, in terms of both). Furthermore, this activity can be either physical or mental, or again both. If a theorist were to argue that knowledge construction is carried out automatically, by the following of some predetermined inflexible routine or by some mechanical process, then his or her work would not count as constructivist; we saw in the case of John Locke that insofar as he postulated that simple ideas were built into complex knowledge by "pre-wired" cognitive processes (to use contemporary idioms rather than Locke's terminology), he could not be regarded as being situated within the general constructivist camp—for although there is a place for mental activity in his model, it is not conscious or deliberate activity *of the knower*.

A nice contrast to Locke is Jean Piaget; he is as individualistic as Locke with respect to how knowledge is constructed (his voluminous writings make only scant reference to the role of the social environment, and Piaget typically depicts the developing child as a lone, inventive young scientist, struggling to make independent sense of the surrounding world). But Piaget does place enormous stress on the fact that the young knower is both mentally and physically active; indeed, knowledge growth is described by Piaget in terms of the dynamic processes of assimilation, accommodation, and equilibration, and the construction and internalization of action schemas (see Phillips 1987, chap. 13, for further discussion).

Another important example of active constructivism is provided by the work of John Dewey and William James. Both these pragmatists (together with latter-day admirers such as Richard Rorty, see Kulp 1992) vigorously attack what they call the "spectator theory of knowledge." In the late nineteenth century James had written a critique of Herbert Spencer's theory of mind, in which he said that mind was not a spectator, but rather "the knower is an actor" (James 1920, 67)—a view that James elsewhere argued was underwritten by evolutionary theory (see, for example, his *Talks to Teachers on Psychology*). Dewey picked up on all this and consistently expounded his own view of knowledge in contrast to the errors of the "spectator theory." (See, for example, Dewey's *The Quest for Certainty*, 1960.)

The spectator theory, as Dewey interpreted it, can be explicated by means of an analogy with football. According to the spectator theory, the way a knower obtains knowledge is analogous to the way a person can learn about football. He or she can learn by watching, by being a spectator; while learning, the spectator remains passive and does not affect the course of the game. In contrast, in the theory held by James and Dewey the knower is an organic part of the same situation as the material to be known. To return to the football analogy, the person learning about football would be playing in the game; he or she would be affecting the game and, in the process, obtaining knowledge about it—the knower would be learning by participating or acting. (It is interesting to note, as an aside, that the spectator theory of knowledge has been largely ignored in the epistemological literature of the last few decades; Kulp, 1992, has produced the only lengthy discussion of it, and although recognizing that it has some strengths, he reaches a generally negative conclusion. See also Phillips 1971.) Lest all this makes Dewey seem unduly individualistic, it is important to note that he also stressed the social nature of knowledge construction, both in individual learners and also with respect to the development of the public bodies of knowledge codified in the various disciplines; but the social activity he depicted was always harmonious and cooperative—he did not pay much attention to the internal politics of knowledge producing communities or the effects of power differentials on the types of knowledge produced.

To turn to the other end of this third dimension, Lynn Hankinson Nelson stresses that knowledge construction is an active process—even a struggle—carried out by groups or communities, not by individuals. In an interesting passage, she writes:

> In suggesting that it is communities that construct and acquire knowledge, I do not mean (or "merely" mean) that what comes to be recognized or "certified" as knowledge is the result of collaboration between, consensus achieved by, political struggles engaged in, negotiations undertaken among, or other activities engaged in by individuals who, *as individuals, know* in some logically or empirically "prior" sense. . . . The change I am proposing involves what we should construe as the *agents* of these activities. My arguments suggest that the collaborators, the consensus achievers, and, in more general terms, the agents who generate knowledge are communities and subcommunities, not individuals. (Nelson 1993, 124)

EPISTEMOLOGICAL VERSUS SOCIOPOLITICAL AND EDUCATIONAL CONCERNS

The previous dimensions along which, I have argued, the various forms or sects of constructivism can be located are all, to a greater or lesser degree, *epistemically related* dimensions. Clearly, all forms of constructivism take a stand on epistemological issues, but we will form a distorted view of all of them if we let matters rest there. For it is clear that while some constructivists have epistemological enemies whom they are anxious to defeat, most also have pressing social and political concerns that motivate their work. It should not come as a surprise, of course, that in the reigning intellectual climate of the changing of the millennia, many of those who held a position that was hypersensitive to the fact that knowledge is produced should also have heightened sensitivity to the sociopolitical conditions under which this production took place. What I am suggesting here is that it would be a mistake to think that when the philosophical concerns of the constructivists have been dealt with, our work is over—the concerns run deeper than this.

Consider several obvious examples: von Glasersfeld, Dewey, and the feminist epistemologists. All of these make epistemological points of varying degrees of sophistication; but all of them also have important educational or social concerns, each of which has a degree of credibility that is independent of the fate of the respective epistemologies. It even could be argued that in these cases the social concerns are more central. (And, of course, a reader can be sympathetic to the educational or social concerns without being a fellow-traveler with regard to the epistemology, or vice versa.)

Thus, von Glasersfeld's epistemology, which I have claimed elsewhere is developed in a flawed way (Phillips 1992, 1997; see also Matthews 1992, 1994, chap. 7; McCarty and Schwandt 2000), is an important springboard from which he and the radical constructivists have launched an important educational movement (see Noddings 1990, for a somewhat similar assessment). His individualism and subjectivism in epistemology lead him (or perhaps were accepted because they allow him) to argue that each individual science and mathematics student is responsible for building his or her own set of understandings of these disciplines; teachers cannot assume that all students have the same set of understandings or that their own ways of understanding are shared by their students. Moreover, it is clear from von Glasersfeld's perspective that everyone studying a field like science has his or her own set of conceptions and preconceptions that influence the course of subsequent learning; teachers should drop the fashionable but misleading talk of student "misconceptions," for this implies that there is a standard set of "correct" conceptions that all learners should have. One result of all this is to highlight the need for individual attention to students and the need to give guidance about how bodies of understanding are built up. *It could be argued here that a weak or at least a controversial epistemology has become the basis for a strong pedagogic policy.* Here is how one prominent researcher in the domains of science and mathematics education summarizes the beneficial influence of radical constructivism:

> When one applies constructivism to the issue of teaching, one must reject the assumption that one can simply pass on information to a set of learners and expect that understanding will result. Communication is a far more complex process than this. When teaching concepts, as a form of communication, the teacher must form an adequate model of the student's ways of viewing an idea and s/he then must assist the student in restructuring those views to be more adequate from the student's and from the teacher's perspective. Constructivism not only emphasizes the essential role of the constructive process, it also allows one to emphasize that we are at least partially able to be aware of those constructions and then to modify them through our conscious reflection on that constructive process. (Confrey 1990, 109)

In the case of John Dewey, epistemology also leads directly to social and pedagogic policies. (In his *Democracy and Education* Dewey specifically claimed that philosophy is the theory of education.) As he saw it, the peda-gogical and social ramifications of his epistemological opposition to the spectator theory of knowledge were quite broad. Starting from the posi-tion that the knower is an actor rather than a spectator, Dewey staunchly advocated the use of activity methods in the schoolroom—for students are potential knowers, yet traditional schooling forces students into the mold of passive receptacles waiting to have information instilled, instead of al-lowing them to move about, discuss, experiment, work on communal projects, pursue research outdoors in the fields and indoors in the library and laboratory, and so forth. Consider this wonderful description of the traditional schoolroom, where his attitude to the spectator theory is crys-tal clear:

> Just as the biologist can take a bone or two and reconstruct the whole animal, so, if we put before the mind's eye the ordinary schoolroom, with its rows of ugly desks placed in geometrical order, crowded together so that there shall be as little moving room as possible . . . and add a table, some chairs, the bare walls, and possibly a few pictures, we can recon-struct the only educational activity that can possibly go on in such a place. It is all made "for listening." (Dewey 1969, 31)

Dewey also had—and it is likely that this predated the development of his epistemology—a deep respect for manual and technical pursuits. He was concerned with the problem of the alienation of labor in the late nine-teenth and twentieth centuries (although he never, to my knowledge, described it this way), and he traced the higher status that is given to re-flective/academic pursuits back to the world of the ancient Greeks. There, because of the social and economic divisions of society, the most highly educated people looked down upon craftsmen—a position that found its reflection in Greek (Dewey almost certainly meant Plato's) epistemology. This is a major theme of his interesting book *The Quest for Certainty*.

The general idea should now be clear enough; the interested reader can try his or her own hand at constructing an analysis of the broader con-cerns that are tied in with Piaget's and Habermas's views on the construc-tion of knowledge (to mention only two of the other most obvious ex-amples). But a third example is worth pursuing here, for it leads in quite a different sociopolitical direction.

Feminist epistemologists such as Sandra Harding and Helen Longino clearly have social concerns that reinforce their commitment to their re-spective epistemologies (the two have philosophies that are similar but by no means identical). In stressing that the knower cannot be conceived as being an artificially objectified, solitary individual devoid of human characteristics and isolated from a sociocultural setting, they wish to highlight the degree to which these previously neglected factors play an epistemological role. Harding stresses that in a society that is stratified "by race, ethnicity, class, gender, sexuality, or some other such politics," the activities of those at the top "both organize and set limits on what persons who perform such activities can understand about themselves and the world around them" (Harding 1993, 54). Such activities, of course, include those in the epistemological arena, and necessarily the knowledge generated by such people is going to be deficient. However, the activities of marginalized people "at the bottom of such social hierarchies" can provide a sounder starting point for epistemological inquiry (Harding 1993, 54). Harding's contention is that people at the bottom can generate more critical questions to guide inquiry, for their position is less "limiting" (Harding 1993, 55). In short, for Harding epistemological considerations lead directly to the issue of social empowerment.

Helen Longino, after citing the influence of Kuhn, Feyerabend, Hanson, and Duhem, goes on to stress the ways in which science is a communal rather than an individual endeavor; scientific knowledge "is constructed . . . by individuals in interaction with one another in ways that modify their observations, theories and hypotheses, and patterns of reasoning" (Longino 1993, 111). She then discusses four criteria that must be satisfied if "transformative critical discourse" is to be achieved—there must be publicly recognized forums; the community must not only tolerate dissent, but its beliefs must actually change over time; there must be publicly recognized standards of evaluation of theories, observations, and so on; and communities must be "characterized by equality of intellectual authority" (Longino 1993, 112–113). Perhaps Longino's overriding concern—which is both epistemological and social—is that "no segment of the community, whether powerful or powerless, can claim epistemic privilege" (Longino 1993, 118).

CONCLUDING REMARKS

I opened the present discussion by identifying the quasi-religious or ideological aspects of constructivism as being *ugly*. The *good*, as I hope I have made clear, is the emphasis that various constructivist sects place on the necessity for active participation by the learner, together with the recognition (by most of them) of the social nature of learning; it seems clear that, with respect to their stance on education, most types of constructivism are modern forms of progressivism. Constructivism also deserves praise for bringing epistemological issues to the fore in the discussion of learning and the curriculum; while I do not agree with some of their specific philosophical points, the level of sophistication of the debates in education journals is much improved as a result of their presence. The *bad*, which I have not been able to document adequately in the present discussion (but which I shall revisit in chapter 11), are constructivist epistemologies that tend (despite their occasional protestations to the contrary) toward relativism and that make the justification of our knowledge-claims pretty much entirely a matter of sociopolitical processes or consensus, or that jettison any justification or warrant at all (as is arguably the case with the radical social constructivists). My own view is that any defensible epistemology must recognize—and not just pay lip service to—the fact that nature exerts considerable constraint over our knowledge-constructing activities and allows us to detect (and eject) our errors about it—which still leaves plenty of room for us to improve the nature and operation of our knowledge-constructing communities, which play a nontrivial role in shaping the nature of *what* is constructed.

Reprinted with permission, and with some changes and additions, from *Educational Researcher* 24 (7) (October 1995): 5–12.

2

HERMENEUTICS AND
NATURALISTIC SOCIAL INQUIRY

INTRODUCTION

Considering only the last three hundred years, from about the time of Vico onward, a massive literature on hermeneutics has accumulated. But in the past two decades there has been a veritable avalanche of material—a poor academician can be driven to the edge of bankruptcy trying to keep pace with the new books.

Unfortunately, this recent material is more a repository of enthusiasm than of enlightenment. There are differing accounts of the nature of the key issues, although what comes shining through is the fact that hermeneuticists manage to reach (via difficult and sometimes nearly impenetrable prose) some far-reaching and important conclusions about the nature of the social sciences. To the skeptical eye, the literature is full of *claims*, but the arguments are left sketchy or unclear (or both); and there is a dearth of concrete examples—Wolfgang Stegmuller (1988, 109) laments that "analysis of examples is totally absent." To add insult to injury, some writers (without much by way of supporting argumentation) extend the scope of hermeneutics—so that, like the Scarlet Pimpernel, hermeneutical issues are claimed to be everywhere. One inescapable conclusion is that hermeneutical activity is called for in order to decipher all the arguments of the hermeneuticists!

The following discussion will attempt to bring some order to this complex domain. First, there will be a distillation of the hermeneuticist case, especially in the form in which it is advanced as a criticism of traditional empirical social science and related fields; then the discussion will focus upon the resulting claims that are made. In general, the center of interest will be the image held by hermeneuticists of both social science and research in applied fields, such as education, and their epistemologies.

19

However, there is one more preliminary matter. Throughout the discussion the terms *hermeneutical* and *interpretive* will be used as synonyms; their use will be varied simply as a stylistic device to maintain the reader's interest. One word derives from Greek, the other Latin; but they mean the same and even, in their classical usage, refer to the same winged messenger of the gods (whose function was to communicate the wishes of the deities in a form that mere mortals could understand).

THE INTERPRETIVIST CASE

The interpretivist case runs as follows, although it must be stressed that what follows is a *general* account and, of course, individuals disagree about many of the details: According to interpretivists, physical scientists deal with objects by explaining their behavior either in terms of external forces or in terms of inner processes that result from their physicochemical microstructure. Notions of force, energy, causation, and natural law are central; and the methods by which knowledge is built up are observational and experimental. The underlying epistemological premise is a form of empiricism. (Many interpretivists would say it is a form of logical positivism.) Until very recently, social science (especially in the United States) has proceeded by mimicking the physical science approach—behaviorism in psychology being one example among many, though also the most notorious.

On the other hand, hermeneuticists would argue, humans are not mere physical objects; people are impelled by ideas, knowledge, and hopes and desires. They harbor intentions. And these things depend upon the use of symbols, as in language; as Gadamer puts it (1977, 29), "language is not only an object in our hand, it is the reservoir of tradition and the medium in and through which we exist and perceive our world." Symbols and language, of course, are impossible without societies. Furthermore, many actions undertaken by individuals are actually *constituted by* public meanings, socially adopted rules, conventions, and the like; thus, to take a fairly trivial example, one cannot understand the game of tennis, let alone play it, unless one understands the rules and conventions that define the valid activities of the game (a serve that is "in," an acceptable placement of a return of the ball, etc.). But activities as diverse as participating in a dinner party, consulting a physician, writing a philosophical paper, and giving evidence in court are no less constituted by sociocultural rules and conventions. John Searle has put this point in an interesting way:

there is a class of social facts having certain logical features that make them quite unlike the phenomena of physics and chemistry. In the case of phenomena such as marriage, money, divorce, elections, buying and selling . . . the phenomena are—to speak vaguely at this stage—permeated with mental components; furthermore, the facts in question are self-referential . . . because they can only be the facts they are if the people involved think that they are those facts. (Searle, 1991, 335–336)

Thus, Searle holds that the "modes of explanation" in the social sciences are "in certain respects" logically distinct from those in the natural sciences (Searle 1991, 334). It seems to follow from all this that to explain the actions of a person (as opposed to the behavior of a physical object), an investigator must uncover the *understandings* of the actor—how the actor interprets the situation he or she is in, how the mores and beliefs of the society in which the actor is located are influential, what the actor sees as being the possible responses that are open (given the social beliefs the actor holds), and the symbolic meaning of the forms of behavior that are open to the actor in that particular setting. In Searle's language, subjective mental states function *causally* in the production of human behavior (Searle 1991, 334). Or, as the social scientist Zygmunt Bauman put it,

Men and women do what they do on purpose. Social phenomena, since they are ultimately acts of men and women, demand to be understood in a different way than by mere explaining. Understanding them must contain an element missing from the explaining of natural phenomena: the retrieval of purpose, of intention, of the unique configuration of thoughts and feelings which preceded a social phenomenon and found its only manifestation, imperfect and incomplete, in the observable consequences of action. To understand a human act, therefore, was to grasp the meaning with which the actor's intention invested it, a task, as could easily be seen, essentially different from that of natural science. (Bauman 1978, 12)

This is the heart of the hermeneuticist or interpretivist position, and it is this that is being referred to by these labels in the subsequent discussion.

It should be noted in passing that a rift occurs at this point between several "schools" of interpretivists. Some believe that it is necessary—as a corollary of the points outlined previously—to pursue the subjective understandings of actors; these can be labeled "phenomenologically oriented hermeneuticists." Others eschew this subjective approach and focus instead upon the *public* meanings together with the observable actions of, and interactions between, people in social settings. There is an accompanying disagreement, therefore, about the methods of inquiry that are appropriate. It is probably true to say that mainstream American social scientists tend to look askance at methods that smack of subjectivism; and philosophers in the English-speaking world have a similar attitude toward theories of meaning that focus upon the "pictures," ideas, or intentions internal to the individual. The dominant contemporary philosophical approach to meaning focuses instead on the public realm, on how people operate with language (and with a pregiven stock of cultural tools)—a view that has clear implications for methodology. Although dominant in North America, this latter orientation is not confined to it (see, for example, Karl Otto Apel 1977, 301). However, it is not the purpose of the present chapter to pursue issues concerning the methodology of interpretive studies; the focus here is unabashedly the theoretical arguments and claims made on behalf of the importance of hermeneutics for the social sciences.

To return to the exposition of the interpretivist case: Human action, according to the very broad position being expounded here, is a type of text (albeit an unwritten one)—for a text is nothing more than a collection of symbols expressing meaning (or even layers of meaning), although this meaning itself may be expressed in terms of metaphors or complex cultural symbols. Hence, it is possible to use the discipline that has developed over many centuries to interpret texts—the discipline of hermeneutics, with its central notion of the hermeneutic circle—to interpret and throw light upon human action. This extension of hermeneutics to cover the nonwritten realm began with the nineteenth-century figures Schleiermacher and Dilthey (see Palmer 1969, part 11); but it reached its apogee with the work of Charles Taylor (Taylor 1977) and Paul Ricoeur in the early 1970s. Thus, in his essay "The Model of the Text: Meaningful Action Considered as a Text," Ricoeur wrote:

> Now my hypothesis is this: if there are specific problems which are raised by the interpretation of texts because they are texts and not spoken language, and if these problems are the ones which constitute hermeneutics as such, then the human sciences may be said to be hermeneutical (1) inasmuch as their *object* displays some of the features constitutive of a text as text, and (2) inasmuch as their *methodology* develops the same kind of procedures as those of . . . text interpretation. (Ricoeur 1971, 316)

Many in the hermeneutics camp have gone on to point out that human societies are full of the "objectifications" of meaning (as Gadamer,

Betti, and others term it)—not only written texts, but social institutions, practices and rituals, and physical artifacts.

Hermeneuticists generally go further than this, however, and stress that interpreters who attempt to grasp the meaning of an actor or to grasp meaning that has been objectified in some way have *their own* understandings shaped by the fact that they themselves are members of a particular culture at a particular historical moment. Interpretation, in other words, is not an act in which a "disembodied" investigator is trying to decipher the (preestablished) meaning of a culturally and historically situated actor or institution; rather, the interpreter, too, must become hermeneutically aware of his or her own historicity (or "preunderstanding," as some writers term it). As David Linge puts it, in his "Editor's Introduction" to a book of Gadamer's,

> This methodological alienation of the knower from his own historicity is precisely the focus of Gadamer's criticism. Is it the case, Gadamer asks, that the knower can leave his immediate situation in the present merely by adopting an (interpretive) attitude? An ideal of understanding that asks us to overcome our own present is intelligible only on the assumption that our own historicity is an accidental factor. But if it is an *ontological* rather than a merely accidental and subjective condition, then the knower's own present situation is already constitutively involved in the process of understanding. (Linge, in Gadamer 1977, xiv)

Interpretivists sometimes use examples such as the following: In the physical sciences, the behavior of objects is explained by bringing to bear physical laws—such as when the orbit of a planet is explained by deducing its behavior from Newton's or Kepler's laws (together with a statement of the initial conditions). On the other hand, the action of Julius Caesar in crossing the Rubicon is not explained by bringing it under a law—for there are no laws of nature pertinent to the voluntary actions of Roman generals standing on the banks of particular rivers like the Rubicon; rather, Julius's action is explained in terms of his intentions and in terms of the symbolic importance of that particular river (which marked the border between divisions of the Roman empire). Julius Caesar's action was not the product of laws of nature (despite the fact that his body was a physical object), but it was voluntary—a result of his consciously reaching the decision to carry out a revolt (a revolt being, of course, a social phenomenon). Furthermore, our attempts to understand Caesar's action are mediated by the historical/cultural milieu in which we, as interpreters, are located; so, as hermeneuticists, we are struggling to understand ourselves at the very same time that we are struggling to understand Caesar. (Gadamer would say that we can achieve objective interpretations, but these are interpretations from within our own cultural and historical setting.)

SOME FAR-REACHING CONCLUSIONS

Before the discussion proceeds, it should be acknowledged that much in the interpretivist position, as just outlined, is compelling. Humans are not mere physical objects; and to understand or explain why a person has acted in a particular manner, the meaning (or meanings) of the action have to be uncovered—and to do this, the roles of language and of social symbolisms and values have to be taken into account. Many philosophers of social science in the English-speaking world have acknowledged variants of this general position for decades (see, for example, Winch 1958 and Simon 1982). Furthermore, it seems uncontroversial that every society contains many "objectifications" of meaning—in rituals, symbolisms, institutions, and so forth. (These sentences are being written in the United States on July 4th amid the festivities, which serves to drive the point home.)

What shall be disputed are some of the very wide-ranging conclusions about research in education and the social sciences that are drawn by some, at least, of the hermeneuticists, conclusions that stray well past what is warranted by the preceding position. These debatable conclusions can be clustered into two major groups.

EPISTEMOLOGICAL CONCLUSIONS

The first set of wide-ranging conclusions can be introduced via reference to Charles Taylor. In his now classic essay "Interpretation and the Sciences of Man" (1971), Taylor reveals himself to be a powerful spokesman for the view that the epistemological foundations of empirical science are an unsatisfactory base on which to erect a "science of man." Taylor refers disparagingly to the ingredients that make up the "epistemological bias" of empirical social science, and he writes that

> many, including myself, would like to argue that these notions about the sciences of man are sterile, that we cannot come to understand impor-

tant dimensions of human life within the bounds set by this epistemological orientation. (Taylor 1977, 106)

Along what seems to be similar lines, Graham Macdonald and Philip
Pettit argue in their *Semantics and Social Science* that the epistemology of
the social sciences is close to that of the humanities: "Social science, insofar as its concern is the explanation of human behavior, begins to look
like a discipline which belongs with the humanities rather than the sciences" (Macdonald and Pettit 1981, 104). This view must come as something of a shock to empirical social scientists; and the shock is exacerbated
by the fact that Macdonald and Pettit are not alone. Thus, somewhat less
pithily, Rabinow and Sullivan assert, in their *Interpretive Social Science: A
Reader*, that

> Interpretive social science has developed as the alternative to earlier
> logical empiricism as well as the later systems approaches, including
> structuralism, within the human sciences. It must continue to develop
> in opposition to and as a criticism of these tendencies. Here interpre-
> tive social science reveals itself as a response to the crisis of the human
> sciences that is constructive in the profound sense of establishing a con-
> nection between what is studied, the means of investigation, and the
> ends informing the investigators. But at the same time it initiates a pro-
> cess of recovery and reappropriation of the richness of meaning found
> in the symbolic contexts of all areas of culture. (Rabinow and Sullivan
> 1979, 13)

So, then, the first set of wide-ranging conclusions that is drawn is
epistemological; and yet detailed and convincing *epistemological* arguments
are in short supply in this literature—for example, it has not been shown
in any detailed way how it is that hermeneuticists actually *know*, that is,
how the products of their interpretive endeavors are warranted. (Once
again, Stegmuller's remark comes to mind; he states that philosophers of
science customarily support their claims about the epistemology of science
by detailed analyses of scientific work, but hermeneuticists do not do the
same in their own fields.) The issues here will be taken up again later.

A different but obviously closely related form in which the epistemological claims surface is in terms of the relation between the human sciences, the natural sciences, and the humanities. The issue can be phrased
as a question: Is hermeneutical or interpretive social science really a science, or is it a branch of the humanities? As Connolly and Keutner put it
in the introduction to their edited volume *Hermeneutics versus Science?* (1988,

1), "Do the hermeneutical disciplines differ in some important way from the natural sciences, i.e., are those disciplines autonomous?" And Alfred Schutz put it extremely clearly when he wrote (1962, 34):

> There will be hardly any issue among social scientists that the object of the social sciences is human behavior, its forms, its organization, and its products. There will be, however, different opinions about whether this behavior should be studied in the same manner in which the natural scientist studies his object or whether the goal of the social sciences is the explanation of the "social reality" as experienced by man living his everyday life within the social world.

A spatial analogy might help clarify this second form taken by the epistemological claims of the hermeneuticists. (This is meant only as a preliminary heuristic device; obviously, it is hard to precisely locate specific theorists, for their thought is usually complex and defies simple accurate categorization.) The humanities, the social sciences, and the natural sciences can be visualized as arranged—in that order—along a continuum. With respect to this continuum, several schools of thought exist:

1. Some scholars have wanted to drive a wedge between the humanities and the rest, by insisting upon the "autonomy" of the humanities; typically, this has been done by stressing the nature of the humanities as interpretive disciplines, in which hermeneutics (and especially the hermeneutic circle) has a central position (see Stegmuller 1988).

2. Others have hammered at the same wedge, by insisting that the sciences are demarcated from the humanities by having a logical character accurately described by the logical positivists.

3. A number of scholars have wanted to remove the wedge entirely. One group has tried to do this by insisting that *all* inquiry, to be genuine inquiry aimed at producing warranted knowledge, must have the same underlying epistemology; usually, the epistemology of science is taken as the model. On some readings, John Dewey, and perhaps Karl Popper, belong to this group. (It should be stressed that in taking science as the paradigm case of knowledge, these thinkers are not necessarily advocating a narrow positivistic view of knowledge; in fact, both Dewey and Popper have a fairly liberal view of the nature of science—a topic on which there shall be more discussion in later chapters of this book.)

4. A different group has wanted to remove the wedge entirely by stressing that all knowledge contains a strong interpretive element. Heidegger and Gadamer, according to some of their remarks, ought ten-

tatively to be classified as members of this group. Thus, Gadamer writes (1977, 38) that "Hermeneutical reflection fulfills the function that is accomplished in all bringing of something to conscious awareness. Because it does, it can and must manifest itself in all our modern fields of knowledge, and especially science."

5. Others, in particular writers like Taylor, Macdonald and Pettit, and Dilthey (1976), wish *at least* to drive a wedge into the continuum between the natural sciences and the social sciences, so that the social sciences end up being grouped with the humanities. Typically, as discussed earlier, the argument is that the social sciences, like the humanities, must give a central place to interpretive methods. It can be seen, therefore, that there is a degree of overlap between the views of those in groups (4) and (5); but (4) is a somewhat more radical position than (5).

CONCLUSIONS CONCERNING THE NATURE OF SOCIAL SCIENCE

The interpretivist case as outlined earlier also embodies within it certain views about the nature and purpose of the various social and human sciences. Humans live in societies, and societies are saturated with objectifications of meaning; and it is with the elucidation of these that the social sciences are centrally concerned. As Dilthey put it,

> Here the concept of the human studies is completed. Their range is identical with that of understanding and understanding consistently has the objectification of life as its subject matter. Thus the range of the human studies is determined by the objectification of life in the external world. Mind can only understand what it has created. . . . Everything on which man has actively impressed his stamp forms the subject matter of the human studies. (Dilthey 1976, 192)

But is it altogether clear that Dilthey is right? And even if the answer to this is in the affirmative, does it follow that the central methods of the "human studies" must be hermeneutical?

SKEPTICAL COMMENTARY

These two groups of far-reaching conclusions both require careful scrutiny. There is some overlap between them, of course, so the discussion of each cannot be kept absolutely watertight. It will make sense to build up to the central issue concerning epistemology, so for want of a better arrangement the discussion will proceed in reverse order.

COMMENTARY: THE NATURE OF SOCIAL SCIENCE

In the view of the interpretivists, the social sciences or "human studies" are almost entirely concerned with meaningful human action together with the objectifications of meaning that are to be found in human societies. Dilthey (1976, 163–167) did allow that a study of nature was also relevant, insofar as natural events are frequently the stimuli for human action and form the focus of mankind's attempts to develop knowledge. But the fact of the matter is that the social sciences are not so concerned with hermeneutical matters as has been supposed by supporters of the interpretivist position. To make this case, it need not be denied that *some* sort of interpretive activity is required in *some* of the social sciences; the point is that there is much else besides.

1. In general, it may be true that the social sciences study phenomena that are *social;* and social phenomena, as the interpretivists claim, are constituted by the use of language and by other symbolic interaction— and thus cry out for hermeneutical analysis. But the "in general" marks an important caveat. The qualification is required because there are many social sciences and they do not constitute a "natural kind"; the category is human-made and is of necessity a somewhat vague one. The point is that there are some social sciences where hermeneutical activity does not appear to be central—witness various branches of psychology and much of economics.

According to some accounts, psychology is a member of the social (and certainly of the human) sciences; and it is clear that psychology includes within its domain the study of mechanisms, such as the cognitive and emotional ones, that underlie individual human performance. Mechanisms like these can be studied in a manner that is as little hermeneutical as is, say, biological research. Cases in point are the use, by cognitive psychologists, of nonsense syllable experiments and designs that focus on performance on nonverbal tests such as Raven's Progressive Matrices.

And then there is economics, which is usually regarded as a clear-cut member of the social sciences—yet much of it can hardly be claimed to be hermeneutical. Some branches of this "dismal science" certainly study the effects of social choices (as in market phenomena), but these choices are conceptualized as being the mathematical aggregate of individual choices. And it is crucial to note that, in general, the individual is treated in the manner of an "ideal type" in physics: the individual is presumed to be fully rational, to be fully knowledgeable, and to have a clear prioritization of needs and desires. Mathematical modeling plays an important role here, but not hermeneutics. (All that this adds up to is merely that economics is not, in essence, a descriptive discipline that aims to discover by historical and interpretive methods either why individuals make the economic choices that they do or the "meanings" thereof.)

2. However, even in those social sciences that *do* focus upon social phenomena—cultural anthropology, political science, and sociology are typical cases—there is something more to study than human actions driven by motives, reasons, and socially determined understandings and interactions. Human actions have *consequences* (both intended and unintended), and the study of these might not always require a hermeneutical stance. Theorists such as Popper place a great deal of emphasis on the unintended consequences of human behavior; indeed, these consequences are seen as a major driving force in history and are part of the reason that it is impossible to accurately predict the future. Popper writes, in italics no less, that *"only a minority of social institutions are consciously designed while the vast majority have just grown, as the undesigned results of human actions"* (1961, 65). A little later he stresses the "unavoidable unwanted consequences of any reform" (67). Sometimes Popper uses a simple economic example to illustrate his point: A person who decides to buy a house does not want the market to suddenly go up, but it will be the unintended consequence of his or her entry into the housing market that prices indeed will rise. The study of the laws of economics, and of how much the price of a commodity will change as the number of individuals in the market changes, seems to be a nonhermeneutical scientific activity. (The broader implications of Popper's insight here will be discussed shortly.)

Consider a noneconomic example: A political party in power in a country might adopt a foreign policy for a set of reasons that requires interpretive elucidation, but the unintended consequences of this policy might be that citizens resident overseas have to return, gasoline shortages might break out as a consequence of disruption of overseas supplies, and there could as a result be a rise in the unemployment rate, which in turn might differentially affect members of minority groups, leading to race riots and the eventual overthrow of the party in power! All of these things can be documented, correlated, and studied without venturing into hermeneutics. (This is not to deny, of course, that some of these issues *could* be studied, for other purposes, from a hermeneutical stance. The point is that they *also* can be studied, and are studied in the social sciences, from non-interpretive stances.)

At this point, if not earlier, an objection is likely to surface: The supporter of hermeneutics is likely to protest that, contrary to the claim that has just been made, of course all these research activities inescapably *do* require the adoption of an interpretive position! But it is hard to resist the conclusion that, in making this counterclaim, hermeneuticists have changed the meaning of the key term involved. Perhaps the point can be made in terms of a distinction between a weak (and almost trivial) sense of "hermeneutics" or "interpretation" and a strong sense. In the weak sense, all endeavors that use the medium of language involve interpretation—from following the directions in a recipe, to understanding an advanced lecture in an academic specialty, the language of the writer or speaker must be comprehended. In this weak sense, hermeneutics is like the Scarlet Pimpernel. Unfortunately, though, this point does not do much to advance the interpretivists' strong case; for it does *not* follow that because physicists or chemists or sociologists use (and must understand) language, the epistemology of their disciplines is somehow suspect or weaker than they thought it to be, or that they are humanists, or that without further evidence they must become adherents of a strong hermeneutical position. This strong program arises, not simply because of the universal human use of language, but because of special problems within this umbrella—the problem of understanding written records of human thought or action (or other objectifications of these things, such as monuments or social practices or ritual) from ages or cultures that are different from the interpreter's own; or from problems arising as a consequence of the fact that all people, even those from the investigator's own culture, react not to their environment but to what they understand or interpret their environment to be.

The issues here are central and are worth pursuing in a little more detail. It is a truism that all scientific investigators must understand language and must engage in some degree of interpretive activity in order to communicate with each other and to be able to comprehend the textbooks and research literature of their field (this is what was labeled as the weak sense of hermeneutics). But only under special circumstances do investigators need to make the strong hermeneutical assumption that *the objects they are studying* have *their* behaviors influenced by meanings and understandings and interpretations. Thus, a physicist does not have to suppose that quarks or atoms have interpretations or preunderstandings that influence the ways they react. The crucial point is that while social scientists investigating *some* problems have to take into account their subjects' understandings and so on, there are numerous *other* problems in social science for which this strong hermeneutical program is not relevant.

3. To pick up the main thread of the argument: Even where the center of attention in a social science is an issue that clearly involves interpretation (in the strong sense), there are many related issues that are nonhermeneutical (in this sense). For example, members of a population might vote in a surprising way at an election, and their actions may require culturally sensitive interpretation (in the strong sense) in order to be understood. (This is the sort of thing that is done or that is attempted by "TV experts" on election night.) But other issues arise in understanding elections—such things as the influence of the weather on the turnout of voters, what are the party preferences of younger versus older voters, and what is the turnout of members of various ethnic groups. To gather information on matters such as these, no strong hermeneutical activity has to be engaged in. Certainly on some matters, the voters might have to be asked for information (for example, in an exit poll of young voters to see which candidates they voted for), but what takes place here is quite unlike the strong hermeneutical activity carried out by literary experts interpreting the meaning of Hamlet's soliloquy, or by historians trying to understand some action of Julius Caesar's, or by a political scientist trying to understand why George Bush surprisingly selected Dan Quayle as his running mate in the presidential campaign of 1988.

4. Finally, it should be noted that in many sciences different levels of phenomena are distinguished—as when physical scientists distinguish between the subatomic level, the atomic level, the molecular level, and so on. The relationship between such levels is a highly debated matter: Can phenomena at one level be "reduced to" (i.e., explained in terms of) phenomena and laws at a "lower" level? Although the issues here are exceedingly complex, it seems clear that explanatory principles used at one level do not always apply at higher or lower levels.

The same holds true in the social sciences and applied areas such as educational research; and it seems that supporters of the interpretivist position would be wise to consider the possibility that the use of hermeneutics might be appropriate at some levels but not at others—leaving at least some phenomena to be dealt with by nonhermeneutic social inquiry. It is worth noting here that the influential Chicago sociologist Herbert Blumer—a critic of quantitative sociology and a prominent proponent of the use of qualitative methods—argued that, nevertheless, statistical methods can be useful in studying "those areas of social life and formation that are not mediated by an interpretative process," and they may result in "unearthing stabilized patterns which are not likely to be detected through the direct study of the experience of people" (Blumer, cited in Hammersley 1989, 117). Blumer's happy expression "mediated by an interpretative process" points to precisely what was called earlier the "strong hermeneutical program"—a program that is required in order to make headway with some social investigations but by no means all.

It has already been seen that economics is an example where the focus of attention is often (at least) on the group or aggregate level rather than on the level of the individual human actors—and at the aggregate level there seems to be a place for nonhermeneutical activity. Thomas Schelling (1978, chap. 1) gives a simple noneconomic example that can be adapted here for illustrative purposes. (Artistic license has been exercised, and a different moral has been drawn from the one Schelling highlights—he is interested in the question of the fruitful coordination of the individual and group levels.) When audience members enter large lecture halls, they seat themselves according to their own individual preferences. That is, the choice of seating is an individual action, and the sitter's knowledge, beliefs, desires, and so forth may all play a role; and the choice of seating may also be a symbolic act, such as one of defiance. Furthermore, a person's choice is affected by the choices made by people who entered the hall earlier. To understand why an individual chose a particular seat, some sort of interpretive inquiry might be appropriate. And yet, if one leaves the individual level of analysis and moves to a "higher" level—the level where audiences in halls, rather than individuals, become the unit of analysis—then it might be apparent that there is a generalizable pattern to the filling of halls, the knowledge of which could be helpful to designers of lecture halls, safety experts, and so on. And to discover this pattern, no hermeneutical methods might have to be used; indeed, it can be put even more strongly—hermeneutical methods could hinder the discovery of the pattern rather than help. (Schelling argues, quite rightly, that the motives and understanding of individuals might have to be considered if any attempt is going to be made to change future seating patterns; but if the aim is not to change the pattern but to use knowledge of it in future planning, then understanding the "micromotives" is not necessary for the comprehension of the pattern in the "macrobehavior.")

Another way to phrase the point just made is that not all of the patterns that are found at the macrolevel in society are "objectifications" of meanings and understandings. And reference to Popper can bolster the point: His argument that often what are most important in social affairs are the unintended consequences of action, in effect, makes the point that there are aspects of society that are *not* objectifications of meaning (for, by definition, unintended consequences do not embody *anyone's* intentions or meanings). Hermeneuticists who assume that all social phenomena *are* objectifications have a distorted view of social phenomena—and at the very least they owe us an argument to justify their position. If they concede the point, they still owe us a discussion of the criteria that can be used to distinguish those phenomena that are objectifications of meaning from those that are not (a debt that, up to the present, they have seemed reluctant to discharge).

The conclusion that must be reached, then, is that although many social science inquiries need to be hermeneutical, because meanings and understandings are constitutive of the phenomena under investigation, many inquiries—perhaps very many—do not have to make this strong hermeneutical assumption. For it appears that the image of social science held by interpretivists is too narrow; it is a view that is colored and limited by their own enthusiasms. *This* conclusion is as far-reaching as those reached by the interpretivists, and it has important implications: it weakens the remaining set of conclusions of the interpretivists. Given that their view of social science is recognized as unduly narrow, it becomes more difficult to insert a wedge between social science (as it really is) and the natural sciences and thereby to group the social sciences with the humanities; and thus it becomes more difficult to sustain an epistemological onslaught. But it is to this remaining broad set of far-reaching epistemological conclusions of the interpretivists that the discussion now must turn.

COMMENTARY: THE EPISTEMOLOGICAL CONCLUSIONS

Two elements require discussion here. In the first place, hermeneuticists often attack the epistemology of traditional social science, which they regard as crudely empiricist, or worse, as a form of positivism. Second, there is the matter of the epistemology of hermeneutical social science itself—that is, what do interpretivists want to put in place of the present "inadequate" epistemology, and is their alternative itself adequate?

To deal with first things first:

1. Clearly, it is a travesty to regard all of mainstream social science, even just in the United States, as being neobehaviorist in spirit. (What of the recent developments in cognitive science, social psychology,

ethnomethodology and anthropology, linguistics, political science, organizational theory, and so on?) In the years around the dawn of the new century it is abundantly clear that neither the natural nor the social sciences have to be viewed as being based on logical positivism; an image of science has emerged over the past few decades according to which it is a more open and more speculative endeavor than had previously been thought. (See the discussion of the work of Kuhn, Lakatos, Popper, Feyerabend, and others in Phillips 1987, part A, or the discussion of postpositivist research in Phillips and Burbules 2000.) It is not stretching the truth to suggest that when hermeneuticists attack the epistemology of mainstream social science, what they have in mind is what Popper has called "misguided naturalism" (Popper, in Adorno et al. 1976, 90–91). In effect, they are attacking what by now is recognized widely to be a straw man.

At least one alternative analysis of the epistemology of science has been offered by Popper himself; hermeneuticists like Taylor do not discuss it, for it seems immune from the sort of charges of positivism that they make. (This is not to say that Popper has all of the answers or even some; his work remains a source of controversy—but in some respects it is clearly an advance over positivism.) Popper denies that human knowledge (including, of course, scientific knowledge) is certain by virtue of the fact that it is erected upon unshakable foundations. His books develop the case for a *nonfoundationalist* epistemology—see, for example, his *The Logic of Scientific Discovery, Conjectures and Refutations,* and *Objective Knowledge—* although it should be stressed that Popper is not alone among twentieth-century epistemologists in regarding foundationalism as outdated. (For an example of a psychologist who holds this epistemology, see Weimer 1979; see also the discussion in chapter 6 of the present volume, and Phillips and Burbules 2000.) That is, Popper and many others do not approach the problem of knowledge in terms of seeking the "rock bottom" and indubitable foundations upon which the certain knowledge of science (and of everyday life, so far as it has certain knowledge) is built by a process of induction. Instead, these luminaries stress that *no* knowledge is unshakably certain and that there are *no* absolutely sound foundations for knowledge. Human knowledge is speculative, it projects tentatively into the future; whatever reason we have to believe the things we do believe, it is not because they are based on absolutely sound foundations. Our beliefs, and the considerations that led us to hold them, are always open to the possibility of revision. (Popper has offered an account of the issues surrounding the "rationality of scientific belief" that arise here, but it is not clear that his resolution of all the problems is acceptable. See Newton-Smith 1981. The relevance of Popper's work to the detailed methodology of research in the social sciences and education is discussed in chapter 8 of the present volume.)

Acceptance of a nonfoundationalist approach to epistemology, in which all knowledge is regarded as tentative, has an additional virtue: it allows a softening of the predicament highlighted by Gadamer (who did not see it as a predicament so much as a too often neglected fact of life), namely, the fact that interpretations must inevitably emerge from the interpreter's own historically and culturally based vantage point. For the nonfoundationalist will put interpretations on a par with the rest of human knowledge—they are tentative, hypothetical, and subject to revision with the passage of time. Acceptance of Popper's brand of nonfoundationalism offers an even stronger response to Gadamer: Popper sees little virtue at all in worrying about the origins of our knowledge-claims. He would acknowledge that, of course, they emerge from the inquirer's own grounding in a particular time and place, but that is not relevant when considering their status as knowledge; what is relevant is how the interpretation (or knowledge-claim) is tested and criticized. For although no knowledge is certain, not all knowledge-claims are equal; some are better warranted than others in the sense that they have survived serious critique and strenuous attempts at overthrow. What is sauce for the scientific goose is also sauce for the hermeneutic gander.

2. Even in those areas of social science that must adopt the strong interpretive program, is there such a great epistemological contrast with science? What do hermeneuticists say about the epistemology of their own domain?

Essentially there are two camps here. One, labeled somewhat misleadingly as "subjectivist," holds that interpretations are always open or "undecidable"—there is no such thing as a "correct" interpretation. While an interpreter has to be able to offer considerations in support of his or her interpretation, in the final analysis many (perhaps infinitely many) defensible readings of a text are possible:

> Texts exist only in being read, and every interpretation gives the text a new reading within a framework constituted by the prejudgements of the reader's time, epoch, or culture; thus there is no such thing as "the one text" capable of serving as the touchstone for the correctness of interpretations from different epochs. This position entails undecidability in principle. (Connolly and Keutner 1988, 26)

Stanley Fish is one prominent literary theorist who holds to this view; in an amusing essay, "Is There a Text in This Class?" (1980), he denies there is one textbook in his class, even though all students purchase the same book! There is not one text, because the book becomes a different "text" for every reader.

It is an easy matter to come up with examples of undecidable interpretations from the humanities. And, of course, the hermeneuticists have a point—if in writing *Hamlet,* Shakespeare depicted a believable person, then as greater understanding of humans accumulates over the ages, the Prince of Denmark can be revisited and new insights gleaned. Thus, interpreters in the twentieth century had new resources compared with their counterparts in the nineteenth (in the form of the work of Freud, Rogers, Jung, and so on) and discussion of the character and motivations of Hamlet were enriched. There is no foreseeable end to this process—it will continue so long as human knowledge continues to grow.

But is this really the issue about hermeneutics that concerns us when we consider the nature of the social sciences? The Italian hermeneuticist Emilio Betti, who is regarded as a member of the "objectivist" school, draws a distinction between *meaning* and *significance* that is helpful here. The question of the meaning of some historical text is one issue, and it concerns the meaning "objectified" by the "other" (the historical figure) and intended to be communicated by him or her; the question of the significance of the document is another matter, one that concerns the uses and the meanings that we can impose on the document from our own perspective in time and space—and this is open-ended (Betti 1980, esp. 68–69). The application of this distinction to literature leads to some controversies—Stanley Fish, for example, would deny that Shakespeare's intentions (the "meaning" of *Hamlet*) *are* important, for what is relevant in literature is what readers can impose or construct for themselves (the "significance," which, of course, Fish would prefer to label "meaning"). However, even in the contentious realm of literary theory the distinction itself is useful and provides terminology that serves to highlight the issues at stake.

In those areas of the social sciences where the strong hermeneutical program seems appropriate, even greater light is shed by Betti's distinction. Consider a person in a social setting who performs some act that draws the attention of a social scientist. (The study of individual human action, it will be recalled from the preceding discussion, is one area where the strong hermeneutical program does seem appropriate in the social sciences.) Betti would have us, in effect, recognize at least two sets of issues: (a) what did the *actor* intend? (that is, what was the meaning of the act for the actor?), and (b) what can the social scientist or interpreter say about the act? (that is, what is the significance of the act?). This is not to say that on every occasion *both* of these matters are of interest, but both are *possible* concerns. Of course, Betti is not alone in pointing to these two things; the philosopher Peter Winch (most notably in his well-known dispute with Ian Jarvie) also makes this point—and Winch argued that the issue having priority was the identification or description of the act, which by conceptual necessity involves the determination of the actor's intentions. Only *after* the act has been identified, Winch suggested, might the social scientist be able to go on and say something about it in terms of his or her own disciplinary perspective (assuming that this second phase is relevant to the particular inquiry) (Winch 1970, 249–259; see also Winch 1958).

What can be said, then, about the epistemological underpinnings of this two-stage interpretive process? The second stage is less problematical, relatively speaking. After an act or document is interpreted as being an instance of X (for example, an expression of jealousy), then it is in principle relatively straightforward (though in practice it is not necessarily easy) to judge if it falls within the domain of some theory T. To be an acceptable theory, T would need to have a warrant that is appropriate—if T is a theory of literary criticism, then it would need whatever warrant is required for reputable status within that field, whereas if T is from sociology or economics, then different types of warrants would be appropriate. Within the social sciences, there is a degree of agreement—although it is far from universal—about such matters as whether a theory T is well-warranted (or if not, why not) and whether phenomenon X falls within the domain of T. (This sounds simple enough on the surface, but, of course, there are many complexities; these, however, are subject to lively debate and investigation within the traditional academic domains. Whether or not one judges the epistemological program sketched here to be reasonable depends upon whether one regards epistemology as a total field as viable or as dead. If the reader judges it to be dead, there is not much more to be said, except that this discussion should have ceased being of relevance long ago!)

The epistemological difficulties of the second phase pale into insignificance, however, when compared to the problems faced by the first. How does an interpreter *know* that he or she has correctly identified the intentions of an actor (or has understood the meaning that has been objectified in some social institution)? Neither Winch, Betti, Gadamer, Dilthey, Taylor, nor the rest of the hermeneutical horde has made much

headway here, although many of them certainly espouse the *ideal* of settling on correct interpretations. Betti is an illuminating figure here, for he
explicitly wants to establish an "objective" position; he writes (1980, 57)
of "the demand for objectivity: the interpreter's reconstruction of the
meaning contained in meaningful forms has to correspond to their mean-
ing-content as closely as possible," and this requires "honest subordination" (i.e., subordination of the interpreter to the "other" whose meaning
is being deciphered). Betti criticizes Gadamer's book *Truth and Method* on
the ground that (unintentionally) it undermines the quest for objectivity,
which Gadamer also espouses. Yet the best that Betti can do himself is to
argue that objectivity arises through the strenuous subjective efforts of the
interpreter to intuitively or empathetically understand the meaning of the
other! This hardly seems an adequate means to achieve the goal he set
out in the form of a methodological canon that he labels, somewhat gran-
diosely, as "the canon of the hermeneutical autonomy of the subject":

> By this we mean that meaningful forms have to be regarded as autono-
> mous, and have to be understood in accordance with their own logic of
> development, their intended connections, and in their necessity, coher-
> ence and conclusiveness; they should be judged in relation to the stan-
> dards immanent in the original intention: the intention, that is, which
> the created forms should correspond to from the point of view of the
> author. (Betti 1980, 58)

From the point of view of the present writer, this canon is fine, but
the epistemological resources with which Betti wants to operationalize it
are, to say the least, deficient.

A case can be made—although it can only be sketched here—that for
the purposes of social science, meanings and intentions can be investigated
using traditional scientific methods. That is, it can be argued that there is
no epistemological difference in kind between gaining knowledge about
the other objects of science and gaining knowledge about meanings and
intentions. Many branches of science can provide cases in which the objects of interest are not directly observable or measurable, but in which
their presence (and their nature) is inferred from what is observable. This
process is hypothetical, and it is not guaranteed to be successful; but it is
self-corrective—by a boot-strapping process involving testing and elimination of errors (which is itself a tentative business), the warrants for the
claims that are made about such objects become stronger (though, many
would argue, never so strong that matters become completely settled).

Again, what is sauce for the scientific goose is sauce for the hermeneutic gander: intentions and meanings can be investigated in the same way. Tentative hypotheses can be checked, if somewhat indirectly; empirical evidence *can* have a bearing on hermeneutical issues; and hermeneuticists can—and do—use the hypothetico-deductive method that is common in the natural sciences (Follesdal 1979; see also Hirsch 1967, 264; and Popper 1972, 185).

CONCLUSION

The net conclusion is that although there are some areas of social science and educational research where the strong hermeneutical program is important—where investigators must take account of the meanings and preunderstandings and so on of the social actors being studied—these areas neither exhaust the scope of the social sciences nor does their existence offer any serious grounds on which to hold that the social sciences and related applied fields are more closely allied with the humanities than with the natural sciences. Those who hold the contrary view and claim that there is a similarity in kind with the humanities, or that empirical social science is completely misconceived, need to offer more detailed and stronger arguments and examples.

Nevertheless, the sometimes exaggerated claims of the hermeneuticists have served a very useful purpose: These claims have forced the adherents of traditional "pure" and "applied" social science to broaden their view of the nature of persons—instead of treating people on a par with inanimate objects, they have been forced to regard persons as *actors* located within social and historical webs of meaning. And this constitutes a watershed.

Reprinted, with minor changes, from the *International Journal of Educational Research* 15 (6). Phillips, D. C. "Hermeneutics: A Threat to Scientific Social Science?" © 1991, with permission from Elsevier Science.

3

HOLISTIC TENDENCIES IN SOCIAL SCIENCE

One of the concerns that motivates those who are dubious about the possibility of producing successful naturalistic social science—social science that in some important respect resembles the natural sciences—centers upon the fact that social phenomena appear to be *holistic*. For a society is a whole or a system; its parts interact and mutually determine each other to such a degree that even to call them "parts" is to use a misnomer. Indeed, the parts seem to be *constituted* by the fact that they are parts of a social whole. In this respect a society is like an organism, which also has parts in dynamic interaction; social organicism has been alive and well in Western intellectual thought at least since the time of Hegel, if not for millennia before then (see Phillips 1976).

Thus, for example, while it is true that a state cannot exist without citizens, it also is true that citizens cannot *be* citizens without the state, and, of course, it is the citizens who, in mutual interaction, actually seem to produce at least some of the features of the state. Nor can a legal system exist without judges, litigants, and so on, but, of course, the judges and litigants are made what they are—*judges* and *litigants*—by their role *within* the state's legal system. (Arguably, judges and litigants are not "parts" of the legal system, they are made what they are *by* the legal system.) John Dewey and Arthur Bentley brought out very clearly the holistic nature of such cases; they wrote that, if the example of a loan of money is considered, it is a mistake to proceed as if there were certain discrete elements in terms of which the situation could be explicated—for there are no "primarily separate items" at all. What seem to be "parts" actually only exist within the framework of a larger "whole," and they called for "transactional" logic to deal with such cases:

> Borrower can not borrow without lender to lend, nor lender lend with-
> out borrower to borrow, the loan being a transaction that is identifiable
> only in the wider transaction of the full legal-commercial system in which
> it is present as event. (Dewey and Bentley 1946, 547)

Except for the fact that he antedated Dewey's and Bentley's work by six
decades, William James might have been parodying this passage (and its
underlying Hegelian or transactional logic) when he wrote these skeptical words:

> Husband makes, and is made by, wife, through marriage; one makes
> other by being itself other; everything self-created through its opposite—
> you go round like a squirrel in a cage. . . . *What, in fact, is the logic of these
> abstract systems? It is, as we said above: if any Member, then the Whole Sys-
> tem; if not the Whole System, then Nothing.* (James 1884, 282–283)

Now, the reason why all this is of concern is that—so it is sometimes
argued—the traditional analytic or mechanistic methods of natural science
are incapable of dealing with such holistic phenomena. Thus, according
to researchers Yvonna Lincoln and Egon Guba,

> ontology suggests that realities are wholes that cannot be understood in
> isolation from their contexts, nor can they be fragmented for separate
> study of the parts (the whole is more than the sum of the parts). (Lincoln
> and Guba 1985, 39)

But herein lies a complex tale.

It is clear that, lumped together here, we have a variety of rather tricky
issues: (1) Ontological issues concerning what actually exists, such as the
question—do social systems and so forth exist, or are individuals the only
existents? And are social properties and phenomena merely "fictions,"
shorthand ways of referring to individuals and their properties and activities? Are individual people the "parts" of a "social whole"? (2) Epistemological issues, such as—can we learn about, or explain, the properties of
"social wholes" by focusing only upon their parts? (3) Methodological issues, such as—is it true that analytic methods are incapable of dealing with
relational properties? To muddy the waters further, several other classic
problems seem also to be involved: (4) The problem of emergence—do
new phenomena and new properties, which are not to be found at "lower"
or individual levels of organization, suddenly and unpredictably emerge
as one moves to "higher" (e.g., social) levels of complexity in nature?; and

(5) The problem of reduction—can the phenomena at the higher levels always be explained in terms of (i.e., reduced to) laws and theories that focus upon the lower levels?

The following discussion will have the unenviable task of disentangling these matters; and given the degree of complexity here, it will be easiest to proceed via a series of simple questions and less simple answers.

QUESTION 1: Where in the social or human sciences can we find examples of this sort of holistic thinking?

ANSWER: We met some cases earlier: A whole society or culture, it has been argued, is a holistic system; the elements or "parts" are determined by the role they play within the whole, and because these elements are in "dynamic interrelationship" with each other, if one were to change, then all others would change (and then, of course, the whole—the overall system—would also change, as William James so nicely pointed out). Within societies, such things as organizations can be interpreted as being holistically structured. Some psychiatrists and clinical psychologists have held that the human psyche has a similar "organismic" nature (see Goldstein 1963, for an influential early statement); Albert Bandura's widely discussed "cognitive learning theory" postulates that there is "reciprocal determinism" between a learner's behavior, environment, and inner "personal" factors—that is, these three form a system and mutually determine each other (Bandura 1978; see also Phillips 1987, chap. 7); social psychology lends itself to holistic treatment (Ford and Ford 1987); an organism in relation to its physical environment seems from some perspectives to form a holistic system; and the authoritative *Handbook of Environmental Psychology* surveys many examples from this developing field (Stokols and Altman 1987, chap. 1). And—as a last example—consider an interesting paper on the methodology of educational research, in which the author (who at the time was the editor of an American Psychological Association journal) states that

> The analytic approach mainly assumes that discrete elements of complex educational phenomena can be isolated

for study, leaving all else unchanged. The systemic approach mainly assumes that elements are interdependent, inseparable, and even define each other in a transactional manner so that a change in one changes everything else and thus requires the study of patterns, not of single variables. (Salomon 1991, 10)

In short, holism is at home whenever there is a situation where an "entity" is *constituted* by its relationship to other entities; an entire "science" even developed to explicate the principles involved in such cases—General Systems Theory (see Phillips 1976, chap. 4; the *locus classicus* is Bertalanffy 1969).

QUESTION 2: In the preceding discussion the impression has been given that holism is a unified school of thought; but I am sophisticated enough to realize that matters are rarely so simple. Do all holists believe the same things?—do they all accept the same principles?

ANSWER: Your intuitions are sound. Like many "isms," holism is far from being a simple position with one core notion. There are a variety of doctrines, and individuals differ over which ones they accept and over how they prioritize them in importance.

In an earlier work (Phillips 1976) I identified three groups of holistic theses, which I somewhat unimaginatively called holism 1, 2, and 3. Although my evaluation of these positions has somewhat changed, the typography is still useful for descriptive purposes. *Holism 1*, or *organicism*, is a set of ideas as follows:

1. The analytic approach as typified by the physico-chemical sciences proves inadequate when applied to certain cases— for example, to society or even to reality as a whole.
2. The whole is more than the sum of its parts.
3. The whole determines the nature of its parts.
4. The parts cannot be understood if considered in isolation from the whole.
5. The parts are dynamically interrelated or interdependent. (Phillips 1970; Phillips 1976, chap. 1)

What ties these together is the Hegelian principle of internal relations, or transactional logic, as we shall see momentarily.

Holism 2 is, in essence, an antireductionist position; it is the thesis that a whole or system, even after it has been extensively studied, cannot be explained in terms of its parts. And *holism 3* is the rather unexceptionable view that it is necessary for the advance of certain areas of science to have terminology that refers to wholes and their properties (Phillips 1976, 36-37 and passim).

The thesis advanced in my earlier work—to which I still subscribe—was that many holists jump from one to another of these sets of ideas as if they are synonymous (which they are not), and as if the arguments in support of one of these positions also automatically support the others. But I should note, before we pursue the issues here in more depth, that other writers give somewhat different accounts of holism. David-Hillel Ruben, for example, characterizes what he calls "metaphysical holism" (a general position that he supports) in terms of its opposition to "methodological individualism" (a position that, with important caveats, I tend to support). He writes:

> Metaphysical individualism, then, can involve either of two distinct doctrines: (1) There are no irreducible social entities; (2) There are no irreducible social properties. In both (1) and (2), the word "irreducible" is important, because metaphysical individualists might not wish to deny that Strathclyde County Council existed, or that there was such a property as that of being an alderman. Rather, they might say that neither case involved the existence of some irreducible social entity or property. (Ruben 1985, 3)

Thus, to turn this account around, metaphysical holists believe that there are some irreducible social entities, or some irreducible social properties, or both. In my view this account narrows the focus too much to what I have called holism 2, and Ruben does not mention Hegel at all.

QUESTION 3: This leads nicely to the next question. A number of times in the preceding discussion the point has been made that, according to your account, holists believe that if entities or "parts" are interrelated, then it follows that if one part changes, all the rest change. This was even labeled as "Hegelian or transactional logic." Could this be spelled out further? Why is Hegel so important?

ANSWER: The key concern of the holists, reflected in the theses of holism 1 but which also carries over into holism 2, is the nature of the relationships that are found in social wholes or systems (and, of course, in organic systems as well). I stated in the opening discussion that, in social wholes, the "parts"— which we are in danger of misconceiving when we label them this way—are constituted by their relationships to each other and to the whole in which they are located. Now, Hegel and his followers have discussed the underlying logic here in some detail. The problem, of course, is that Hegel is perhaps the most difficult, the most obscure, of all the major philosophers to read; but despite this—or because of it—he has been extremely influential. And, matters are not made easier by the fact that the topic of relations that concerns us here is far from simple.

Hegel and his followers regarded the whole of reality as forming a *system*, the parts of which were *organically* or *internally related*. Being a system, reality could not be studied successfully by dividing it into parts each of which was studied in isolation. For when a part was isolated from the whole system, its nature changed—it was no longer a part of the whole, and it became an inaccurate guide to the nature of the whole. (To revert to an earlier example, a judge or a litigant, when removed from the context of the legal system, is no longer a *judge* or a *litigant*.) It therefore seemed apparent to the neo-Hegelians that the Hegelian theory of organic or internal relations was directly opposed to the analytic or mechanistic method of the leading natural sciences—a method that they characterized as depending upon isolating elements or units for investigation. (That this view carried over at least to the late twentieth century is illustrated by the earlier quotations from Lincoln and

Guba, and from Salomon—and, I also would argue, by Bandura's work.)

The theory of internal relations is based upon the supposition that entities (such as the parts of a system) are altered by the relationships into which they enter. If A, B, and C are the interrelated "parts" of a system, then A gains properties x and y as a result of its interrelations with B and C, and these "parts" in turn gain relational properties as a result of their interactions within the system. But if A is removed for study, then its relational properties x and y will disappear, and we will no longer have A (because A is made what it is by its properties, and two of these have now been changed). A similar argument can be developed if a new entity, D, is added to the whole or system; A, B, and C will now gain new relational properties, and they will no longer *be* A, B, and C but will have become instead E, F, and G. This is the logic underlying all the theses of holism 1—the parts are dynamically interrelated; the whole system has properties that are greater than the properties of the parts (because outside the system the "sum" of the properties of the "parts" no longer include the relational properties x, y, and so on); and a change in one part changes the whole! In this spirit the twentieth-century human scientist Andras Angyal wrote in a discussion of the logic of systems (he uses the term *aggregate* to refer to a *collection*, a "heap" of entities that are not internally related):

> It should also be kept in mind that "part" means something different when applied to aggregates from what it means when applied to wholes. When the single objects a, b, c, d, are bound together in an aggregate they participate in the aggregation as object a, object b, object c, etc., that is, as lines, distances, color spots, or whatever they may be. When, however, a whole is constituted by the utilization of objects a, b, c, d, the parts of the resulting whole are *not* object a, object b, object c, etc., but α, β, γ, δ . . . (Angyal 1969, 26)

QUESTION 4: As you have just explained it, the principle of internal relations does seem to throw light upon what is taking place within systems. I might play a role within an organization, for example, and key features of this role will depend upon my interrelation to the roles of other individuals within the same system; and if any one person's role within the organization were to change dramatically, all the rest—including my own—would undergo concomitant alteration. Furthermore, I do not have that role when I leave the system! So I'm impressed, but yet I infer from the tone of your discussion that you are critical of Hegel's principle.

ANSWER: Yes—it seems to me that the principle goes too far in suggesting that if *one* relational property of an entity were to change, the entity's entire nature would change—*A* would change to α. In more technical philosophical language, the principle of internal relations requires that *every* relation into which an entity enters determines a *defining characteristic* of that entity. However, modern discussions of relations recognize that entities are not defined by a specific set of relational properties—some relations can change without us wanting to say that the entity has transformed into something entirely different. (That is, we do not accept that all relations determine a defining characteristic; for further discussion, see Phillips 1976, chap. 1.)

A concrete example might be helpful here. Consider the controversial nomination of the conservative Clarence Thomas to the U.S. Supreme Court in 1991 (it may be recalled that there were allegations that he was not a strong legal scholar and that he had engaged in sexist behavior). It was clear from the outset that if Mr. Thomas were to become a member of the Court, he would be adopting a new role within a new system, and thus he would gain new relational properties. But, as the public furor made clear, most people believed that he would take with him into this new role the characteristics that he already possessed—he would not become an entirely different person. These "old" characteristics would remain and would influence his work as a member of the Court. Indeed, even more strongly, people on both sides of the controversy believed that much of his work on the Court could be predicted by the characteristics that he already possessed. Both supporters and detractors of Mr. Thomas agreed about this; the issue was, what *were* the characteristics that he possessed—was he a good enough legal scholar, did he have an acceptable attitude toward civil rights and affirmative action, was he a political and social conservative, was he a decent person or was he sexist, and so on? His supporters, including President Bush, thought that he had admirable characteristics, which he would continue to possess and display upon his becoming Justice Thomas; while his critics thought he was not admirable and would continue not to be admirable when he took on his new role. A strict Hegelian, however, would seem to be committed to opposing this commonsense view and to hold instead that we could not predict, from Mr. Thomas's characteristics before joining the Court, what his likely characteristics would be after taking his seat upon it—for the principle of internal relations holds that he would gain a new defining characteristic upon joining the Court, and so *all* his (interrelated) characteristics would change, and thus he would change from α to A (that is, Justice Thomas would be a different individual from Mr. Thomas)!

QUESTION 5: That was a helpful example, but I still have lingering concerns. Surely in order to understand an entity within a system, and to explain why that entity is the way that it is, we *have* to take into account the fact that the entity *is* part of, or is located within, a system that exerts an influence over all its parts or members?

ANSWER: Of course, but nobody has denied this—certainly, I have never argued against the position you have just outlined. The point is, we can agree about this *without* having to subscribe to the principle of internal relations or accept the "through-and-through" logic (as William James called it) of holism 1. To revert to our previous example, in order to understand what Clarence Thomas will be doing when he becomes Justice Thomas, it is uncontroversial (and indeed verges on being a truism) that we have to understand something about the U.S. legal system and in particular about the Supreme Court and how its various members function. It is quite apparent that only in terms of this sort of understanding can we determine which of Mr. Thomas's prior characteristics are relevant for predicting his behavior as Justice Thomas. (Of course, we might make mistakes here, but making predictions is *never* certain.) But there is nothing mysteriously holistic about any of this, just as there is nothing mysteriously holistic about the fact that to understand the way a chess-piece moves on the board, we have to understand the system of rules that constitute the game of chess!

QUESTION 6: But why, then, do some people hold that the methods of natural science somehow run into serious problems when faced with systems whose parts are interrelated? Why are so-called "holistic phenomena" sometimes touted as blocking the way to developing naturalistic social science?

ANSWER: I'm not sure that I can give you a full answer—why intelligent people believe all the things that they do believe is often something of a mystery! But part, at least, of the answer is that holists—especially supporters of holism 1—have tended to give oversimplified accounts of what they are prone to call the mechanistic or analytic methods of naturalistic science. (Something of this was illustrated in various earlier quotations.)

The fact is that holists do not carefully delineate the "logical" conditions that are necessary for the analysis of the behavior of any complex system, organic or inorganic. Thus, in the first place, holists have not emphasized that the laws or generalizations applicable to the system need to be known (this covers the Justice Thomas case); and second, that the initial conditions of the system have to be described. To refer to the simple example of the behavior of gases in physics (this example is often used by social scientists—see the discussion in chapter 12): To be able to predict the future state of a sample of gas, or to explain the state after it occurs, the relevant gas laws and theories must be known (e.g., Boyle's and Charles's Laws and Kinetic Theory), and so must the initial conditions (the present values of key variables such as pressure, volume, and temperature). Only then is it possible to proceed with precise predictions and explanations. Now, while scientists can state the relevant laws and initial conditions for many physico-chemical systems, it is much more difficult to do so in the biological and human sciences; and opponents of naturalistic methods take any failure in these cases not as a sign of the difficulties that are present, but rather as a sign that the analytic endeavor is *mistaken in principle!*

In other words, the critics conveniently forget the conditions that must be met for successful naturalistic explanation and prediction, and they go on to give an oversimplified and hence invalid account of the analytic method of the natural sciences, which they often label with such epithets as "the simpleminded epistemology of Galileo" (see Boudon 1971, 13). A particularly clear example of this is to be found in Andras Angyal's classic book on personality theory:

> Since the basic idea of the holistic attitude is quite generally known, it will be sufficient here to indicate its meaning with but a single example. Let us draw on a surface a horizontal line A, and an oblique line B in such a manner that the two lines intersect. One can study and describe the properties of line A and those of line B. However, a knowledge of the whole resulting from these two lines, namely of the angle which the two lines form, does not emerge from such a study. The angle is something entirely new, and its properties cannot be derived from the properties of the lines which constitute it. . . . Just as complete information concerning the two lines which form an angle does not give us any knowledge about the angle itself, so knowledge of physiology, psychology, and sociology cannot result in a science of the total person. (Angyal 1941, 2-4)

Thus, by *defining* the method of analysis as neglecting relations, Angyal can reach the conclusion that naturalistic science cannot deal with relations! But by what exercise of the imagination does he conclude that the direction of the two lines, or their spatial juxtaposition, is not to be included in "the complete information" about them? (By a similar feat, no doubt, he would be able to accuse nonholists of holding that complete information about Justice Thomas did not include the fact that he was a Justice of the U.S. Supreme Court.) But, of course, mechanists or analysts (or atomists, as they are sometimes labeled) have always considered such relationships between the parts as vitally important—a point that holists choose to overlook. Edward H. Madden has argued this at length in connection with Gestalt psychologists (who seem to accept the principles of holism 1), and he has shown that in classical Newtonian dynamics (one of the high points of analytical naturalistic science) relational factors such as position and velocity (movement in a given direction) of the various elementary particles were considered to be vital pieces of information (Madden 1962, chap. 1).

To sum up, then, the analytic methods of naturalistic science are not so simple-minded as they are made out to be. Now, I don't want to deny that understanding "organic" wholes or systems is a very complex matter, and sometimes our attempts to explain or to predict the functioning of the "parts" of such systems run into trouble. But one of the strengths of science is that it is self-corrective; if our attempts to understand fail, we go back and do some more work, and then we try again. To say that the methods of naturalistic science are *bound* to fail is to severely underrate them!

QUESTION 7: Perhaps it is time to turn our attention to holism 2. As I recall, those who hold this position believe that properties or characteristics of wholes or systems cannot be explained in terms of the properties of their parts; you identified Ruben as a supporter of this holism, who argues that there are at least some irreducible social entities. Could you explain the antireductionism that is at the core of the issues here?

ANSWER: Reductionism is a doctrine concerning the explanatory relation that holds between various branches of science. A contemporary philosopher explains it as follows:

> For obvious reasons, issues concerning reduction loom large in all the nonphysical sciences (biology, psychology and the social sciences). *It is accepted on all sides that the ultimate constituents of the phenomena discussed by the various special sciences are physical in nature.* Biological organisms, for example, are built up of cells, which in their turn are built up of complex molecules, which may be built up of simpler molecules, and so on, until we reach the level of phenomena that it is the aim of the physical sciences to explain. *But . . . does this mean that theories in the special sciences ultimately reduce to theories in physics?* (Gasper 1991, 546, emphasis added)

To which might be added—does this mean that theories in sociology ultimately reduce to theories in psychology (for individual people are the "constituents," it is often argued, of sociological phenomena); do the theories of psychology ultimately reduce to theories in biology (on the grounds that people are biological organisms); can consciousness and its characteristics be reduced to biochemistry and ultimately physics (as so many natural scientists seem to suppose at the moment); and so on?

Now, opponents of reductionism often treat it as an "all or nothing" position: you are either a reductionist, or you are not. But, of course, this is far too crude; for one can believe that chemistry, for instance, can be reduced to physics, without holding that sociology or psychology can be reduced to biology. The point is that whether or not reduction of one science to another is feasible depends upon the state (and nature) of knowledge in those two branches of science. There was a time when the laws and theories of chemistry could not have been explained in terms of the laws and theories of physics; but with the growth of knowledge, the reduction in this instance did become feasible. At the moment it clearly is not possible to reduce the social sciences to psychology or biology, and there are considerations that suggest (but do not absolutely prove) that this may *never* be possible.

Ruben, for example, argues that individual people are *not* the parts of social wholes; individuals may be *members* of systems or wholes, but that is a different matter (Ruben 1985, esp. chap. 2). If he is right about individuals not being parts, this would mean that we cannot be successful in attempting to explain the properties of social wholes in terms of the properties of individuals—that is, we cannot hope to reduce social science to psychology or biology. John Dupre also makes a point that strengthens this conclusion: In essence he shows that a science at one level will often produce theories in terms of certain entities or abstractions that are quite different from the entities or abstractions involved in the theories at the next "lower" level—in short, the two branches of science might "carve" reality up (or conceptualize it) quite differently. Hence, it will not be possible to reduce the theories of the first science to the second (Dupre 1983). Chemistry can be reduced to physics because the ways they carve up their realities are similar; but the same is not true of the social sciences and psychology, or of much of psychology and biology, or of much of biology (for example, evolutionary biology) and physics and chemistry. I made a point similar to this in chapter 2, when I argued that at the "macro" level in society, there might well be explanatory laws and theories that do not refer to the motives or reasons that the individuals who constitute the society have for acting; and I referred to an example from Schelling (which in chapter 2 I had used for a slightly different purpose) about how audience members fill a lecture hall—each individual has his or her own reasons for sitting in a particular seat, but nevertheless there might be a general descriptive law that covers how the hall gets filled. The philosopher Harold Kincaid put all this very nicely:

> The positive picture of the social sciences I shall defend is one that I believe is generally true of whole-part or macro-micro relations in the sciences. That view holds that wholes are, of course, composed of or exhausted by their parts and do not act independently of them; that, nonetheless, theories at the level of the whole can be confirmed and can explain at that level, without a full accounting of underlying details; that theories at the level of the whole may have only a messy relationship to how microlevel theories divide up the world, thus making macrolevel theories irreducible; that searching for lower-level accounts can be informative as a complement to, but not as a substitute for, more macro investigations. (Kincaid 1996, 142)

Clearly, then, reductionism involves many complex issues; and it should be apparent from the preceding discussion that one's views about it are logically independent of one's position with respect to holism 1—they are not merely two sides of the same coin. And there is one final point that needs to be stressed: wherever one comes down with respect to the controversies about holism 2 or reductionism makes no difference to the general issue that we are pursuing—the possibility of having a naturalistic social science. For, although in many branches of science a reductionist ideal is reasonable, in many other reputable branches of science it is more problematical.

Thus, whether a science holds reductionist pretensions or not cannot be taken as an indication of its viability *as* a science. The fact that reduction does not (at present) seem a reasonable goal for the social sciences does not indicate that they are any less *sciences*—just as the fact that evolutionary biology does not seem to be reducible does not make it any the less a viable natural science!

QUESTION 8: Holism 3 still remains to be discussed; earlier, you seemed to dismiss it rather quickly as being unproblematical. What is it, precisely?

ANSWER: As branches of science uncover new phenomena, suitable terminology—and often new concepts—have to be devised. When Röntgen discovered a new form of radiation in his laboratory, he called them "X rays"; and when particle physicists discovered new orders of particles with hitherto unknown properties, they coined names such as "quarks," "charm," and "color." Similarly, investigators studying systems of dynamically interrelated parts have argued that special terminology and special concepts are required here. Arthur Koestler, to cite one example, was particularly eloquent in arguing that systems are integrated hierarchies, in which the "parts" have a feature that hitherto had not been noticed—they are *holons:*

> The point first to be emphasized is that each member of this hierarchy, on whatever level, is a sub-whole or *"holon"* in its own right. . . . They are Janus-faced. The face turned upward, toward the higher levels, is that of a dependent part; the face turned downward, towards its own constituents, is that of a whole of remarkable self-sufficiency. (Koestler 1979, 27)

Now, whatever one makes of Koestler's interesting new concept of entities that are both parts and wholes, it surely seems uncontroversial that as sciences progress, they *will* have to advance conceptually and terminologically. And many remarks of people who seem to be holists can be interpreted as nothing more than a very reasonable plea to recognize the new phenomena that the study of systems qua systems has turned up. But again, there is nothing here that threatens the possibility of producing social science (or even a science of systems) that is naturalistic.

QUESTION 9: I'm not sure whether this next question—which is my last—is a red herring or not. I have noticed that the words *holism* and *holistic* have been used in a variety of ways in the contemporary literature. One common usage, which clearly is different to—and less specialized than—the senses outlined in the foregoing discussion of holism 1, 2, and 3, is in the health sciences, where there are discussions of holistic medicine, holistic treatment, and the like. Here it is clearly the intention to refer to "the whole person," but there is no desire to conjure up troublesome Hegelian issues of relations of parts to wholes. But another common context is more confusing for me—indexes of contemporary works in philosophy of science frequently have entries on "semantic holism." Where does this fit into the picture you have given of the various types of holism?

ANSWER: Semantic holism pertains not to social or organic systems but to symbolic or linguistic systems. Nevertheless, it is of wider interest than this might imply—for example, a good case can be made that semantic holism is very relevant to discussions of the nature of theories in science—for scientific theories, of course, are symbolic systems. Thus, semantic holism is tied up with the assessment of Thomas Kuhn's notorious thesis of incommensurability between paradigms in science (Kuhn 1962)—a thesis that has been particularly influential in the social sciences (Phillips 1987, chap. 3). And it also is involved in discussions of whether or not we can understand different cultures (and translate their beliefs into our own terms). Furthermore, semantic holism certainly does raise many of the issues that were discussed earlier.

To start at the beginning: Dating back a long time in philosophy of science, there has been a problem about the meaning of the terms that appear in scientific theories. For, as was realized by the logical positivists and others (see chapters 9 and 12), these terms cannot be fully translated into observation language—for example, there is no simple set of observation statements that is equivalent to "there are electrons moving along this wire" or "the electron has a complex structure consisting of . . . " One way out of the problems here is to deny that statements about theoretical entities such as electrons are literally meaningful (Skinner, to cite an example from the human sciences, sometimes gives the impression that this is his position about "inner psychological variables"); it is possible to argue that theoretical statements have the status of *instruments* that are useful shorthand and that can aid in calculations and making predictions, but that are not to be taken as giving an account of actual reality. Another stratagem is to hold that theoretical terms gain some degree of meaning because of the *role* that they play within a theory—they have "systematic import." In the writings of such diverse philosophers as Hempel and Quine (see chapters 6, 9, and 12), scientific theories are seen as *webs* or *networks*, wherein each theoretical term is caught up in a number of complex relations to other terms, thereby (and insofar) gaining meaning. This, essentially, was the position adopted by many of the logical positivists, whose verifiability theory of meaning (see chapter 9) raised the problem for them of the status of theoretical terms. And, in essence as well, this is semantic holism; for, as described by Fodor and Lepore, this is the

> doctrine that only whole languages or whole theories or whole belief systems *really* have meanings, so that the meanings of smaller units—words, sentences, hypotheses, predictions, discourses, dialogues, texts, thoughts, and the like— are merely derivative. (Fodor and Lepore 1992, x)

Now, semantic holism has the following interesting consequence, one that exactly parallels a central thesis held by all those enamored of holism 1: namely, that if one element of a linguistic or theoretical system undergoes change, or if a new element is added to the system, then all the other interrelated "parts" of the system will undergo change (for, everything in the systemic net will now be related to this new element, and hence the "systematic import" will have changed—it will be recalled that this is what James meant when he said "if any Member, then the Whole System"). In terms of a scientific theory, this means that if a theoretical term is changed, or deleted, or added, all the other terms in the theoretical system will undergo change in meaning. The philosopher Newton-Smith refers to this as the thesis of "radical meaning variance," and he shows how this leads to Kuhn's stance on the incommensurability of different paradigms:

> Consequently, both so-called theoretical terms and so-called observational terms are treated as being implicitly defined by the theory in which they occur. In this event Newton and Einstein cannot even communicate about the observational consequences of their theories. . . . [for] they mean something different by "mass" . . . and so on. . . . Given this thesis that in theory change the meanings of all terms change . . . all theories will be incommensurable and there will be no possibility of making rationally grounded theory choice. (Newton-Smith 1981, 12)

Several further points need to be made with reference to semantic holism. First, it is not recognized by most of those in the social sciences who have been greatly stimulated by Kuhn that they owe a great debt to the logical positivists and their theory about the meaning of theoretical terms; on the contrary, admirers of Kuhn usually think of themselves as dyed-in-the-wool opponents of positivists! Second, while, of course, it may raise our suspicions to be reminded of the affinity between semantic holism and the views of the logical positivists, it will hardly do as a "knock-down" criticism; but it would seem that a fair bit of (negative) weight ought to be given to the counter-intuitive consequence of this holism that two "rival" theories are supposed to be incomprehensible to each other's adherents. Furthermore, we are not forced to accept semantic holism for lack of alternatives, as there *are* other theories available concerning the meaning of theoretical terms. Newton-Smith, for example, supports the so-called "causal theory" of meaning that derives from the work of Hilary Putnam (see Newton-Smith 1981, chap. 7). According to this theory, theoretical terms get introduced into science as a means of referring to causes of phenomena—*electron*, for example, refers to whatever entity or mechanism it is that is causally responsible for certain observable phenomena such as wires getting hot when connected to batteries. When our theories about electricity change, the term *electron* does not change meaning—as Kuhn and the semantic holists suppose—for it still refers to the purported cause of the phenomena; what *does* change is the account we give of the properties or nature of this causal entity, the electron.

But, as a last word, I would stress that the various types of holism are logically independent. One might accept, or reject, holism 1 with respect to social phenomena, without being committed to a position with respect to semantic holism; and one's views on these matters do not entail a commitment to a particular stance about the possibility or impossibility of the reduction of the social sciences to some "lower level" science (holism 2). And—most important of all—the viability of pursuing a naturalistic program in the social sciences does not seem to be threatened by any of the things we have discussed.

4

NARRATIVE RESEARCH:
TELLING STORIES ABOUT STORIES

It is tempting to study important social activities such as teaching by collecting and ruminating upon the narratives told by those who are engaged in the activities; but such research is often based upon faith. In *The Devil's Dictionary*, Ambrose Bierce defined "faith" as "belief without evidence in what is told by one who speaks without knowledge of things without parallel" (quoted in Rogers 1983, 173); although narrative research had not become popular as a mode of social science and educational research in Bierce's day, his definition of "faith" was prescient. It is the theme of the following discussion that too many (although, of course, not all) researchers who make use of narratives as sources or data do not pay enough attention to the issue of evidence or warrant—in practice, they rely too heavily on faith, they trust too much that those who provide the narratives that they collect know what they are talking about and are talking "straight." (At the outset of this discussion I shall ignore the distinction that is drawn in the literature between analysis of narratives—which is what I am mainly talking about—and narrative analysis; see Polkinghorne 1995.)

An important train of thought that lies behind the rise in interest in narrative is the following: It has been stressed in recent years that one reason human activities are meaningful is that they can be seen in narrative terms—we make our own actions, and the actions of our fellows, meaningful by presenting a descriptive narrative. Thus,

> People ordinarily explain their own actions and the actions of others by means of a plot. In the narrative schema for organizing information, an event is understood to have been explained when its role and significance in relation to a human project is identified. This manner of explanation is different from that favored by logico-mathematical

reasoning, where explanation is understood to occur when an event can be identified as an instance of an established law or pattern of relationship among categories. (Polkinghorne 1988, 21)

Jerome Bruner would add to this account the insight that the culture to which an individual belongs provides the characteristic categories and concepts in terms of which that person will explain his or her own actions and the actions of others—"he is jealous," "she is angry," "he does not understand," "I am ambitious," and so on. These concepts constitute the categories of "folk psychology" that many researchers mistakenly try to replace with talk of "deeper" cognitive mechanisms and the like:

> All cultures have as one of their most powerful constitutive elements a folk psychology, a set of more or less connected, more or less normative descriptions about how humans "tick." ... We learn our culture's folk psychology early, learn it as we learn to use the very language we acquire and to conduct the interpersonal transactions required in communal life. (Bruner 1990, 35)

And he notes that

> Antimentalistic fury about folk psychology simply misses the point. The idea of jettisoning it in the interest of getting rid of mental states in our everyday explanations of human behavior is tantamount to throwing away the very phenomena that psychology needs to explain. (Bruner 1990, 14)

As a result of this kind of support, in a short period of time the use of narratives has become fashionable among researchers. As Kathy Carter has noted,

> Story has become, in other words, more than simply a rhetorical device for expressing sentiments about teachers or candidates for the teaching profession. It is now, rather, a central focus for conducting research in the field. (Carter 1993, 5)

Carter goes on to identify what various researchers have claimed to be the virtues or strengths of narratives; and she states that, in general, these views about narrative "ring very true" (Carter 1993, 8). But, deep into her paper, she recognizes that use of narratives provokes "a very serious crisis for our community" (Carter 1993, 8). One of the aspects of this crisis that she touches upon a couple of times in her remaining pages is the one that has been of central concern to me:

> an extreme view of teachers' voice endows their stories with an authenticity that is simply unwarranted. . . . Stories, including those told by teachers, are *constructions* that give a meaning to events and convey a particular sense of experience. They are not videotapes of either reality, thought, or motivation. Thus, we cannot escape the problems of veracity and fallibility in our work by making special claims for teachers' constructions of their practice. (Carter 1993, 8)

She adds, a little later, that it is difficult to tell if a particular story that is told is a reflection of the facts of the case or whether it has been shaped (by the storyteller) in order to meet the demands of "narrative coherence" (i.e., in order to make it a *good story*, according to the informal rules of storytelling that are current in our society) (Carter 1993, 9). Her words serve as a nice segue into the next sections, where the problems she points to are pursued in more depth.

HOW ISSUES OF EPISTEMOLOGICAL WARRANT ARE HANDLED

A researcher who has been convinced by Bruner and others, and who has decided to pursue use of the/a narrative method in order to understand the actions of individuals who are of interest (teachers or students or school administrators, for example), will eventually come face-to-face with the issue: "Will any old story suffice?" In traditional science, it is *not* the case that "any old explanation will suffice"; and although from time to time the criteria for judging the adequacy of explanations has been a controversial matter, nevertheless, various "communities of practice" within science usually reach a workable degree of consensus about what the criteria of adequacy are—and why, indeed, these are the criteria at all. Similarly, it might be expected that members of the "community of narrative practice" have some shared understanding of criteria of adequacy or of epistemological warrant. And they *do*—although it will be argued in the following section that the criteria they claim are important are hardly unproblematic. But before turning to critique, it is necessary to engage in some exposition of their views. (I will focus only upon one narrow but nonetheless vital issue; for a broader bibliography of work centered around narratives, see Carter 1993.)

In his book published in 1990, Bruner himself has little to say about the form that research, or "disciplined inquiry," should take in these new realms—how narrative explanations are to be *warranted or assessed as knowledge* is an issue that is not specifically addressed. He makes one very brief remark to the effect that verifiability in the hard-nosed positivist sense is not appropriate, and he states that plausibility is a key notion (Bruner 1990, 108). He also has a suggestive page or so critiquing the assumption made by many psychologists that what a person *does* is more important and revealing, and is scientifically more significant, than what that person *says* about what he or she is doing (Bruner 1990, 16). But that is all. In an earlier work published in 1986, Bruner also says little on this topic that moves beyond the level of vague generality; narrative is a "different way of knowing" than science, which prizes "well-formed argument" (Bruner 1986, 11), for in narrative what is valued is not truth but "verisimilitude" (which, as we shall see in a moment, was a notion that was taken up by later writers). A story, whether allegedly true or allegedly fiction, "is judged for its goodness as a story by criteria that are of a different kind from those used to judge a logical argument as adequate or correct" (Bruner 1986, 12). Good narrative leads to "good stories, gripping drama, believable (though not necessarily 'true') historical accounts" (Bruner 1986, 13). And, in a significant passage, he stresses:

> Physics must eventuate in predicting something that is testably right, however much it may speculate. Stories have no such need for testability. Believability in a story is of a different order than the believability of even the speculative parts of a physical theory. If we apply Popper's criterion of falsifiability to a story as a test of its goodness, we are guilty of misplaced verification. (Bruner 1986, 14)

Donald Polkinghorne adds very little in his book published in 1988 (one of his later works will be discussed in detail further on); in the only entry on validity he states that:

> Narrative research, by retaining an emphasis on the linguistic reality of human existence, operates in an area that is not limited by formal systems and their particular type of rigor. The results of narrative research cannot claim to correspond exactly with what has actually occurred—that is, they are not "true." . . . Research investigating the realm of meaning aims rather for verisimilitude, or results that have the appearance of truth or reality. . . . Narrative research, then, uses the ideal of a scholarly con-

sensus as the test of verisimilitude rather than the test of logical or mathematical validity. (Polkinghorne 1988, 176)

Clearly, these accounts raise more questions than they settle.

In a recent article on "teacher research," Lytle and Cochran-Smith define research as "systematic, intentional inquiry," which they say is based upon Stenhouse's definition in terms of "systematic, self-critical enquiry"; but it is noteworthy that although they discuss "systematic" and "intentional" at greater length, they do not comment at all on "self-critical"—a significant sin of omission that enables them to bypass altogether the issue of the validity of the findings of teacher-researchers (Lytle and Cochran-Smith 1990, 84). These authors include teachers' journals, essays, oral inquiries, and classroom inquiries as items in their typology of teacher research (and, of course, many of these have a narrative form). Jardine, in discussing interpretation of narratives, seems to reject the notion that there might be a true version and instead holds that the aim of interpretation is to "playfully explore what understandings and meanings" the particular narrative "makes possible" (Jardine 1992, 56). He specifically asks, "How do I *know* that this reading I have given of this instance is reliable?"; his answer is not phrased as lucidly as the question itself, but in essence it is this: "Put more sharply, for an interpretation to engage, the text and I must be allowed to 'play.' . . . The interpretation is thus unavoidably linked to *me*" (Jardine 1992, 57). But the fact that you can "play" with an interpretation of a story hardly justifies the claim that the interpretation, or the story, passes muster *epistemically*—for, clearly, many works of sheer fantasy can stimulate "play."

In the *Educational Researcher*, Connelly and Clandinin explicitly raise the question "What makes a good narrative?"; their answer, in essence, is that we have to go "beyond reliability, validity and generalizability," although they pass the buck by stating that the specific criteria are currently "under development in the research community" (Connelly and Clandinin 1990, 7). They suggest that a good narrative is one that can be lived vicariously by others; they advocate use of the criteria of adequacy and plausibility, and they cite (apparently approvingly) Spence's dictum that "narrative truth" consists of "continuity," "closure," "aesthetic finality," and a sense of "conviction" (Connelly and Clandinin 1990, 8). In similar vein, they affirm that "time and place, plot and scene, work together to create the experiential quality of narrative" (Connelly and Clandinin 1990, 8).

In his book on the nature of "human science" (a phenomenologically and hermeneutically oriented narrative endeavor), Max van Manen holds a similar position:

The aim is to construct an animating, evocative description (text) of human actions, behaviors, intentions, and experiences as we meet them in the lifeworld. . . . Those entering the field of human science research may need to realize that the very meanings of "knowledge," "science," "theory," and "research" are based upon different assumptions. (van Manen 1990, 19-20)

Finally, in an essay also in *Educational Researcher,* Thomas Barone advocates the widespread use of narratives or stories, particularly about schoolpeople (and he even suggests, in a "throw-away" remark, that it is about time that novels were accepted as doctoral dissertations in the field of educational research). He writes, in a section on "quality control" (which we must assume is his locution for such things as "reliability" and "validity"):

This enhanced professionalism will require the educational research community to maintain quality control over its stories. Accessibility, compellingness, and moral persuasiveness will serve as criteria for judging the professional worth of educational stories. All three will be present in a good popular narrative. Accessible and compelling stories that fail to offer empirical, nonstereotypical portraits of schoolpeople will not be judged professionally worthy. On the other hand, neither will a carefully researched, morally sensitive story that is dull, malformed, and unattractive to a broad audience. (Barone 1992, 21)

It is high time to turn to some attractive, well-formed, and far from dull critical commentary directed at these accounts of what constitutes an adequate narrative for the purposes of research.

CRITIQUE: WHY NARRATIVES NEED
TO MEET EPISTEMIC CRITERIA

The foregoing material raises many issues requiring critical comment. To keep the discussion manageable, it will be set out in the form of a number of points.

a. At the outset it must be acknowledged that there is much in this literature that is admirable. Of particular importance is the point hammered home by Bruner (assisted, of course, by many others) concerning the central role of folk psychology in shaping how individual members of a culture understand each other—and themselves. Although it is an area still shrouded in controversy (see, for a critique of folk psychology, Stich 1985), many of us regard it as incontrovertible that we impute motives and beliefs and values and knowledge to our friends (and even to strangers), and we try to understand their actions (and our own) by composing narratives in these terms. And we not only *try*—we succeed, or at least we *believe* we succeed (for when we have constructed a narrative that fulfills an explanatory purpose, we very often rest content and stop our inquiries).

The issue that concerns me is: What follows from this? Are things like "adequacy," "plausibility," and an engaging "plot" themselves adequate criteria for judging narrative explanations or accounts? What role is left for scientific inquiry here? It is worth noting in this context that anthropologist Clifford Geertz, a clear supporter of "interpretivism" and an opponent of "positivism," is unhappy with these criteria; he points out that a "paranoid's delusion or a swindler's story" have coherence, they hang together, and they are put forward with great assurance! (Geertz 1973, 18). As a scientist, Geertz wants more than this. But the point can be put even more strongly: There are very serious grounds of concern with respect to using a criterion like plausibility. Sir Cyril Burt could tell a plausible story about his research on the intelligence of twins reared apart (which later turned out to be in large part fraudulent); alchemists had a story that many regarded as plausible, and present-day racists convince many about the reasonableness of their narratives; Freudians can tell a plausible tale about the etiology of autism in any particular case (and, indeed, here they also have an intriguing plot about parental sexual repression and so on).

b. Whenever a narrative explanation for some phenomenon/event is considered, a difficulty immediately surfaces. For it is clear that *many rival narratives* can be devised by an individual to account for a given action, just as, in the natural sciences, many rival hypotheses can be invented to account for any finite body of data. And if there are many, the issue will often arise as to which one—or which ones—of the alternatives is or are true.

I have chosen the language here carefully, for it is not *always* the case that we need to know which narrative is true; sometimes we are content to hit upon a serviceable or satisficing explanation for a person's behavior, and we accept the first one that surfaces and we then get on with our lives without pushing the matter further—for as indicated previously, we might feel that we have achieved sufficient understanding. And as a further complication there can be several narratives about the same matter that are all true; for example, an account of a car accident that focuses upon the physics of the incident can be true, but so can an account that focuses on the legality or otherwise of the driver's actions. In these latter cases the different true narratives are "orthogonal" to each other, to borrow a graphical term.

It is worth stressing that in many cases the importance of a narrative or story does not depend upon its being true. Fairy stories amuse and educate and often teach important morals; legends inspire and sometimes promote national or ethnic cohesion; hasidic tales instruct. A soldier may be inspired by a propaganda story about the enemy and be led to act in a heroic manner; and a teacher might be inspired by a psychologist's story about her students and be led to take heroic action in the classroom. (These latter examples are somewhat borderline, for the teacher and the soldier *believe* the stories to be true, even though they may not be; but only the grossly unsophisticated take a fairy story or a legend to be true. Where a false story is passed off as being true, we speak of ideology and the production of false consciousness, and this is not intended as a compliment. But the point remains: To be useful or effective or of instructional value, it might be quite irrelevant whether the story is true or not.)

But clearly there are times when it *is* important to ascertain the *correct* narrative or narratives. It is hard to give a precise definition of such occasions; they are likely to be occasions when something of significance hangs in the balance, when further action or intervention is called for, when policy is about to be made, and so on. The point is that if action is taken upon the basis of an incorrect narrative, then, even if disaster does not always ensue, at least it will be likely that we will end up with consequences that we neither anticipated nor desired—we are more likely to act successfully if we act on the basis of correct information. Some simple examples will serve to make this issue clear: A newly baked apple pie has disappeared, and the likely culprit—the only child in the house—has offered a narrative that purports to explain the mystery; but if the child is lying, we wish to take the opportunity to teach a moral lesson. A patient in therapy has given a narrative to explain why she has a particularly destructive relationship with her mother; the future course of the therapy hinges upon knowing whether this account is true or not (and not simply whether or not the patient currently believes the story to be true). An inspector from the Internal Revenue Service is interviewing a businessman about why he failed to declare certain income on his tax return; whether or not the businessman is prosecuted may depend upon whether or not his story is judged to be true. A teacher has provided a researcher with an account of why he did certain things during a successful calculus lesson; if the researcher swallows the story, she might write it up and publish it in a "case study" book on "teacher thinking" that will be used in the training of new teachers. (There is another, and possibly more important, issue in this last example; the researcher might sometimes want to know if the actions the teacher performed, or claimed to perform, were causally efficacious in producing student learning—to which end the researcher will have to go *beyond* the narrative and study its match, or the interaction of elements cited in the narrative, with the world.)

In each of these examples, the narrator of the story could have given a number of quite different narratives; and even though only one narrative was presented in each case, the most likely alternatives probably would spring to the mind of the tax inspector, or the hungry parent, or the therapist—for these people would have had to face the question: "Was the story's narrator (the child, the patient, or the taxpayer) presenting me with the *correct* narrative?" One would hope that the educational researcher would not be the most naive of the bunch and would not swallow the teacher's story without this type of critical reflection!

Although the point probably is clear enough at this stage, one last example is worth citing—it is one that Gilbert Ryle used but that the anthropologist Clifford Geertz takes much further (Geertz 1973, chap. 1). A young man at a party notices an attractive young woman winking at him and takes appropriate action. What an embarrassment if it turns out she was only blinking! The man in question needs to be sure that his narrative "The woman is winking at me" is the *correct* narrative. Geertz rejects the view that the meaning of such things is *private;* and although we cannot have absolute certainty here, neither are we forced into a subjectivist position:

> I have never been impressed by the argument that, as complete objectivity is impossible in these matters (as, of course, it is), one might as well let one's sentiments run loose. As Robert Solow has remarked, that is like saying that as a perfectly aseptic environment is impossible, one might as well conduct surgery in a sewer. (Geertz 1973, 30)

c. Now, it does not seem adequate to say that such important narratives are acceptable if they have an enticing plot or if they are well-formed or coherent. For the point is that a narrative can have these features and still not be true. (As I know from long-ago personal experience, a child who has illegally appropriated a pie can be extremely inventive in devising a well-formed and enticing story that can deflect the blame elsewhere!) To put it bluntly, these features are *not epistemically relevant*. And when a lot hinges upon whether or not a narrative is true (recognizing the point made earlier, namely, that this is not always the case), we are not well-served by criteria that lack epistemic relevance. Writers on the use of narrative systematically neglect the fact that the acceptance of a narrative can have important practical consequences and that on some (but by no means all) occasions it is important that the narrative be true; rather, they seem to regard acceptance of a narrative as hinging only upon whether or not the story produces a warm positive feeling of familiarity or comfort—and they neglect the fact that, for such a "psychological" purpose, an untrue narrative may be just as functional as a true one.

The same case can be made against the criterion of "credibility" or "plausibility" that we saw earlier was advocated by supporters of narrative inquiry. The fact that a story is credible tells us nothing—*absolutely* nothing—about whether it is true or false (or even a good or bad story, for each category contains both credible and incredible examples). For a true story might be credible, or it might be incredible; and similarly for a false story. Once again, credibility, or lack of it, is not an epistemically relevant criterion.

As a test, consider the following story: An observer, walking down a high school corridor that has little traffic, notices through the glass door of a history classroom that the teacher is sitting and apparently dozing at the front table, while at the back of the room some of the students have a crowing rooster on one of the desks. Presuming that this is a pretty incredible tale, can one tell, *from this*, whether it is true or not? The truth or otherwise of the story depends upon whether the events it recounts actually happened, and not upon any factors internal to the story, nor upon any degree of psychological impact or degree of surprise that the story has upon the reader. (The reader with sufficient motivation will find whether or not the story is true in an explanatory addendum at the end of the chapter.)

d. At this point another matter needs to be clarified. Various advocates of narrative were cited earlier as making use of the notion of "verisimilitude," and occasionally in this context Karl Popper's name has been mentioned. Unfortunately, there seems to be complete misunderstanding of Popper's work on verisimilitude and its significance. Supporters of narrative inquiry have said that a narrative must have verisimilitude, in the sense that it must have "the appearance of truth or reality" (Polkinghorne 1988, 176). It should be clear, in the light of the previous argument, that this will not do—for a false story can *appear* to be true. (If all false stories appeared to be false, and only true stories appeared to be true, it would be an epistemological blessing. But as the history of virtually any field of human inquiry bears witness, this is sheer fantasy.)

Popper presented a detailed theory wherein verisimilitude was regarded as *approximation to* or *closeness to* truth. (This is an entirely different matter from *appearing to be* true, for clearly a plausible error also appears to be true. To the men and women of medieval times, it appeared to be true that the Earth was flat—a viewpoint that had very little verisimilitude, for the Earth is not even close to being flat!) In Popper's view, although science may never attain the truth, it can aim at getting closer to it; the process, of course, is one involving the testing of our hypotheses and the rejection of those that turn out to be inadequate, and the replacing of them by hypotheses that are better in the sense of being able to survive new tests (Popper 1985, chap. 14; see also the discussion in chapter 8 of this present volume). Unfortunately, it turns out that there are technical problems with Popper's theory of verisimilitude—it cannot be true! But it may be close to the truth. (For an account of these problems, and a suggested revised account of verisimilitude that preserves Popper's sense of the term, see Newton-Smith 1981.) At any rate, Bruner's remark that the demand that narratives be tested or warranted in some rigorous way is "misplaced verification" (Bruner 1986, 14) is itself misplaced. Those narratives that need to be true (or close to the truth) in order to be accepted and acted upon *must* have faced—and survived—some epistemically relevant test or examination.

e. To return to issues raised by the earlier examples of narratives that might not be true: I do not want to suggest that we are always faced by people who deliberately lie when they present us with narratives to explain some actions or states of affairs. In the cases of the child and the pie, and the businessman and his taxes, it might well happen that deliberately false stories are put forward; but in the cases of the patient in therapy and the teacher of calculus, it might well happen that the individual concerned *believes* that the narrative he or she is telling is true, even when it is not. As the ethnographer Renato Rosaldo points out, when discussing the accounts given by indigenous informants in a culture, "natives can be just as insightful, sociologically correct, axe-grinding, self-interested, or mistaken as ethnographers" (Rosaldo 1987, 93).

Bruner, for one, in places seems to suggest that if the narrative-teller believes what he or she is relating, then the story is acceptable. And if he *is* saying this, then Bruner is both right and wrong. Bruner is right in the following sense: People do not act on the basis of what is true, they act according to what they *believe* to be true. I might be in need of some ready cash, and I might believe that you are both rich and generous, so I approach you for a stake. You, being poor but generous, might be startled by my action—how could I possibly ask someone as poor as yourself for such a large loan? My action is not explained by the true state of affairs—your poverty—but by my (mistaken) belief about the state of affairs, namely, my belief that you are rich. So, if what a narrative inquirer is concerned about is to understand conscious, voluntary human action, that inquirer must ascertain the beliefs of the actor—that is, the beliefs that the actor truly holds (but they need not be beliefs that are true). It is important to note the proviso here—"beliefs that the actor truly holds"—for acceptance of this will entail that the researcher cannot always accept at face value the narrative that the actor provides. (One reason for such caution is discussed a little later.)

But Bruner is wrong in this sense: A person might produce a narrative that he or she genuinely believes to be true and that he or she believes can explain some action that this person has recently performed. In other words, the narrator might not be lying. However, it is possible for the narrative to be mistaken, that is, it is possible for the narrative not to be true. An example that occurred in one of my own classes a couple of years ago will serve to illustrate the point. A visiting lecturer—a psychiatrist—put several students under hypnosis and instructed them that later in the lecture, even though they would be out of their trances, they would stand and perform certain embarrassing actions (such as barking loudly like a dog). Not only did the students do these things, they all were able to offer a narrative to explain why they had acted this way! But, of course, their narratives were not true, for none of them mentioned posthypnotic suggestion.

Consider another case, one of a type that is very common in the social sciences, although it is somewhat more controversial: An anthropologist doing fieldwork might elicit a narrative explanation from a native informant about some exotic custom in the host culture, and the informant might truly believe this "emic" account that he is giving; but the anthropologist's social science knowledge might suggest a much more adequate "etic" account. (Think of how we would try to explain some strange custom in our own society; most of us could come up with some account, and maybe even a believable account, but an expert in social customs and social history might come up with the *correct* account—which might, of course, be quite unfamiliar to many of us whose custom it is!) There are many cases in the social sciences (including educational research) where the beliefs—and resulting narratives—of the individuals concerned are not particularly insightful or causally enlightening. But it should be stressed here, and again, that whether we want to push to discover the true account will depend upon what our research purpose is. If we want to know what a person believes that makes her behave in a certain way, it might be of little consequence to us that her key beliefs are unfounded (although probably it remains crucial that *our* research narrative of such a case *is* true); but if we are planning therapeutic intervention to change her behavior, it might be very relevant to discover, as well, whether or not her motivating beliefs are true or not. Narrative researchers seem cavalierly to reject the latter situations, where the truth of narratives is relevant, and to reduce all situations to the former category where truth is irrelevant.

Although examples should not be multiplied beyond necessity, there is another case that is illuminating and that will return us to the main theme: Once, in a debate with the psychotherapist Carl Rogers over the nature of human psychology and the inadequacy of behaviorism, B. F. Skinner "conditioned" or "shaped" the behavior of Rogers by leaning forward and showing intense interest whenever Rogers performed the desired action. (My memory is failing, but I think it was putting his hand in his pocket.) At any rate, within a few minutes Rogers was constantly acting in the manner Skinner wanted! If he had been questioned about why he was doing this, I think it not at all unlikely that Rogers would have given a narrative that he believed but that clearly was erroneous. The point of this example, and of the cases of hypnosis and emic/etic explanation, is that we do not always truly know why we act the way we do, although we usually have strongly held beliefs about why we are acting that way. For some purposes, a social science investigator only needs to know what these beliefs are, but on other (important) occasions, as argued earlier, it is necessary to uncover the *real* reasons. Furthermore, although it is dubious that individuals always (or even often) understand the roots of their own actions, it is nevertheless true that humans have an enormous capability to devise narratives that can be believed to be true—tall stories as well as short ones are easy to come by.

f. There is another reason why we should be cautious in dealing with narratives, whether those of other people, or our own. As argued in several earlier places, it is naive to assume that narratives are always explanatory in purpose or that they are primarily directed at giving a true account of the event or phenomenon they have as their subject. Narratives can serve at least one other major function in addition to the ones already discussed: They can be *justifications or rationalizations.* Thus, I might react sarcastically toward a colleague behind his back, and my narrative explanation might suggest that I took this action because I am a man of principle who is committed to opposing hypocrisy and class-consciousness wherever I meet it; but this might simply be a story that functions to excuse or to justify my action—for, in reality, this colleague might make me feel uncomfortable or inferior, and my sarcasm was merely a way of my venting my feelings. Or a teacher might present a narrative to show that she was acting on deeply held pedagogical principle when she introduced a lesson in a certain way, whereas in reality she acted this way in panic or because she once saw another teacher do this and could think of nothing better herself when the time came to teach this topic. Unfortunately, human nature is such that we have a pronounced tendency to readily believe that the considerations we offer by way of justification of our own actions were the factors that actually led us to act that way; and it might take a very refined degree of self-understanding for some of us to realize that we have become victims of self-delusion. So, once again, the interviewer or researcher cannot accept a narrative at face value. (In traditional "positivistic" social science, researchers who rely on questionnaires and interviews know—or, at least, at their best they know—that many factors can influence the types of answers that are given, and techniques have been devised to ensure that the resulting data are reliable and valid, in various senses of these terms. Not everything that is "positivistic" is bad!)

g. Earlier in my discussion I strove to be fair in summarizing the range of epistemological points that have been made, by supporters, about narratives and narrative inquiry in the educational research literature. But it is striking that on such an important matter—the status of narrative as a knowledge-bearing or explanation-giving genre—the supporting arguments turned out to be so scanty. From evidence internal to their writings I surmise that researchers who are pronarrative have tended instead to have sociopolitical rather than epistemic grounds for their enthusiasm: They have stressed that narrative is a basic human cognitive style or mode of thought or inquiry; or they give the impression that they support narrative in order to break the illiberal hegemony of positivism (and its descendants) in the research community; or they have argued that by making narratives more central in research, the barriers (including status differentials) between university researchers and schoolpeople will diminish, and the resulting work will be of more direct relevance to practitioners so that the perennial problem of linking research and practice will disappear; or they stress that professional university researchers have much to learn from the insights and stories of teachers (Lytle and Cochran-Smith 1990). Max van Manen hopes that his "human science" will be conducive to the production of "an action sensitive pedagogy" (which is the subtitle of his book); Polkinghorne stresses in his preface that "practitioners work with narrative knowledge. They are concerned with people's stories: they work with case histories and use narrative explanations to understand why the people they work with behave the way they do" (Polkinghorne 1988, x); and Connelly and Clandinin wrote in the concluding paragraph of their influential article:

> We need to listen closely to teachers and other learners and to the stories of their lives in and out of classrooms. We also need to tell our own stories as we live our own collaborative researcher/teacher lives. Our own work then becomes one of learning to tell and live a new mutually constructed account of inquiry in teaching and learning. . . . for curriculum, and perhaps for other branches of educational inquiry, it is a research agenda which gives "curriculum professors something to do." (Connelly and Clandinin 1990, 12)

Almost as revealingly, Barone talks about "the politics of method" (Barone 1992, 22); and in one place he asks why narratives are not accepted by traditional "positivistic" researchers, and he gives as his answer the style and the vernacular language that is used—in other words, he completely ignores the possibility that there might be *epistemological* objections to narrative research (as presently conducted) of the kind discussed in this present chapter (Barone 1992, 19).

Many, or perhaps all, of these "political" points might be true—teachers might be more comfortable with narratives, and narratives might narrow the gap between research and practice, and so on—but none of these points serves to establish that narrative *ought* to be regarded as trustworthy or deserving of a central place in educational research. It is like arguing that because in many human situations the telling of lies is functional, in that it can help you gain some desired goal or advantage, therefore you *ought* to tell lies; the functionality, even if true, hardly by itself serves to justify the adoption of such a weighty policy. Narrative will often need to be *epistemically* respectable—even though, as I have indicated earlier in my discussion, there are some quite common contexts where the use of narrative is both essential and clearly warrantable on theoretical grounds without having to meet the criterion of being true. The "bottom line" is this: There are many contexts where the issue of the truth of narratives needs to be dealt with more thoroughly before widespread use can be condoned.

ANOTHER EXAMPLE

At this stage it might be helpful to illustrate some of the points that have been made with another and more lengthy example. In 1781 one of the great personal narratives of the modern era was published—the autobiographical *Confessions* of Jean-Jacques Rousseau. Something of the tone of the volume is revealed in the famous words found in the opening pages: "I was born, a poor and sickly child, and cost my mother her life. So my birth was the first of my misfortunes" (Rousseau 1781/1953, 19). Rousseau gives lively, engaging, and (usually) internally consistent accounts of his many adventures, deeds, and misdeeds. But the following issue is forced upon the reader's attention: Are his accounts always (or perhaps ever) to be believed? Probably Rousseau himself believed his narrative accounts, for he had developed and had internalized a particular image of himself that he skillfully promulgated in powerful prose. Most of his stories about his own actions are believable (although often they are extraordinary), and certainly they make for an engrossing read; for most of us, it matters little whether the stories actually are true or not—they are entertaining and beautifully written, and they reveal something about the author's personality. But an eighteenth-century historian engaged in a research project centered upon one or other of the events described in the book might want to know whether or not Rousseau's accounts are true.

Consider Rousseau's narrative about his period as a secretary to the French ambassador in Venice. He described the filthy conditions in which he was forced to live and the discourtesy with which he (and the other secretaries) were treated. Rousseau continued with the account:

> I was the only one in the house who said nothing outside, but I complained loudly to the ambassador, not only of our treatment but of his own conduct. Prompted in secret, however, by his evil genius he daily offered me some new affront. Though compelled to spend freely in order to keep up with my colleagues, and to live up to my position, I could not touch a penny of my salary; and when I asked him for money he

spoke to me of his esteem and confidence, as if that could have filled my purse and provided for everything. (Rousseau 1781/1953, 290)

Was Rousseau telling the truth? Was it true that he spent money "to keep up appearances," or was this a justification of his freeness with money (in other words, was he merely trying to justify or gloss over his profligate habits)? Was he in fact owed money by the ambassador? Was the ambassador truly a rogue, or had he and Rousseau suffered some kind of falling out that had colored Rousseau's opinion of him? (Perhaps the ambassador had criticized the quality of Rousseau's work, and so the latter's account was merely a case of "sour grapes.") Was the account of eating dinner with dirty linen and cutlery (which occupied a central place in Rousseau's account of life in Venice) a representative occurrence, or was it merely one incident that happened to stick in Rousseau's mind?—after all, there is a human tendency to remember unusual or aberrant incidents, and to overestimate their frequency. Was, in fact, the linen and cutlery quite as filthy as Rousseau made out? I am not suggesting here that Rousseau was consciously lying (although he might have been); rather, as all perception is known to be theory-laden (see chapter 6), perhaps Rousseau's (genuinely believed) account was colored by his negative attitude toward his employer. The account, in other words, might (but also might not) represent what Rousseau *believed* to be true, although it might in fact actually *not have been* true.

Now, on some occasions we might only be interested in Rousseau's reported perceptions and beliefs, whether they were true or not; but on other occasions we might be interested in the truth—was the ambassador *really* the rogue Rousseau made him out to be? In short, on some occasions (and maybe there are many such occasions) the *truth* of the narrative might be of relevance. Once again, the parallels with narrative research in education should be obvious, and one moral leaps out: *Those whose stock-in-trade is narratives need to make clear, in each specific instance, whether it matters to their inquiry if the narrative is true; and if not, they need to explain why not.*

POLKINGHORNE'S LATER DISCUSSION OF NARRATIVE

The earlier discussion made heavy use of Donald Polkinghorne's book published in 1988, but a few years later he made another major contribution to the topic of narrative in the form of an essay in the *International*

Journal of Qualitative Studies in Education (1995). In this paper Polkinghorne makes many interesting points and draws some useful distinctions, but nevertheless his treatment of the issue of the truth of narrative inquiry is unsatisfactory. He certainly makes a number of concessions to the need for truth (or "validity," as it is often misleadingly called), but on each occasion he quickly "shoots himself in the foot" and either takes back or seriously modifies what he has just said. Nevertheless, his paper is important, and I discuss it at some length as I suspect there are many in the social science and educational research community who hold similar views.

Polkinghorne's paper is complex, and I will not attempt to give a comprehensive summary; instead, I will comment on a number of his points that directly relate to the themes I developed earlier.

a. Polkinghorne rightly stresses the importance of *plot* in narrative research, and he recognizes that it plays a crucial role in configuring various events into a story. (Here he is focusing on narratives that a researcher constructs about some phenomenon that has been investigated, rather than on the narratives that might be told *to* the researcher.) The plot delimits a "temporal range which marks the beginning and end of the story," it provides "criteria for the selection of events to be included in the story," it allows temporal ordering of the events leading up to the conclusion, and it makes explicit "the meaning events have as contributors to the story as a unified whole" (Polkinghorne 1995, 7). But there is an obvious problem here, one I alluded to in the earlier discussion: The conditions that the need for a clear plot imposes upon a story are *epistemically irrelevant.* The plain fact of the matter is that unification of the narrative, having a clear conclusion to which the narrative coherently leads, and so forth, can all be achieved without the story being true. These are conditions imposed, perhaps, by the genre of narrative itself, but they have little if any epistemological justification; very often narratives must satisfy *both* masters—they are answerable to the standards of the genre but *also* to epistemic standards.

Furthermore, there is the strong danger that once a narrative researcher becomes set in his or her own mind about what the plot is going to be of a particular story he or she is telling, the subsequent selection of "events" to include is likely to be "plot driven," not "truth driven"—after all, the demands of the narrative genre become central if one is engaged in constructing a narrative! (One only has to go to the movies in order to come across examples of this—Oliver Stone's *Nixon* is a good example of how the plot line can determine what events will be presented as factual, even though there is not a scintilla of evidence in favor of them.)

To all this it might be replied that the same danger exists across the physical, biological, and social sciences, and yet we do not feel that the narratives produced here (which we glorify with the name "scientific explanations") are particularly deficient; in *all* the sciences, data is selected from vast pools of facts, events, and so forth that are potentially relevant. Undoubtedly this retort is correct, but, nevertheless, there is a crucial difference between the narratives or accounts produced in the sciences and those that too commonly are found in fields like education. In any discipline that is (or aspires to be) a science, or wishes to tell the truth, or to offer true explanations, any story that is told is—to put it crudely—shaped to an important degree by nature (see also the discussion in chapter 11); the person telling the story certainly has significant input concerning the direction that it will take, but nevertheless he or she is constrained by what is happening in that portion of the world that is under investigation. In so-called narrative research, however, the constraints are imposed by the needs of the *story* and its *plot* (as pointed out by both Polkinghorne and Carter 1993). Indeed, Polkinghorne seems to suggest, in one part of his essay where he gets somewhat bogged-down and where his discussion is difficult to follow, that narrative analysis is not accountable to the same standards as science (which for some reason he prefers to call "paradigmatic inquiry" or "paradigmatic cognition"; see, for example, Polkinghorne 1995, 9ff and 15). He stresses that "all of these data need to be integrated and interpreted by an emplotted narrative" (Polkinghorne 1995, 15).

It should by now be clear to the reader that it has been the nub of my discussion in this chapter that distinctions of the sort that Polkinghorne and others wish to draw are mistaken: there are many occasions on which the stories used in narrative research, no less than scientific explanations, need to be true or at least have a significant epistemological warrant—it is not only "paradigmatic inquiry" that has to face the demand for truth.

b. The same problem arises with the other notable distinction that Polkinghorne draws. He distinguishes between "analysis of narratives" (where a researcher, for example, collects various narratives via interviews or questionnaires and then subjects these to coding and analysis, the fruits of which frequently are reported in tabular or statistical form) and "narrative analysis," where an account or analysis is constructed by the researcher and presented in narrative form (as, for example, is done by historians trying to account for some event such as the start of the First World War).

Helpful as this distinction is, an important caveat needs to be entered. This is merely a repetition of the point I made earlier: Polkinghorne is mistaken if he thinks that only the analysis of narratives has to satisfy the epistemic canons of science; accounts presented in narrative form might have to meet the canons of the narrative genre, but they *also* have to satisfy the scientific ones as well—what use is it to produce a gripping story about the origins of the First World War if this has the same epistemic status as a fairy tale?

c. At this stage a complication arises. I mentioned earlier that Polkinghorne on one hand makes some concessions about the need for truth (without, of course, using this term), but on the other hand, he rapidly reneges or says something quite at variance. A clear example of this occurs toward the end of his paper. His concession is the following:

> In producing the story, the researcher draws on disciplinary expertise to interpret and make sense of responses and actions. Because the story is offered as a scholarly explanation and realistic depiction of a human episode, the researcher needs to include evidence and argument in support of the plausibility of the offered story. (Polkinghorne 1995, 19)

Although this concession is moving in the right direction, it does not go nearly far enough; as argued earlier in the discussion of Rousseau and elsewhere, *plausibility* is far too weak a requirement—we have all heard the expression "plausible rogue" spoken of someone whose stories are not to be trusted. Because the story "is offered as a scholarly explanation," the warrant that is offered ought to indicate the likely *truth* of the story, whether it is plausible or not. (Technically, I doubt whether plausibility is even a necessary condition for the acceptance of many stories; there are innumerable examples of true stories that appeared quite *im*plausible when they first appeared—think of the reception of the Copernican account of the universe by the Catholic Church and Galileo's fate for championing it. I also remind the reader of the implausible tale of the crowing rooster that I told earlier—does its implausibility mean that the story is not true?)

"Plausibility" is the key to Polkinghorne's backing away from the promising requirement that evidence is needed to support narratives. Within twenty lines of the concession made previously, the following passage appears in a context where it is clear that the focus is upon the criteria that narratives must meet in order to carry out their "explanatory function"; the paragraph opens with the sentence "The function of narrative analysis is to answer how and why a particular outcome came about." Then, two sentences later:

The plausibility of the produced story is in its clarification of the uncertainty implied in the research question of why the happening occurred. The explanation needs to satisfy the subjective needs of the reader of the report to understand how the occurrence could have come about. The story has to appeal to the reader's experienced general sense of how and why humans respond and act. It needs to be compatible with the reader's background knowledge or beliefs in characteristic behavior of people or nature in order for the reader to accept the explanation as possible. (Polkinghorne 1995, 19)

Here the satisfactoriness of a narrative *as an explanation* (and not as an instance of the narrative genre) is defined in terms of its ability to meet the "subjective needs" of the reader; furthermore, according to Polkinghorne an effective narrative should not challenge a reader's background beliefs or assumptions. Once again, the epistemic defects are easy to discern—there is no reason to think that a narrative that satisfies its readers' needs and that does not shake any of their prior convictions is likely, because of these factors, to be true. (I doubt whether at this stage an example is needed, but I include one to bring out the horrendous consequences of Polkinghorne's position. The narratives told by racists to justify discrimination or even genocide certainly seem to satisfy the subjective needs of their audiences, and these stories do not challenge any prior convictions but are fully compatible with the racist assumptions held by members of the audience. Are we to say, then, that because these narratives meet Polkinghorne's desiderata they are satisfactory as explanations of genocide? Apart from their moral bankruptcy, racist narratives are not *true;* they make use of faulty notions of genetic superiority and of race, they refer to the mythical virtues of blood and breeding, and they often contain distortions of history. They do not stand up to critical empirical and theoretical scrutiny, and so they are defective as *explanations.* Polkinghorne's desiderata completely miss the point.)

d. The plot thickens even more! On the very next page of his essay Polkinghorne makes further concessions:

In judging the credibility of a story, a distinction can be made between the accuracy of the data and the plausibility of the plot. It is the researcher's responsibility to assure that the reported events and happenings actually occurred. The use of triangulation methods . . . can help in producing confidence that the event occurred. . . . Researchers need to treat interview-based data with care. Recollection of past events is

> selective and produced from the present perspective of the respondent. (Polkinghorne 1995, 20)

Here Polkinghorne is making points rather similar to some of those I made previously in my discussion of Rousseau. The only fault is that he makes these points in the name of "credibility," which is a psychological and relativistic criterion; accuracy and veracity of data may or may not increase credibility in the eyes of members of the audience for the story (as I argued earlier), but these factors are certainly appropriate to consider when making a judgment about the truth or falsity of an account.

However, at the end of the very next paragraph, Polkinghorne states:

> Nevertheless, because configurative analysis is the researcher's construction, it is inappropriate to ask if it is the "real" or "true" story. (Polkinghorne 1995, 20)

As I stated earlier, I believe Polkinghorne is on quite the wrong track here; asking these questions is *highly* appropriate. For if we ask for an explanation of some event, action, or sequence of events, we often want the *true* explanation, and we do not want to be fobbed-off with a credible fiction. If we ask about the causes of the First World War, or about President Nixon's motives for going along with the Watergate cover-up, or why a teacher acted so harshly toward a student, or who stole the apple pie, presumably we want the *true* account, the *real* reasons. If not, if we would be happy with a credible fiction, we have no need to ask but often could invent it for ourselves.

But there is another objection to this last statement of Polkinghorne's: It is a non sequitur. It does not follow that because stories and analyses are made by researchers, they therefore cannot be "real" or "true." Stories can be both *made*, and *true*, at the same time! Humans made the stories that the Earth is round, that Hitler and Stalin were psychopathic monsters, and that mass-murders of civilians have occurred in the recent Bosnian conflict; does the fact that these are human constructions rule out the possibility that they also are true?

e. Perhaps what is clouding the issue here, for Polkinghorne and many who hold similar views, is—as discussed earlier—the fact that it is difficult to decide, beyond all doubt, whether or not many narratives *are* true. We cannot know for certain the truth of any psychological diagnosis of Hitler and Stalin; we cannot tell whether Rousseau's stories about the French ambassador are correct. Certainly, much of what humans consider to be knowledge is conjectural, but this does not mean that the beliefs we hold are neither true nor false. It simply means that we cannot know for sure if the things we believe, if the stories and explanations we accept as being true, actually *are* true. Often our goal is to find the truth, and we do the best that we can, using the strongest epistemic warrants that are available to us. The fact that this is difficult work, and that we are not assured of success, is no grounds upon which to abandon the quest or to settle for accepting narratives that are "credible" when there are better tests available.

****

Explanatory addendum concerning roosters: The story of the teacher and the rooster was true, as most readers will have guessed—guessed not because the story is credible or incredible, but because it was surmised that the present author is more likely to want to impress his readers with a true story than with an invented one. The event described occurred many years ago; I was the observer; the history teacher concerned was close to retirement, was having severe disciplinary problems with his classes, he was stone deaf—and he was in the habit of setting his class to read a chapter of the textbook, whereupon he would turn down his hearing aid and have a snooze. Now, here, of course, I have given an elaborated version of the story, which some might think makes the story more credible; but confidence tricksters often know that to make their lies more believable, a certain amount of credible detail has to be appended! What makes the story true is that the event *actually took place;* you should believe the story, not because it is credible or incredible, but because my eyewitness testimony is epistemically relevant. Which does not, of course, mean that my testimony cannot be challenged—after all, I might have been intoxicated, or I might be a psychotic liar; and we know from contemporary philosophy of science that *no* evidence is absolutely certain. Whether or not the story is true does not affect its value as an entertaining anecdote; but if the school's principal was planning to chastise the teacher on the basis of this story, it would have been wise for her to have made some effort to ascertain that it was true.

This chapter incorporates material from two previously published papers: D. C. Phillips, "Telling It Straight: Issues in Assessing Narrative Research," *Educational Psychologist* 29 (1) (1994): 13–22, reprinted with permission; and D. C. Phillips, "Telling the Truth about Stories," *Teaching and Teacher Education* 13 (1) (1997): 101–109, reprinted with permission from Elsevier Science.

5

NATURALISTIC IDEALS IN SOCIAL SCIENCE

It is a common human practice for us to label past ages in such a way that we can neatly but oversimply categorize their intellectual achievements (or lack of such)—the nineteenth century was "the age of ideology," the medieval period was "the age of faith," and so forth. (A series of widely read books of readings in the field of history of ideas was organized in this fashion; see Aiken 1956, for one of these volumes.) Egoistically, perhaps, many of us do not regard *ourselves* as living in an "age"; it is as if each of us believes that intellectual history stopped (or reached fruition) on the day of our own birth. However, many of the contemporary theoretical and philosophical disputes about the nature of the social sciences become explicable if—by an out-of-the-body exercise of the imagination—we look at ourselves as living in an age when the naturalistic ideal has migrated from the physical and biological sciences into the social sciences, where it is not receiving a uniformly warm reception. (The existentialists and phenomenologists, for example—not to mention many hermeneuticists— can be seen as opposing any kind of naturalism that might have the effect of diminishing the distinction between humans and other parts of nature. See Husserl 1970.)

The terms *naturalistic* and *naturalism* suffer from the fact that they have a range of meanings, covering a variety of things from the Romantic submission to nature or the collecting of butterflies to the practice of sunbathing on the beach clad only in one's birthday suit. In the social sciences, these terms are often as not used to refer to studies in which—in contrast to experimental work—the researcher does not interfere with the situation that is under scrutiny. The (philosophical) sense of these terms as used in the present discussion is somewhat different: In general, a naturalist is a scholar who attempts to explain phenomena that occur within the realm of the physical universe in terms of concepts and explanatory hypotheses that themselves refer to this same "natural" realm; in other words, the naturalist eschews explanations in terms of (literally) *super*-natural or *meta*-physical entities, or that appeal to a priori principles. Applied more specifically to the social sciences, the meaning is narrower still: A naturalist is a person who holds that, in some fashion that he or she is under an obligation to make precise, the social sciences are similar to the natural sciences (see Thomas 1979). It will be noted that an important condition has been built into this account—each naturalist has to make clear the respect in which he or she believes the natural and social sciences are similar. Because different people give different accounts in this important area— they see the similarity in different terms—there is not *one* naturalistic ideal for the social sciences; rather, there are several. And thereby hangs our present tale.

THE SPREAD OF NATURALISM: A THUMBNAIL SKETCH

It is not entirely clear when the naturalistic ideal emerged in the physical sciences, but there is little doubt that it was well on the way to being established by the time Galileo's work was done. His observations through the telescope helped to remove the distinction between the (perfect) heavens and the (imperfect) Earth; for he displaced them both from places of special privilege and significance in the universe. But, probably more important, his investigations with the inclined plane demonstrated what could be accomplished with careful laboratory manipulation and measurement and the use of mathematical analysis coupled with rigorous argumentation. (For a readable and relatively nontechnical account of these contributions, given by a physicist, see Rogers 1960.) Galileo died in 1642; in 1644 Descartes published the *Principles of Philosophy*, in which he stated boldly that all he required in order to explain "all natural phenomena" were the concepts of matter and motion (Descartes 1963, 221). In this work he also expressed his indebtedness to the idea of machines; and he stated that natural phenomena work on the same principles as man-made machines, except that the parts of natural phenomena are so small that "they utterly elude our senses" (Descartes 1963, 236). By the end of Newton's lifetime, the picture of the universe (in its physical aspects) as a vast mechanism akin to clockwork was well on its way to general acceptance among the intelligentsia. The Creator was revealed to have been a mechanic and mathematician, Who absented Himself from active participation after having set the cosmic machinery into motion. As the historian of science Herbert Butterfield put it,

> a subtle intellectual change was giving people an interest in the operation of pure mechanism; and some have even said that this came from the growing familiarity with clocks and machines, though it would be impossible to put one's finger on any authentic proof of this. . . . One thing is clear: not only was there in some intellectual leaders a great aspiration to demonstrate that the universe ran like a piece of clockwork, but this was itself initially a religious aspiration. It was felt that there would be something defective in Creation itself . . . unless the whole system of the universe could be shown to be interlocking, so that it carried the pattern of reasonableness and orderliness. (Butterfield 1957, 119)

The naturalization of the physical worldview (or mechanization, as some have preferred to call it—see Dijksterhuis 1961; also Randall 1976, chap. 10) has just about run its course in our own times. In the late 1980s the noted physicist Victor Weisskopf, a former president of the American Academy of Arts and Sciences, gave an address to the Academy on the topic "The Origin of the Universe." In masterly style he summarized the relevant recent work in the fields of astrophysics, cosmology, and particle physics; and finally, arriving at the "Big Bang," he argued that this occurred as a consequence of the fact that the laws of quantum physics still operated when *nothing* existed:

> According to the fundamental tenets of this well-established theory, there is nothing in nature that remains quiet. Everything, including the true vacuum, is subject to fluctuations—in particular to energy fluctuations. . . . Thus, at one moment a small region somewhere in space may have fluctuated into a false vacuum. This would happen very rarely but cannot be excluded. That region almost instantly expands tremendously and creates a large space filled with energy according to the properties of a false vacuum. (Weisskopf 1989, 36-37)

Perhaps to soften the impact of this news on any deists in his audience, Weisskopf arranged for the opening bars of Haydn's oratorio "The Creation" to be played as he concluded his lecture. Stephen Hawking, the contemporary occupant of Newton's Chair at Cambridge, holds what appears (to a relative layman) to be a similar position, but in his best-selling *A Brief History of Time* he goes a little further and asks whether this account leaves room for God to exert any influence at all—for even the Deity cannot transgress the laws of physics (Hawking 1988). God has moved from being a mechanic, architect, and mathematician, to being a passive spectator—a triumph for the process of naturalization. (For a philosophical critique of these recent ideas from physics, see Grunbaum 1989.)

A similar process has been at work in the biological sciences. It is probably unnecessary to recount the spread of naturalism from Harvey on the role of the heart as a pump to Crick and Watson on the biochemical mechanisms underlying gene replication, although it should be made clear that the spread was not an easy accomplishment nor was it without setbacks. (To cite two examples: the spread of vitalism in the biology of the late nineteenth and early twentieth centuries seems in large part to have been a reaction as the complexities of living organisms became apparent—especially the complexities of cell-division—which no "natural" mechanism conceivable at the time could explain; and the Romantic movement of the late eighteenth and early nineteenth centuries was to a significant degree a reaction to what was taken to be the sterility, dehumanization, and lack of historical consciousness of the mechanical science of the Enlightenment.) The words of the intellectual historian John Herman Randall, Jr., are worth citing as a reminder of the critical role of Charles Darwin in widening the scope of naturalism to encompass humans:

> Of all the consequences that followed from the new evolutionary world of science, what seemed most momentous was the definite inclusion of man within the scope of the cosmic process. Not only was man an integral part of Nature, bound by her laws and subject to her forces. . . . after Darwin, however, there could be no further blinking of the fact that man was a product as well as a part of nature. (Randall 1976, 497)

(It also is worth noting here that we humans can be a part of nature, of course, without the scientific methods useful in studying the *other* parts necessarily being appropriate for studying *our* affairs! In other words, while the Darwinian placement of humans firmly into the natural order makes it easier to defend naturalism in the sense defined at the beginning of the chapter, it does not absolutely seal the case.)

Although again it is difficult to be precise, during the first half of the nineteenth century naturalistic ideals started to motivate some, at least, of those who wished to study human affairs in a more rigorous fashion—a phenomenon that was driven, in large part, by the success that naturalism enjoyed in other domains. (The hermeneutic school, as discussed elsewhere in the present volume, can be regarded as in general resisting this trend.) In the early decades of the century social statistics had been collected by the Belgian scholar Quetelet (Quetelet 1968) in an attempt to find precise measurements of social forces; and also in the 1830s and '40s Auguste Comte argued that what he called the "positive philosophy" would spread successfully into the new field of "social physics" (for further discussion, see the discussion of positivism in chapter 9). At close to the same time, John Stuart Mill, in the sixth book of *A System of Logic* (see Mill 1988, chap. 3), offered the opinion that the difficulties standing in the way of developing a science of human affairs were analogous to the difficulties barring an accurate and fully predictive science of the tides (i.e., they were difficulties concerned with obtaining accurate initial data—in the case of tides, about the precise slopes of beaches, wind strength, and so on—they were not what we might call difficulties in principle). Herbert Spencer, the influential essayist and proselytizer for scientific naturalism, produced a volume, *The Principles of Psychology*, in 1855; he had modestly (but, as it turns out, mistakenly) written to his father that this volume would "ultimately stand beside Newton's *Principia*" (Spencer, quoted in Kennedy 1978, 47). Around this time, too, Karl Marx believed that he had produced a scientific and materialistic account of the dynamics of history; and Darwin, who had declined the invitation to write the "Introduction" for the former's *Capital*, reluctantly turned his attention explicitly to humans in both his *Expression of the Emotions* and *The Descent of Man* (1871). (Darwin's *Origin of Species*, in 1859, only implicitly dealt with humans, but nevertheless his readers jumped to the conclusion discussed earlier—humans are animals and thus part of the natural order.)

Experimental psychology also originated in this era; one of its first achievements was Fechner's "psychophysical law," which purported to show the mathematical relationship between (objective) "outer" stimuli and (subjective) "inner" sensations—in other words, the law seemed to mathematically relate matter with mind, a neat trick if only valid (see contributions by Fechner and others in Dennis 1948). What now is acknowledged to be the first great textbook of modern scientific psychology, William James's *The Principles of Psychology*, was published in 1890.

In the last few decades of the nineteenth century there was another significant development: statistical analysis started to blossom as a research tool in science (its origins go back further, of course; see Hacking 1990) and began its rapid development to become the cornerstone of much twentieth-century social science. While some statistical techniques were imported into the social sciences from agriculture and even brewing

("Student," as the inventor of the notorious "t test" chose to identify himself, was an employee of the Guinness brewery), some were developed by researchers specifically interested in human affairs. Early work on what is now called the curve of normal distribution talked about "the curve of errors"—nature was picturesquely conceived as making mistakes as it aimed to produce individuals with all the same measure of the same characteristic (height of adult males in a population, for example). Darwin's cousin, Francis Galton, used various human and social examples to illustrate this notion together with the idea of correlation (which he originated); and in what must have been to some extent a mischievous tongue-in-cheek example (Galton 1872), he even used his nascent statistical techniques to investigate "the efficacy of prayer." (Briefly, Galton argued that the British national anthem—"God Save the Queen"—was a prayer for the longevity of the monarch; so he took the ages at death of British monarchs and statistically compared them to a sample of other nonrelated members of the nobility. There *was* a "significant" difference, but in a distasteful direction—prayer seemed to be killing off the royal family prematurely! Although this example was—presumably—mainly intended as an engaging illustration of the possibilities of the new statistical tools, there may well have been some intent to attack the clergy (see Forrest 1974, chap. 8), and as might be expected, there was a public controversy. Galton's knighthood did not come until the new century!

During the early decades of the present century the naturalistic program became firmly entrenched in the human and social sciences, especially in North America. B. F. Skinner was the leading spokesperson for one particular (and, it must be said, narrow) version of the naturalistic program; one crucial chapter of his book *Science and Human Behavior* (Skinner 1953) displays its author's naturalism even in the title (which may have been a Freudian slip)—"Why Organisms Behave." For the point is, of course, that the organism of chief interest to Skinner was "Homo Sapiens," but clearly as a convinced naturalist he was planning to make no distinctions within the animal kingdom! He wrote:

> We undertake to predict and control the behavior of the individual organism. This is our "dependent variable"—the effect for which we are to find the cause. Our "independent variables"—the causes of behavior—are the external conditions of which behavior is a function. Relations between the two—the "cause and effect relationships" in behavior—are the laws of a science. A synthesis of these laws expressed in quantitative terms yields a comprehensive picture of the organism as a

behaving system. This must be done within the bounds of a natural science. We cannot assume that behavior has any peculiar properties which require unique methods or special kinds of knowledge. (Skinner 1953, 35-36)

This passage is saturated with notions that would have seemed fantastic one and a half centuries ago (if they don't seem far-fetched enough now): Human and animal behavior are of a kind, behavior can be predicted, the laws of behavior can be determined, behavior is best conceptualized as a dependent variable, behavior does not differ in kind from physical phenomena. . . . These are the elements of Western naturalism that Skinner wove into his own particular program of research. But Skinner's is not the only naturalistic game in town.

NATURALISTIC STRATEGIES

As indicated earlier, several general strategies are open to naturalists, for there are a number of ways in which the social sciences can be held to be similar to the natural sciences. This is an important point that often escapes those who are inclined to be opposed to naturalism—the easiest path for opponents to take is to set up a straw man by focusing on a narrow, outmoded, or very limited view of the nature of natural science, whereupon it is an easy matter to show that the social sciences are not like *that*. (The point is, of course, that the natural sciences are not like that either!) Popper put the point well when he wrote that when critics

denounce a view like mine as "positivistic" or "scientistic," then I may perhaps answer that they themselves seem to accept, *implicitly and uncritically*, that positivism or scientism is *the only philosophy appropriate to the natural sciences*. (Popper 1972, 185)

Another example is provided by the work of the philosopher and political theorist Charles Taylor, whose classic paper "Interpretation and the Sciences of Man" (1971) became an important document for the development of the hermeneutical or interpretive approach to the social sciences on the North American continent (as discussed in an earlier chapter of the present volume). It is clear from the examples used that in 1971 Taylor considered behavioristic social science to be *the* form of naturalism that needed to be combated. Now, while behaviorism was still common and relatively prominent at the time Taylor was originally writing—although even then it was in clear decline—it is not apparent that in his later essays he abandoned or updated his views about its fitness to serve as the sole representative of naturalism. Worse still, many of those who have been influenced by Taylor over the intervening decades, and who should know better the state of play across the full range of the social sciences, make a similar mistake. For the fact is that, considered as an overarching approach to the study of human affairs, behaviorism is almost universally recognized as flawed and is relatively easy to dismiss (this is not to deny that in some areas behaviorism has led to impressive results—for example, in the treatment of some severe behavioral symptoms in disordered patients).

What, then, are the general possibilities open to a supporter of naturalistic social science? In what general ways can the social sciences be held to parallel the natural sciences? In the following discussion four of the strategies that have been tried in the past century and a half will be discussed, but it should be stressed at the outset that it is not being claimed that these are fully independent—clearly, they are not mutually exclusive, as some of the illustrative examples should make clear.

a. The use of certain favored concepts and findings from the natural sciences. It is not uncommon for human inquirers, when faced with a puzzling phenomenon in some new area, to try to impose intellectual order by bringing to bear ideas that worked well in other fields. This, of course, is related to the use of those powerful intellectual tools, metaphor and analogy—and some might want to argue that it is related to the phenomenon common throughout the animal kingdom of using well-established behavioral patterns in new domains. But the transfer of ideas from one intellectual domain to another is not a matter of mere reflex; it is a process that often requires great ingenuity and intellectual persistence.

Thus, with the great success of certain core notions in the physical sciences, it is no great surprise to find that from time to time they have been taken and applied in the domain of the social sciences, with the expectation that this would be the key (or at least one key) to making a scientific breakthrough in the new domain. Two examples should suffice. Herbert Spencer, to whom passing reference was made earlier, spent the greater part of his adult life developing his "synthetic philosophy" and attempting to unify the known branches of science, including the social sciences. He produced a volume on psychology at the early date of 1855, and this was followed by a series of very influential volumes on the infant (if not embryonic) field of sociology—*The Principles of Sociology*—which were published between 1876 and 1896. But he also wrote on biology, education, anthropology, and a host of other topics. The key to Spencer's unification of these disparate domains was the law of progress, which he believed was the same in all fields—physical, biological, and human. In turn, this universal progress was underwritten by a physical mechanism, namely, the fact that every force produces more than one effect (Spencer 1949, especially 176-177). To the modern reader, Spencer's train of argument seems bizarre, but his contemporaries found him stimulating (at least for a time). Thus, at one time or another, he could number among his admirers John Stuart Mill, Thomas Henry Huxley, William James, Ivan Pavlov, the multi-millionaire Andrew Carnegie, and a generation or two of American social scientists and political theorists who were adherents of what we would now call "Social Darwinism" (Hofstadter 1955).

The second example of the first naturalistic strategy is probably better known. Sigmund Freud was trained in medicine at a time when the "mechanistic" ideas of Helmholtz and his followers were dominant; German medical research at the time was committed to finding naturalistic explanations and, furthermore, to finding explanations that would preserve Helmholtz's law of conservation of energy. Reflecting these influences, Freud approached the human psyche in terms of the conservation of "psychic" energy—this is why he believed that treating only the symptoms of mental disorder was a strategy doomed to failure, for energy denied one outlet would merely seek another and would thus display itself in some new set of symptoms. (This use of Helmholtz's law is particularly apparent in the lectures Freud gave in the United States in 1910; see Freud 1989, especially lectures 1 and 3.)

It is difficult to avoid the feeling that this first naturalistic strategy can be pushed to extremes. Certainly, one can never tell, beforehand, whether a borrowed idea will prove to be fruitful in a new domain, but it is also the case that each domain probably will require concepts that are faithful to the new and unique phenomena that it contains. Furthermore, and more seriously, the application of ideas taken from the physical and biological sciences—no matter how inventive or fruitful—does not seem sufficient to cement the naturalist's case. For it is apparent that the use of such borrowed ideas only makes intellectual sense if the borrower is *already* committed to the view that there is no relevant difference between the natural and social or human sciences. Freud and Spencer were able to apply ideas from the physical and biological domains because they already had a commitment to universal naturalism. (The same case can be made about others who adopt this first strategy, such as the behaviorists Watson and Skinner.)

b. The use of the "deeper" presuppositions of natural science. The four figures already mentioned—Spencer, Freud, Watson, and Skinner—all made use of this second strategy in their extension of naturalism. They shared a strong belief that the human phenomena that were of concern to them were marked by causation as strictly deterministic as it was in physical mechanical systems. They also shared the belief that nature was regular—natural laws were to be found in the human or social domain as well as in the physical. The differences between them were due to the way they played out these fundamental metaphysical commitments in practice—they were interested in somewhat different phenomena, and the mechanisms that they saw at work in nature and that they generalized were different in their four cases: Spencer latched onto the fact that forces produced more than one effect, Freud focused on conservation of ("psychic") energy, Watson adopted the Pavlovian mechanism of classic conditioning, and Skinner took over the idea of operant conditioning that had made an appearance in E. L. Thorndike's work with imprisoned cats. (For more details on some of these examples, see Cleverley and Phillips 1986.)

To cut what could be a long story short, then, it seems incontrovertible that at least some branches of the modern social sciences have taken over the metaphysical underpinnings of the natural sciences (or what has commonly been thought to be those underpinnings): nature is regular, in the sense that there are lawlike generalizations waiting to be discovered (or, more accurately, invented); causal language is appropriate in the social sciences (although often this is disguised, as when researchers talk of dependent and independent variables, or when they use locutions such as "this event happened as a result of . . . "); and even in social affairs there is a "fact of the matter," a "social reality," that is independent of what the researcher happens to believe. The fact that these days there is no shortage of writers who attack these assumptions as being out of place in the social sciences only goes to prove the point that they *are* present. (For merely one example, see the exchange between Phillips and Guba in Eisner and Peshkin 1990.)

Are these assumptions reasonable? Are there good reasons for following this second strategy? Clearly, the issues here are very complex. Some writers would say that all inquiry necessarily must have a soft underbelly of assumptions—Kuhn, for example, would hold that in natural science there always will be paradigmatic assumptions (although, to throw a wrench in the works, Kuhn doubted that there were any paradigms in the social sciences); for Lakatos, there is a set of "hard-core" assumptions at the heart of every research program (Phillips 1987, part A). From the vantage point of one of these perspectives, then, it would come as no surprise that some naturalists take over into the social sciences the hard-core assumptions they believe to be present in the physical or biological sciences; the only alternative to borrowing would be to devise a new set and start *ab initio*. There is, of course, no way of *establishing* the soundness or otherwise of metaphysical assumptions; but on the other hand, as people like Popper have insisted, such items can be discussed and criticized, and it certainly is possible for us to reach the conclusion that some assumptions are—given the considerations that have been advanced—more reasonable than others (see Popper 1985, chap. 16).

But it also remains possible for a person to be a naturalist and to believe that in some respects the social sciences resemble the natural sciences (or vice versa), *without* subscribing to the view that the metaphysical underpinnings of natural science must be replicated in the social sciences. (What becomes really crucial here is precisely *what* these metaphysical foundations are taken to be.) Thus, for example, it would seem possible to hold that the physical notions of law and of causation are out of place when human voluntary action is the object of inquiry—humans act for reasons, not as a result of impressed forces (hermeneuticists, as discussed in an earlier chapter, develop this position in some detail). But it still could be held that human-oriented inquiry can be subjected to naturalistic study—the point being that some *other* naturalistic strategy would thereby be favored, rather than the second one that has been the subject of attention here. (Some members, but by no means all, of the hermeneutical school also believe that their program, with its rival conception of the nature of the human person as meaning-maker, can be investigated in a disciplined and even "scientific" manner.)

c. The adoption of "structural" features of natural science. The mature natural sciences have developed an impressive structure consisting of empirical laws related through the medium of theories. Thus (as discussed more fully in chapter 12), the laws of gas behavior that bear the names of Boyle and Charles are subsumed under the Kinetic Theory of Gases, from which they can be shown to follow deductively (given certain reasonable linking assumptions). But the theory also was able to generate predictions that could be tested and that led to the discovery of phenomena that were completely unexpected on the basis of knowledge of only Boyle's Law and Charles's Law. Carl Hempel paints the situation in the following manner:

Theories are usually introduced when previous study of a class of phenomena has revealed a system of uniformities that can be expressed in
the form of empirical laws. Theories then seek to explain those regularities and, generally, to afford a deeper and more accurate understanding of the phenomena in question. To this end, a theory construes those
phenomena as manifestations of entities and processes that lie behind
or beneath them, as it were. These are assumed to be governed by characteristic theoretical laws, or theoretical principles, by means of which
the theory then explains the empirical uniformities that have been previously discovered, and usually also predicts "new" regularities of similar kinds. (Hempel 1966, 70)

The logical structure of theories is currently a matter of intense debate among philosophers of science (see chapter 12), but Hempel's account
is a classic formulation of what the literature calls the "received view"
(Suppe 1974).

Whatever the outcome of the debates over the "structure" of natural
science, there has been no shortage of social scientists who are impressed
by one or other of the accounts of this structure and who have lusted after a social science that would be similar. The field of economics, to cite
the most notorious example, is packed with theories that resemble the
structure of the Kinetic Theory of Gases (and that go so far as to treat
individuals rather like molecules, even to the length of endowing them
with properties as unrealistic—or more charitably, as idealized—as are the
properties possessed by the molecules of classic Kinetic Theory). Organization Theory, too, is a field marked by the development of theories on
the model of the physical sciences.

The work of the sociologist Robert Merton deserves special mention
here. In his celebrated discussion of "sociological theories of the middle
range" he writes, in a passage that closely resembles the work of Hempel:

> the term *sociological theory* refers to logically interconnected sets of propo-
> sitions from which empirical uniformities can be derived. Throughout
> we focus on what I have called *theories of the middle range:* theories that
> lie between the minor but necessary working hypotheses that evolve in
> abundance during day-to-day research and the all-inclusive systematic
> efforts to develop a unified theory that will explain all observed unifor-
> mities of social behavior, social organization, and social change. (Merton
> 1967, 39)

Merton continues with these significant words: "One speaks of a theory
of reference groups, of social mobility, of role-conflict and of the forma-

tion of social norms just as one speaks of a theory of prices, a germ theory of disease, or a kinetic theory of gases" (Merton 1967, 39-40). Here, then, it is clear that the third naturalistic strategy is at work; indeed, it sits so comfortably with Merton that he does not even consider justifying his assumption that it is *possible* to produce sociological theories that are logically parallel to Kinetic Theory.

In advocating the quest for middle-range theories, Merton was concerned to combat the work of "grand theorists" such as Talcott Parsons—the physical science analog of grand theory being, perhaps, Einstein's unified theory or contemporary particle physicists' "theory of everything" (neither of which have been successfully produced). Merton's discussion of why the production of grand theory is a mistaken enterprise highlights further how well-entrenched the naturalistic ideal had become by the 1950s and '60s. In an argument that unabashedly draws on the physical sciences, Merton suggests that "the attempt to create total systems of sociology" rests on three mistakes about science: first, that systems of thought (i.e., grand theories) can be erected before a great mass of "basic observations has been accumulated" (Merton 1967, 46); second, that all branches of inquiry existing at the same time have the same level of maturity (Merton 1967, 47)—that is, for example, that contemporary social science is in the same state of development as contemporary physics; and third, that physical science has, indeed, produced grand theory that can serve as the inspirational model for social scientists (Merton 1967, 47). The point here is not, of course, whether Merton's analysis is right or wrong, but rather the way in which he assumes *without argument* that what is sauce for the physical science goose is also sauce for the social science gander. (And again, the point is not so much to challenge this assumption, but merely to highlight that it is there—the third naturalistic strategy has become, as it were, internalized.)

d. Cementing the hegemony of scientific method. This fourth naturalistic strategy is, perhaps, the most widespread of all—the methods of science, which, of course, must be given credit for the great success of the natural sciences, can be used fruitfully in the social sciences. The naturalist who takes this route must, of course, follow through and put on the table an analysis of precisely what the scientific method *is* (a task that is simpler in the describing than in the doing). It is giving away no secrets for me to indicate that I have much sympathy for the position espoused by the philosopher Harold Kincaid, who recently wrote the following about some of his deep convictions:

(1) that pressing social problems such as poverty, discrimination, and inequality are not simply the result of individual characteristics but result instead from larger social structures; (2) that scientific methods are the most powerful tools available for replacing superstition and prejudice with knowledge *and thus that we can and ought to study those social structures with the methods of the natural sciences, broadly construed. . . . Naturalism is thus the belief that social phenomena are part of the natural world and accordingly amenable to the methods of the natural sciences.* (Kincaid 1999, xv; emphasis added)

This fourth position is so familiar that it is probably unnecessary to swamp the reader with examples. Two will suffice. In 1910 John Dewey published *How We Think,* which he revised in 1933; the volume opens with the statement that some ways of thinking "are better than others," and the reasons why they are better "can be set forth." He calls the better way "reflective thinking" rather than scientific thinking (Dewey 1971, 3), but a rose by any other name still smells as sweet. He was less circumspect in 1916, when he wrote of science as "authorized conviction," and he stated that "without initiation into the scientific spirit one is not in possession of the best tools which humanity has so far devised for effectively directed reflection" (Dewey 1966, 189). (It is worth noting that Dewey was a contributor to the *International Encyclopedia of Unified Science,* which produced nineteen monographs before its demise; the title of the series—sometimes called *The Foundations of the Unity of Science*—is self-explanatory.)

Another example of the fourth line that can be taken by naturalists is provided by the work of Auguste Comte. He believed the key method of science was, indeed, the only intellectual method that could produce *real* knowledge:

All competent thinkers agree with Bacon that there can be no real knowledge except that which rests upon observed facts. This fundamental maxim is so evidently indisputable if it is applied, as it ought to be, to the mature state of our intelligence. (Comte 1970, 4)

Again, this is not the place to undertake a detailed assessment of such arguments, but it can be suggested, without undue prejudice, that this fourth strategy involving the generalization of scientific method is probably (to mix the metaphor) an easier row to hoe than the previous three. Certainly, it is not particularly restrictive or threatening—various social science fields can maintain their individuality, and researchers in these fields are not severely handicapped, if a Deweyan (or, for that matter, a

Popperian) "scientific" intellectual methodology is adopted (there is further discussion of Popperian methodology in chapter 8). Indeed, as Follesdal (1979) and Hirsch (1978, 151-152) have both argued, the hypothetico-deductive method of science can readily be found in the humanities.

There is no need for a grand concluding statement. The purpose of the foregoing discussion was simply to establish two points, namely, that the push for naturalistic social science is part of a major trend in Western intellectual thought over the past few centuries, and that naturalism is not a simple position—there are a variety of naturalistic strategies. Thus, those who see themselves as opponents of the quest to develop naturalistic social science are under an obligation to avoid being simplistic: it does not suffice to refute naturalism (if refutation of such a broad spectrum of positions is the appropriate thing to aim for) to refute or severely criticize merely *one form* of naturalism.

6

NEW PHILOSOPHY OF SCIENCE

It is arguable that recent advances in the philosophical understanding of science have vindicated many of John Dewey's views on the matter. Scientific reason is not marked off from other forms of human intellectual endeavor as a sort of model of perfection that these lesser activities must always strive (unsuccessfully) to mimic. Rather, science embodies exactly the same types of fallible reasoning as are found elsewhere—it is just that scientists do, a little more self-consciously and in a more controlled way, what all effective thinkers do. As Dewey pointed out more than half a century ago, he believed that intellectual inquiry,

> in spite of the diverse subjects to which it applies, and the consequent diversity of its special techniques has a common structure or pattern: that this common structure is applied both in common sense and science. (Dewey 1966, 101)

Thus, it is no surprise that Dewey contributed to the "unified science" movement of the early to middle decades of the twentieth century (a matter commented upon further in the previous chapter). Recent work has shown that scientists, like workers in other areas, are in the business of providing reasonable justifications for their assertions, but nothing they do can make these assertions absolutely safe from criticism and potential overthrow. (There are no absolute justifications, hence the somewhat misleading name sometimes given to recent epistemology—"non-justificationist." This is misleading because it suggests that if there are no *absolute* justifications, there are no justifications at all.) It is salutary to remember that Dewey preferred not to use the term *truth*, but rather *warranted assertibility*, and he recognized that different types of assertions required different warrants. Furthermore, this change of language highlighted the fact that a warrant is not forever; today's warrant can be rescinded tomorrow, following further inquiry. Karl Popper, too, expressed a similar view; and in impassioned prose he pointed out that "the question of the sources of our knowledge, like so many authoritarian questions, is a *genetic* one. It asks for the origin of our knowledge, in the belief that knowledge may legitimize itself by its pedigree" (Popper 1985, 52). A little later he added:

> So my answer to the questions "How do you know? What is the source or basis of your assertion? What observations have led you to it?" would be: "I do not know: my assertion was merely a guess. Never mind the source, or the sources, from which it may spring. . . . But if you are interested in the problem which I tried to solve by my tentative assertion, you may help me by criticising it as severely as you can." (Popper 1985, 53)

Criticism, for Popper, includes the offering of disconfirming (refuting) experimental data. (For further discussion of Popper's relevance for the conduct of social science research, see chapter 8.)

It should be clear, therefore, that none of this means that science is *unbelievable*, or that "anything goes" or "anything may be accepted," or that "there is no justification at all for scientific claims," or that "there are no standards by which the truth or adequacy (or both) of a piece of science can be judged." It simply means that it no longer can be claimed that there are any *absolutely authoritative foundations* upon which scientific knowledge is based. Hence, the other title often given to contemporary epistemology—"nonfoundationalist."

This account of science fits comfortably with the view that many scientists themselves hold—especially, perhaps, action researchers in the applied social sciences and evaluators of social programs; these latter *are par excellence* fields of "the believable," of building the "good case," but where even the best of cases can be challenged or reanalyzed or reinterpreted. Nothing is more suspicious in the field of program evaluation, for example, than a report that is presented with the implication that it has the status of "Holy Writ." Researchers in the "pure" sciences, and in the more laboratory-oriented of the social and human sciences, now have to accept that good science is a blood brother if not a sibling to what transpires in these messier and more open-ended fields of endeavor.

What happened in philosophy of science to build this new and modest view? Or, alternatively, what destroyed the older view?

AN OUTLINE OF RECENT DEVELOPMENTS

The new view of science could not get off the ground until the foundations of the dominant older view, positivism, had been shown to be untenable. The role that had been ascribed to observation—being the rock-bottom foundation of science and at the same time being the final arbiter of what could be believed—was reevaluated; and the relation between scientific theories and evidence was shown to be more complex than had been thought. The related view that science grows by steady accumulation of findings and theories was challenged by the work of Thomas Kuhn and subsequent scholars such as Lakatos and Feyerabend. Obviously, these matters are too complex to discuss in encyclopedic detail, but a few of the crucial issues can be highlighted.

1. It is clear (to all except some of the more radical social constructivists—see chapter 11) that if the aim of science is to establish bodies of knowledge about the world, then somewhere in the process of doing science the world must be allowed to constrain or discipline our theories. But it has been recognized for many decades that the positivistic and operationalistic view that all theoretical terms of science must be reducible to (i.e., definable in terms of) observational language is quixotic. The status of operationalism in the behavioral sciences was a hot issue in the decade immediately following the Second World War, and there were international symposia on the matter. A consensus was reached (except, of course, for a few diehards—an old story). The point was driven home that the theoretical concepts of science have meanings that transcend definition in observational terms; if this was not the case, science would have trouble in growing and extending into new areas. And it was realized that if the positivist/operationist view was accepted, it would have a chilling effect on theorizing about unobservable mechanisms such as the subatomic events that have won Nobel Prizes for so many physicists. (See the discussion of positivism in chapter 9.) Some logical positivists and fellow travelers even softened their views to make room for meaningful theoretical terms; thus, Carl Hempel, a somewhat "lapsed" logical positivist, drew the following enticing picture, which makes absurd the strict operationalist notion that concepts can each be reduced to a set of observation statements:

> Scientific systematization requires the establishment of diverse connections, by laws or theoretical principles, between different aspects of the empirical world, which are characterized by scientific concepts. Thus,

the concepts of science are the knots in a network of systematic inter-
relationships in which laws and theoretical principles form the
threads. . . . The more threads that converge upon, or issue from, a conceptual knot, the stronger will be its systematizing role, or its systematic import. (Hempel 1966, 94)

(It should be noted that there is another—perhaps even more attractive—
account of theoretical terms, an account that realists can embrace but that
positivists have to avoid. See Newton-Smith 1981, especially chapter 2.
See also the discussion of the "causal theory" of the meaning of scientific
terms near the end of chapter 3 in the present volume.)

But there is another issue about the role of observation. It has often
been held that it is the "neutral court" that adjudicates between rival scientific claims; together with this has usually gone the belief that science
is actually built upon the foundation of indubitable observation. (The
operationalist thesis discussed before concerned the *status* of theoretical
concepts, not their *origin*.) The crucial critical work here is that of N. R.
Hanson, whose *Patterns of Discovery* (1958) has taken on the status of a
classic. Hanson was not the first to have said the things that he said;
Wittgenstein used the key illustration that Hanson used, and even Dewey
made much the same point. But it was Hanson's work that for some reason fired imaginations.

Hanson's thesis may be stated in one sentence: "The theory, hypothesis, or background knowledge held by an observer can influence in a
major way what is observed." Or, as he put it in a nice aphorism, "There
is more to seeing than meets the eyeball" (Hanson 1958, 7). Thus, in a
famous psychological experiment, slides were made from cards selected
from a normal deck, and these were projected for very short periods onto
a screen in front of observers. All were correctly identified, except for a
trick slide that had the color altered (for example, it might have been a
black four of diamonds). Most commonly, this slide was *seen* as a blur or
as a black suit (spades or clubs). A Hansonian interpretation is that there
is an interaction between the visual stimulus and the observers' background knowledge ("diamonds are red"), so the final result is that a blur
is observed.

Subsequent writers have drawn a variety of conclusions from Hanson's
thesis of theory-laden perception (although it should be noted in passing
that some special cases where it does not hold—such as optical illusions—
have been discussed in the recent literature; see Fodor 1984). For instance,
many have taken it as supporting relativism—"There is no such thing as

objective truth, for what observers take to be true depends upon the framework of knowledge and assumptions they bring with them." Sometimes an example is given that comes from Hanson himself: He imagined the astronomers Tycho Brahe and Johannes Kepler watching the dawn together; because they had different frameworks, one would see the sun moving above the horizon, while the other would see the Earth rotating away to reveal the sun. However, a closer reading of Hanson provides no succor for such an extravagant relativism, for he explicitly acknowledged that *both* astronomers would agree that what they actually *observed* during the dawn was the sun increasing its relative distance above the Earth's eastern horizon (Fodor 1984, 23). This acknowledgment is evidence that Hanson realized people with different frameworks have some views in common, views that can serve as the basis for further discussion and clarification of their respective positions—something a dedicated relativist has to deny.

A less extreme interpretation of Hanson, then, is that while we must be aware of the role played by our preconceptions, and while we have to abandon the view that observation is "neutral" and theory-free, there is nothing to force us to the conclusion that we cannot decide between rival claims and, therefore, cannot arrive at consensus about which viewpoint (or which observations) seem to be most trustworthy under the prevailing circumstances. Israel Scheffler put it well:

> There is no evidence for a general incapacity to learn from contrary observations, no proof of a preestablished harmony between what we believe and what we see. . . . Our categorizations and expectations guide by orienting us selectively toward the future; they set us, in particular, to perceive in certain ways and not in others. Yet they do not blind us to the unforeseen. They allow us to recognize what fails to match anticipation. (Scheffler 1967, 44)

2. Over the last few decades it has become increasingly clear that scientific theories are "underdetermined" by nature; that is, whatever evidence is available about nature, it is never sufficient to rule authoritatively between the merits of rival theories. Or to put it in yet another way, a variety of rival theories or hypotheses can always be constructed that are equally compatible with whatever finite body of evidence is currently available. An implication of this, of course, is that we can never be certain that the particular theory we have accepted to account for the evidence is the correct one. (Some radical or "strong" social constructivists make

much of this point, which they misinterpret—see chapter 11.) Recently, however, Laudan has pointed out that it must not be assumed that all the rival or alternative theories that are *logically possible* will be equally plausible—in other words, he cautions that the argument from underdetermination might be overblown (Laudan 1990).

Several issues here are worthy of further comment (these are discussed at greater length in Phillips 1987):

a. The first point is illustrated by Nelson Goodman's notorious example of "grue and bleen" (Goodman 1973). A large amount of observational evidence has accumulated over the ages concerning the color of emeralds; all that have been studied thus far have been found to be green. It might be supposed, then, that this amounts to irrefutable evidence for the hypothesis "all emeralds are green." But the *very same* evidence also supports the hypothesis that "all emeralds are grue" (where "grue" is the name of a property such that an object is green up to a certain date, for instance, the year 2000, and blue thereafter—a thesis that readers of the new edition of this *Bestiary* will be able to empirically test!). The fanciful nature of this example is beside the point; it nicely illustrates the underdetermination of theory by available evidence, for it shows that a general theory ("emeralds are green—i.e., always have been, and always will be") necessarily goes beyond the finite evidence that is available ("the finite number of emeralds observed to date have been green"), thus leaving open the possibility that some ingenious scientist will come up with an alternative explanation for the very same finite set of data (maybe the crucial date is the year 3000!).

b. A related issue here is that when new evidence necessitates that *some* accommodatory change has to be made in whatever theory is currently the favored one, there is *no one specific change that is necessitated*. Different scientists may change different portions of the theory—they are free to use their professional judgment and their creativity. It would be a mistake to interpret this as indicating that scientific theories are a matter of mere whim or individual taste; to stress that judgment is required is not to throw away all standards, it is just to stress that decisions cannot be made using some mechanical or algorithmic procedure. It is appropriate to point out here that John Stuart Mill had inklings of this point as long ago as the mid-nineteenth century; for, according to Hilary Putnam, Mill said

> that one cannot do science by slavishly following the rules of Mill's *Logic*. (There is no general method, Mill remarked, that will not give bad results "if conjoined with universal idiocy.") (Putnam 1987, 73)

This general point is often made in terms of the "Duhem-Quine" thesis. Scientific theories, indeed vast areas of science, are interrelated; the image of science as a huge fishnet is a predominant one in much recent writing. It is this network as a whole, rather than little portions of it, that has to withstand the test of dealing with whatever evidence is gathered. Thus, it might appear that a piece of recalcitrant data offers a serious challenge to one particular section of the net, but the threat cannot be localized in this way; one scientist may react to the data by altering the "obvious" portion of the net, but others might want to preserve this piece and so might advocate changing some other portion of the net so as to accommodate the new information.

c. It might even be the case that when some counter-evidence turns up, scientists might decide to make no accommodatory changes at all—a course of action (or rather, a course of inaction) that receives the blessing of the new philosophy of science. For one thing, it might well be the case that one of the auxiliary assumptions that have to be made in any piece of scientific work is faulty, and scientists can blame one or other of these rather than accept the counter-evidence at face value and be forced to change their net. In doing laboratory work, for example, it is often assumed that the chemical samples that are being used are pure, or that there were no temperature fluctuations, or that the testing equipment was reliable, or that an observer was unbiased, or . . . (See Popper 1985, chap. 10, for an early discussion of auxiliary hypotheses.)

On the other hand, scientists might ignore the counter-evidence in the hope that "something eventually will turn up that will explain it." It was a traditional tenet of methodology that a scientist must abandon a theory, no matter how attractive it might appear, once some counter-evidence became available. It now appears, however, that there are good reasons to suppose that it can be quite rational to adhere to the theory even under these adverse conditions. Paul Feyerabend has been the most forceful writer on this and related issues:

> The idea of a method that contains firm, unchanging, and absolutely binding principles for conducting the business of science gets into considerable difficulty when confronted with the results of historical research. We find, then, that there is not a single rule, however plausible, and however firmly grounded in epistemology, that is not violated at some time or other. It becomes evident that such violations are not accidental events. . . . On the contrary, we see they are necessary for progress. (Feyerabend 1970, 21-22)

Even Popper, the arch proponent of falsification, has stressed that negative or refuting evidence is never absolutely binding; the scientist has to make a methodological decision to *accept* the evidence as valid—and sometimes it is reasonable not to take this action. But, of course, Popper recommends that we adopt the rule that, in general, refuting evidence *be* accepted (see Popper 1985, chap. 10). Imre Lakatos devised his "methodology of scientific research programs" in an alternative attempt to gauge when changes made in an ongoing research tradition were progressive or degenerative (Lakatos 1972).

3. Perhaps the most famous feature of the new philosophy of science, however, has been its focus upon the dynamics of science. The process of scientific change has come under increasing investigation since Kuhn's work on scientific revolutions popularized the notion of "paradigm clashes." Science is not static; theories come and theories go, and new data accumulates and old findings are interpreted in new ways. As Newton-Smith put it, "viewed *sub specie eternitatis* scientists (even physical scientists) are a fickle lot. The history of science is a tale of multifarious shiftings of allegiance from theory to theory" (Newton-Smith 1981, 3). And involved in all this is the question of the *rationality* of change—what justifies scientists in throwing out old ideas and accepting new ones? There has been much debate here, but little consensus—witness, for example, the work of Kuhn, Popper, Lakatos, Feyerabend, Toulmin, Laudan, and Newton-Smith (see previous citations, plus Laudan, 1977; and Newton-Smith 1981). It will suffice to quote a brief passage from Popper to illustrate this major theme in the new *postpositivist* philosophy:

> I assert that continued growth is essential to the rational and empirical character of scientific knowledge; that if science ceases to grow it must lose that character. It is the way of its growth which makes science rational and empirical, the way, that is, in which scientists discriminate between available theories and choose the better one. (Popper, 1961, 215)

QUESTIONS AND ANSWERS

There are some who have drawn a dangerous moral from the developments just outlined. Science has fallen from its pedestal; and if no knowledge can be justified totally and unchallengeably, then no claims to have attained knowledge can be disbarred. The rocky road to relativism is embarked upon. But it is possible to retain a hopeful outlook and even to relish the challenge that this new picture of science presents. It is here that we can obtain succor from the fields of program evaluation and action research in the applied social sciences. Investigators here do not lose heart, yet they are faced with a reality that (we now realize) closely parallels that of "pure" scientists; and some even thrive on the uncertainties of their field. The ideal that is embraced seems to be this: Seekers after enlightenment in any field do the best that they can; they honestly seek evidence, they critically scrutinize it, they are (relatively) open to alternative viewpoints, they take criticism (fairly) seriously and try to profit from it, they play their hunches, they stick to their guns, but they also have a sense of when it is time to quit. It may be a dirty and hard and uncertain game, but with no fixed algorithms to determine progress, it is the only game in town.

Although to the present author this seems a modest, nondoctrinaire, unsurprising, and eminently reasonable position, there are many who feel uneasy and who continue to raise questions about it. So it might be fruitful to grapple with some of these directly.

QUESTION 1: In what sense is the new position that has been outlined here "postpositivistic"? Isn't it merely a weaker form of positivism in disguise? It may have come *after* positivism, and that is the only reason for calling it "post"positivism.

ANSWER: In no sense is the new philosophy of science—broad and ill-defined though it is—closely akin to positivism (or, more especially, to the most notorious form of positivism, logical positivism). Logical positivism became discredited in the years immediately following the end of the Second World War; few if any philosophers these days subscribe to its core tenet, the "verifiability criterion of meaning," according to which a statement is meaningful only if it is verifiable in terms of sense experience (excepting logicomathematical propositions). (For more discussion of this topic, see chapter 9.) One of the serious problems associated with the use of this principle in science was that it made theoretical terms meaningless, for the fact is that many theoretical entities cannot be verified in terms of sense experience; but there are few today who would want to argue that the discourse of subatomic particle physicists or of black hole theorists is meaningless! The fact of the matter is that the logical positivists were, by and large, antirealists who held—or came close to holding—some form of instrumentalism.

QUESTION 2: Aren't contemporary postpositivists clinging to an old and outmoded realist paradigm?

ANSWER: This question embodies a serious confusion. The old positivist view was antirealist; as explained in the previous answer, the logical positivists (on the whole) denied the reality of theoretical entities and indeed claimed that talk of such entities was literally meaningless (some took refuge in a position about theories similar to the one cited earlier from Hempel). Modern realism is a recent, postpositivistic development. Furthermore, there is little consensus within the philosophical community; whether or not realism is viable is a hotly debated topic—many contemporary philosophers are for it, but many are against it. (A leading postpositivistic antirealist is Bas van Fraassen 1980; but his *grounds* for antirealism are not those of the logical positivists.) There is even controversy about the precise definition of realism: Arthur Fine has written:

> Given the diverse array of philosophical positions that have sought the "realist" label, it is probably not possible to give a sketch of realism that will encompass them all. Indeed it may be hopeless to try, even, to capture the essential features of realism. (Fine 1987, 359)

There is a nice passage in Hilary Putnam's "Paul Carus Lectures" that highlights these complexities:

> Thus, it is clear that the name "Realism" can be claimed by or given to at least two very different philosophical attitudes (and, in fact, to many). The philosopher who claims that only scientific objects "really exist" and that much, if not all, of the commonsense world is mere "projection" claims to be a realist, but so does the philosopher who insists that there *really are* chairs and ice cubes . . . and these two attitudes, these two images of the world can lead to and have

led to many different programs for philosophy. (Putnam 1987, 4)

QUESTION 3: Well, old or new, many influential post-positivists are realists. Aren't they overlooking the fact that multiple realities exist, and aren't they overlooking the well-known fact that each society *constructs* its own reality? If you accept these two points, you cannot be a realist! Consider merely one example; Egon Guba has written that social scientists are studying phenomena that are

> *social* in nature. There is no need to posit a natural state of affairs and a natural set of laws for phenomena that are so-cially invented—I shall say socially constructed—in people's minds. I suggest an ontology that is relativist in nature. It begins with the premise that all social realities are con-structed and shared through well understood socialization processes. It is this socialized sharing that gives these con-structions their apparent reality. (Guba 1990, 89)

ANSWER: There are several important issues here, some of which were touched upon in the earlier discussion. (See also the discussion in Bunge 1992, section 9.)

1. In the first place, this question seems inspired by an ex-treme reading of Kuhn—the view that all of us are trapped within some particular paradigm and that we cannot converse rationally with those in other paradigms because our beliefs are incommensurable. Even the later Kuhn—the Kuhn of *The Es-sential Tension*—did not accept this extreme relativism. (Fur-thermore, such relativism seems contradicted by everyday ex-perience within science. Freudians do understand—but, of course, disagree with—Skinnerians, and neo-Marxist social scientists understand colleagues of more conservative bent, and vice versa.)

2. Second, there are a number of things that get run to-gether illicitly in discussions about "reality." First, there is a simple confusion here between, on the one hand, the fact that different people and different societies have different views about what is real (a fact that seems undeniable) and, on the

other hand, the issue of whether or not we can know which of these views is the correct one (or, indeed, whether there is a correct one at all). From the fact that we might not be able to reach agreement (an epistemological matter), it does not follow that there is more than one "reality" (an ontological matter). Second, it is clear that on some issues what is *regarded or judged* to be "real" depends upon which conceptual apparatus is available—one group, for example, may only have concepts or classificatory schemes that recognize three types of snow, while a different group might make distinctions between ten types, and the result will be that the two groups differ with respect to the question "How many types of snow exist?"

Now, the relativist seems to be committed to the view that *all* such differing views are correct—that is, there *really are* three types of snow and ten types of snow; whereas the realist is only committed to the minimal (and more informative) view that something, "snow," really exists although different groups conceptualize it differently. The realist (qua *realist*) is not forced to say which of these conceptualizations is "correct"; indeed, it is a viable position for the realist to say that it is a silly question to ask which conceptualization is correct, for different conceptualizations do different work in different communities.

There is, however, another type of situation where the realist will want to take a stronger stand. This is the (perhaps rare) situation where groups or different individuals are using terms in the same sense. To make this a little more precise: Suppose that one social group believes that "X is the case," and another group believes—in the very same sense of X—that "not-X is the case." The realist holds that both of these views cannot be correct, although, of course, some people *believe* one or the other of these to be true; it is either the case that X or not-X, but not both, is true. (The realist does not have to believe that we can always settle which of these views, X or not-X, is true; the issue is whether both or, at best, only one *can* be true.) The relativist has to hold that, in this situation, there are multiple realities—that reality is both X and not-X—for if the relativist does not hold this, then his or her position dissolves into the realist position. Stated thus boldly, it can be seen that the relativist case here hinges on obscuring the distinction between "what people believe to be true" and "what really is true, whether or not we can determine this truth at the moment." (This confusion is discussed further in Phillips and Burbules 2000; and, of course, here are many other problems with relativism—see Siegel 1987.)

3. Third, it is important to note that this issue dividing realists from relativists is not the same as the issue (discussed earlier) that separates realists from antirealists; the second of these is the issue (broadly speaking) of the reality or otherwise of theoretical entities (that is, the status of the entities referred to in theories such as those found in the field of particle physics). There is, as might be expected with such complexities, a tendency for the neophyte to run these two sets of issues together! (See, for the second of the two issues mentioned, Leplin 1984.)

4. Finally, this third question raises the very important matter of the social construction of reality, touched upon briefly earlier (and discussed in more detail in chapter 11). Certainly, there is nothing in postpositivism, per se, that requires denying that societies determine many of the things that are to count as real for their members; what things are *taken* to be real depends upon the concepts and classifications available within those societies. Thus, a "primitive" society may define certain spirits as being real, and the members of that society might accept them as real and act accordingly. A similar thing certainly happens in our own society and not just with spirits. All a postpositivist would want to insist upon is that these matters can be open to research: We can inquire into the beliefs of a society, how they came about, what are their effects, and what is the status of the evidence that is offered in support of the truth of the beliefs. And we can get these matters right or wrong—we can get our descriptions of these beliefs right or wrong, or we can be right or make mistakes about their origins or their effects. It simply does not follow from the fact of the social construction of reality that scientific inquiry becomes impossible or that we have to become relativists. And certainly, it does not follow from the fact that a tribe of headhunters socially determines its own reality, that we thereby have to

accept that reality as *true*. What is true—if we have done our research properly—is that the members of that tribe actually do *believe* in their own "realities." But that is a different issue, one that raises no great problem of principle for postpositivists. Thus, Popper, one of the major postpositivists (and the man who claimed to have been the person who killed positivism), stressed that his philosophy "assumes a physical world in which we act," although he added that we may not know very much about it. But, he wrote, it was also necessary to "assume a social world, populated by other people, about whose goals we know something (often not very much), and, furthermore, social institutions. These social institutions determine the peculiarly social character of our social environment" (Popper 1976, 103). Popper includes laws and customs among "institutions."

QUESTION 4: Given the acceptance by postpositivists of Hanson's thesis concerning the theory-ladenness of perception, and given the general nonfoundationalist tenet that nothing can be considered as absolutely certain, and so forth, does it not follow that postpositivists have to abandon the notion of objectivity? Hasn't it been stripped of any meaning that it might have had?

ANSWER: Certainly not! The notion of objectivity, like the notion of truth, is a regulative ideal that underlies all inquiry. (For further discussion of this issue, see chapter 7.) If we abandon such notions, it is not sensible to make inquiries at all. For if a sloppy inquiry is as acceptable as a careful one, and if any inquiry that is careless about evidence is as acceptable as an inquiry that has taken pains to be precise and unbiased, then there is no need to inquire—we might as well accept, without further fuss, any old view that tickles our fancy.

Now, it is true that the fact that an inquiry is objective does not guarantee its truth—it was shown earlier that *nothing* can guarantee that we have reached the truth. Perhaps an analogy will help to clarify matters: Consider two firms that manufacture radios; one is proud of its workmanship and backs its products with a strong guarantee; while the other firm is after a quick profit, practices shoddy workmanship, and does not offer any warranty to the buyer. A consumer would be unwise to purchase the latter's product, but nevertheless it is clearly understood that the first firm's guarantee does not absolutely mean that the radio will not break down. The fact that this situation exists is not taken by consumers as invalidating the notion of a warranty, nor is it seen as making each purchase equally wise. And the very same situation exists in science.

The Popperian account of objectivity is widely, though not universally, accepted by postpositivists. The following sentences capture the essence of his approach:

> What may be described as scientific objectivity is based solely upon a critical tradition which, despite resistance, often makes it possible to criticize a dominant dogma. To put it another way, the objectivity of science is not a matter of the individual scientists but rather the social result of their mutual criticism, of the friendly-hostile division of labour among scientists, of their cooperation and also of their competition. For this reason, it depends in part, upon a number of social and political circumstances which make criticism possible. (Popper 1976, 95)

[handwritten marginalia: Function of what science is]
[handwritten marginalia: Cultural values as advanced as necessary components of]
[handwritten right margin: Central to regulation ideas of what sci. is.]

CONCLUSIONS

[handwritten: — open, free debate ~ Western values]

It can be seen from the foregoing that postpositivism is a broad, complex, and dynamic approach to understanding the nature of science. There is little unanimity on important issues among its "adherents" (if people can be said to adhere to so amorphous a position)—but this is a healthy feature and not a weakness. Paul Feyerabend wrote, more than a quarter-century ago, that unanimity of opinion may be fitting for some church, or for the followers of a tyrant, but it is most unfitting for science (Feyerabend 1970, 33).

The danger to postpositivism comes not from internal dissension, but from outside—from those who draw false, and often oversimple, conclusions from some of the very same developments that have produced postpositivism itself.

D. C. Phillips, "Postpositivistic Science," in E. Guba, ed., *The Paradigm Dialog.* © 1990 by Sage Publications, Inc. Some minor changes have been introduced. Reprinted by permission of Sage Publications, Inc.

7

OBJECTIVITY AND SUBJECTIVITY

You do not have to read very widely in the contemporary methodological or theoretical literature pertaining to research in the "pure" and "applied" social sciences in order to discover that the topic of objectivity is causing great *angst*. Some scholars think that objectivity is dead or a ghost from a modernist past; others—more sophisticated, perhaps—see that the account that we give of objectivity needs to be rethought. Sometimes when the term happens to be used, it is set in quotation marks—"objectivity"— to bring out the point that a dodolike entity is being discussed. On other occasions, "there is no such thing," authors confidently state, unmindful of the dilemma this puts them in: For if they are right, then the reader does not have to break into a sweat—because if there is no such thing as objectivity, then the view that there is no such thing is itself not objective; but, then, if this view is the subjective judgment of a particular author, readers are entitled to prefer their own subjective viewpoint—which, of course, might be that objectivity is *not* dead!

A couple of illustrations should suffice to set the stage; the first is from Gunnar Myrdal:

> The ethos of social science is the search for "objective" truth. The faith of the student is his conviction that truth is wholesome and that illusions are damaging, especially opportunistic ones. He seeks "realism," a term which in one of its meanings denotes an "objective" view of reality. . . . How can a biased view be avoided? (Myrdal 1969, 3)

After an interesting discussion of the deep-seated sources of bias and opportunism in belief, Myrdal suggests that some techniques exist to help achieve at least a degree of objectivity. A second example comes from the sociologist Robert Nisbet, writing in 1974; even then objectivity was under severe attack, a phenomenon that Nisbet regarded as "unbelievable" and potentially fatal to the social sciences. He pointed out that many were arguing "that objectivity of inquiry is not even a proper end of the social sciences" (Nisbet 1974, 16) and that these people also argued that an

> objective understanding of social behavior is impossible; such understanding will always be limited by the political, or ethnic, or social and economic position one occupies in the social order. Its embedded values must become the values of the investigator and, hence, the bias of his conclusions. There is nothing that can be done about this. (Nisbet 1974, 17)

These views attacking—or modifying—objectivity did not die out during the 1970s. Thus, to cite one later example, on the occasion of receiving an honorary doctorate in 1986 the prominent American educational researcher Elliot Eisner stated that

> What I have even more quarrel with is the view that a scientifically acceptable research method is "objective" or valuefree, that it harbors no particular point of view. All methods and forms of representation are partial. (Eisner 1986, 15)

Or consider the fact that during the '80s and '90s, some postmodern and feminist scholars struggled to develop a new view of objectivity (realizing, perhaps, the dilemma with which this chapter opened—if your view is not "objective," why should others pay attention to it; and yet if you do accept objectivity as a criterion, then one seems to have become very "modernist"). The postmodernist James Scheurich writes that he can accept even a "strong" view of objectivity (of which more later), but

> I strongly resist the idea that this criterion is not historically mediated. I can see that this criterion is useful and meaningful for the social struggle to establish equitable social arrangements, but I cannot see that arguing that this criterion is itself unmediated by socially located truth games is helpful to that struggle. (Scheurich 1997, 40)

It is interesting to note that he does not mention the *epistemic* need for research to be objective—he only stresses the consequences for social struggle. (One might be excused for thinking this puts the cart before the horse—which is not to say that the horse is more important than the cart, but it is strange to think that it should not take the lead!)

It is not intended that the present chapter will develop into a paradoxical discussion of the self-referential puzzles generated by critiques of objectivity. But it is the intent, at the outset of the inquiry, to point out the oddity of trying to write an essay for an academic volume—a paradigm case of an exercise in the marshaling of objective considerations—if, indeed, there is no escape from subjectivity. It would be too quixotic; and it would be better to take the bull by the horns and proceed by using rhetoric (much as is being done now), or special pleading, or appeals to the readers' baser motives.

Believing the task not to be quixotic, the present author is inspired to inquire into the intellectual reasons for objectivity sinking into such disrepute and to investigate whether—as an ideal—it deserves the fate that has befallen it. (Nisbet focused his discussion on the *political*, and not the *intellectual*, grounds of the attack on objectivity.) The issues, then, are these: Why do some have doubts that research can be objective, and are these doubts reasonable? What notion of objectivity is involved here? Are critics correct in suggesting that it is naive to hold objectivity as a goal for social inquiry? If all views are subjective, are they all on a par, or are some more subjective than others? (The closely related issue of the precise role of value judgments in the social sciences is pursued in chapter 13.)

One further point remains to be made in this prelude. It is clear that—despite the attacks—in normal parlance the term *objective* is commendatory, while *subjective* carries negative connotations. After all, the "person in the street" does not think it is a good thing for a judge, a physicist, an anthropologist, or a professor to be subjective. It is even worse to be *biased*—this latter term being sometimes used to mark the contrast with objectivity. Myrdal seems to use *bias* in this way throughout his book (Myrdal 1969). (Such negative evaluations are likely to change over time, of course, if it turns out that objectivity is dead and that there is no option but to be subjective.) In what follows, the discussion will attempt to avoid using the terms in a judgmental way—at least until it has been established, objectively, that either term can justifiably be so used.

THE INTELLECTUAL ROOTS OF THE ATTACK ON OBJECTIVITY

The fields of philosophy of science and epistemology have undergone something of a revolution in recent decades. As recounted in the previous chapter, the traditional foundationalist or justificationist approach to epistemology has largely been abandoned in favor of a nonfoundationalist

approach; in philosophy of science, the work of Popper, closely followed
by that of Kuhn, Hanson, Feyerabend, and Lakatos, has been the center
of much debate. Acting under these influences, some individuals have
moved in the direction of relativism (although this is not what had been
intended by most of the individuals just mentioned). But the very same
forces—supplemented by one or two others—have also given rise to the
strong attack on objectivity. It will be as well to discuss the major influences in turn.

a. Nonfoundationalist Epistemology

Traditional epistemologies, whether of rationalist or empiricist persua-
sion, were foundationalist or justificationist in the sense that they regarded
knowledge as being built upon (or justified in terms of) some solid and
unchallengeable foundation. It was the presence of this solid foundation
that served as the justification for the knowledge claims that were made.
Where the traditional schools of epistemology fell out with each other was
over the issue of what, precisely, constituted this foundation. Empiricists
(like Locke, Berkeley, and Hume) saw the foundation as being human
experience—sense impressions or some such item. Rationalists (like
Descartes) claimed it was human reason; the starting place for the construction of knowledge (Descartes termed it the "Archimedian point") was
to be those beliefs that appeared indubitable after scrutiny in the light of
reason.

In the twentieth century there has been a steady erosion of foundationalism of both varieties. It is now recognized that there is no absolutely
secure starting point for knowledge; nothing is known with such certainty
that all possibility of future revision is removed. All knowledge is tentative. Karl Popper is probably the best-known advocate of this newer perspective, but he is not, by far, a solitary figure. In his words:

> The question about the sources of our knowledge . . . has always been
> asked in the spirit of: "What are the best sources of our knowledge—
> the most reliable ones, those which will not lead us into error, and those
> to which we can and must turn, in case of doubt, as the last court of ap-
> peal?" I propose to assume, instead, that no such ideal sources exist—
> no more than ideal rules—and that all "sources" are liable to lead us into
> error at times. And I propose to replace, therefore, the question of the
> sources of our knowledge by the entirely different question: "*How can
> we hope to detect* and *eliminate error?*" (Popper 1968, 25)

It is important to note that abandonment of the notion that knowledge is built on an unshakable foundation does not mean that the traditional notion of truth has been abandoned. Popper constantly reminds his readers that truth is an essential "regulative ideal." He offers this nice image:

> The status of truth in the objective sense, as correspondence to the facts, and its role as a regulative principle, may be compared to that of a mountain peak which is permanently, or almost permanently, wrapped in clouds. The climber may not merely have difficulties in getting there—he may not know when he gets there, because he may be unable to distinguish, in the clouds, between the main summit and some subsidiary peak. Yet this does not affect the objective existence of the summit. . . . The very idea of error, or of doubt . . . implies the idea of an objective truth which we may fail to reach. (Popper 1968, 226)

It makes little sense to search for a summit if you do not believe that a summit exists; and it makes little sense to try to understand some situation if you believe that *any* story about that situation is as good as any other. In this latter case, to inquire is to waste one's energy—one might as well have just invented any old story. But if some stories are regarded as being better than others, then this belief, upon unpacking, will be found to presuppose the notion of truth as a regulative ideal. (For the application of this insight to narrative research, see chapter 4.)

The crucial point for the present discussion is that it does not follow from any of these developments in epistemology that the notion of objectivity has been undermined. This "unbelievable consequence" would only follow if objectivity were equated with certainty. This is to say that the following argument is a *non sequitur*, at least until some further premise is added to link the antecedent to the consequent: "If no knowledge is certain, then there is no possibility for any viewpoint to be objective." (It might be objected here that Popper himself referred to the real existence of his cloud-covered mountaintop, and he said it might never be possible to know that one had reached it—showing that attainment of "objective truth" might not be possible. But it is crucial to note that here he was not discussing "objectivity," he was discussing "truth"; certainly, Popper was speaking for most of us when he stressed that we may never know when—and if—we have stumbled across the truth. When we abandon foundationalism, we abandon the assurance that we can know when we have reached the truth; but, as Popper's story also illustrates, we do not have to abandon the *notion* of truth or the quest for it, and we do not abandon the view that some types of inquiries are better than others.)

Leaving aside the notion of truth, and returning to the issue of the objectivity of inquiries: *There is good reason to hold that certainty and objectivity should not be linked.* For if they were, all human knowledge would thereby become subjective (for no knowledge is certain), and this would have the effect of washing out the following vital distinction. Consider two researchers in a classroom in which a science teacher has been conducting a lesson on a difficult topic. One researcher claims to have noticed that the students did not understand the material, but the only evidence she gives is that "I did not understand the material myself"; the other social scientist also claims that the students did not learn but offers by way of evidence the test scores of the students, a videotape of the classroom showing the puzzled demeanor of the students, and interview protocols that a panel of readers agree show that a random sample of the students were rather confused about the topic. The new epistemology would have us recognize that neither of these two views is absolutely certain; but it is not the consequence of the new nonfoundationalist epistemology that we would have to judge both views as being equally "subjective." For it is evident that one of the researchers was greatly influenced by her own personal reactions to the lesson, and this unduly affected how she perceived the classroom ("unduly" signifying here that this researcher's personal biases or inclinations were not, in this situation, epistemically relevant—for the issue under study was: what was happening in the *classroom*). In contrast, the other social scientist had taken pains to marshal epistemically relevant evidence (even if that evidence was not absolutely incorrigible). In a straightforward and nontroublesome sense, all normal users of the English language would regard the view of the first researcher as a subjective one, and the second researcher's opinion would be regarded as being more objective (even if the opinion later turned out to be wrong).

This example suggests the following hypothesis: "Objective" *seems to be a label that we apply to inquiries that meet certain procedural standards*, but objectivity does not guarantee that the results of inquiries have any certainty. (It implies that the inquiries so labeled are free of gross defects, and this should be of some comfort—just as a consumer prefers to buy an item that has met rigorous inspection standards, although this does not absolutely ensure that it will not break down.) The other side of the coin is that a biased, bigoted person who jumps to some subjective conclusion about, say, a political candidate who happens to be of different ethnicity, may not always be wrong. His or her biased judgment may turn out to be true (just as a consumer who purchases a shoddy piece of merchandise occasionally "lucks out" and never has any trouble with it). To use a historical example, in its heyday Newtonian physics was supported by a wealth of objective evidence, that is, evidence that was free from personal "contamination" and that was, in large part, accepted by an international community the members of which had subjected it to critical scrutiny and cross-check. Nevertheless, in our day, evidence has accumulated that makes it difficult to maintain the view that the Newtonian framework is anything but a reasonably good approximation to the truth (but not as good, for example, as the Einsteinian framework, which itself is probably not absolutely true). Thus, those scientists of earlier times who rejected Newton for their own personal (subjective) reasons turned out to have been right in doing so, although we can say that they were not *rationally justified* in so doing.

To put the point pithily, neither subjectivity nor objectivity has an exclusive stranglehold on truth. As Brian Fay puts it,

> Given fallibilism, an acceptable account of objectivity cannot tie it directly to the notion of truth. . . . Thus "objective" cannot mean "objectively true" if objectivity is to remain an ideal. If objectivity does not characterize the outcome of research, what else might it characterize? Fallibilism suggests an alternative account of objectivity, one which construes objectivity not as a property of the results of inquiry but as a property of *the process of inquiry itself.* (Fay 1996, 212)

This is a segue into a vital issue: Why, then, should objectivity be preferred if it is not guaranteed to lead to the truth? The answer is implied in the previous discussion: At any one time, the viewpoint that is the most objective is the one that currently is the most *warranted* or *rational*—to deny this is to deny that there is any significant difference between the warrants for the views of the two classroom researchers in the earlier example. If we give up this distinction, if we hold that a biased or personally loaded viewpoint is as good as a viewpoint supported by carefully gathered evidence, we are undermining the very point of human inquiry. (This is why Nisbet, for example, was so concerned.) If a shoddy inquiry is to be trusted as much as a careful one, then it is pointless to inquire carefully. The philosopher Ernest Nagel put it well:

> those attacks on the notion that scientific inquiry can be objective are tantamount to an endorsement of the view that the grounds on which conclusions in the sciences are accepted are at bottom no better than are

the grounds on which superstitious beliefs are adopted. Those attacks
may therefore . . . justify any doctrine, no matter how unwarranted it may
be. (Nagel 1979, 85)

In the light of these remarks, it would seem that the educational researcher Elliot Eisner (used as an example earlier) was both right and
wrong when he stated that "To hold that our conceptions of reality are true
or objective to the extent that they are isomorphic with reality is to embrace a hopeless correspondence theory of truth . . . " (Eisner 1979, 214).
He was right to criticize the identification of objectivity with "isomorphic
with reality"; however, he was wrong to treat "objective" and "true" as
synonyms, and he was wrong to suggest that nonfoundationalism leads to
the rejection of the correspondence theory of truth. It is worth comment-
ing here, to forestall a philosophical misunderstanding, that the correspondence theory of truth is firmly entrenched in contemporary philosophy,
and it is supported by weighty—but not by absolutely conclusive—considerations. Eisner runs together two issues that philosophers keep separate for good reasons: The first of these issues is concerned with what account best clarifies the *meaning* of the term *truth*, and it is here that the
correspondence theory is alive and well, as Popper's story of the cloudy
mountain illustrates; the second issue is what test or criterion we can rely
upon in order to judge if a theory actually is isomorphic with reality. On
this second matter, nonfoundationalists would answer that there is no such
test or *criterion*, as once again Popper's allegory illustrates. Eisner and others have reasoned backward, invalidly, from the (correct) negative response
to the second issue, to a negative judgment about the first. (A similar confusion bedeviled critics of William James's work. See D. C. Phillips 1984.)

b. Hansonism

It is now widely accepted that observation is always theory-laden. Due
largely to the work of N. R. Hanson (although Wittgenstein and Popper
could claim priority), researchers are aware that when they make observations they cannot argue that these are objective in the sense of being
"pure," free from the influence of background theories or hypotheses or
personal hopes and desires. (Hanson's work and its general impact—and
the ways in which it has been misinterpreted—are discussed in Phillips
1987; see also chapter 6 in the present volume.) Qualitative researcher John
Ratcliffe reflected this view when he wrote "most research methodologists
are now aware that *all* data are theory, method, and measurement depen-

dent" (Ratcliffe 1983, 148). And he went on to turn this point into a thinly veiled attack on objectivity: "That is, 'facts' are determined by the theories and methods that generate their collection; indeed, theories and methods create the facts" (Ratcliff 1983, 148). If the observer's prior theoretical commitments do, indeed, determine what he or she sees as being the facts of a situation, and if there can be no criticism of one observer's results by others holding different theoretical backgrounds, then subjectivity or at least some form of relativism would seem to reign supreme.

It is here that the distinction between low-level and higher-level observation becomes relevant. The distinction is similar to the one that research psychologists have in mind when they speak of "high inference" and "low inference" variables. While observation is never theory-free, it does not follow that many (or most) observations are such that people from a wide variety of quite different theoretical frames will be in total disagreement about the facts of the case. There are many situations where all frameworks are likely to lead to the same results—they overlap, as it were. This is particularly so in cases of low-level observations, such as "there is a patch of red" or "the object on the left is heavier." Even people who do not share the same language can agree on such matters, for the only problem they face is the relatively trivial one of translation. Thus, my Korean students might not understand when I speak of "a patch of red," but with the help of a bilingual dictionary they can quickly come to comprehend and to agree with me. Or, to take an example from the philosopher Hilary Putnam, it may well be the case that there are different logical systems that may lead to different answers being given to the question: How many objects are here? Putnam shows that, in the cases he considers, one group might answer three, and another group answer seven. It does not make sense, Putnam argues, to ask how many objects there *really* are. And, of course, he is right—the answer you give depends upon how you count and what you regard as objects; in other words, it depends upon the rules of counting and classification that you use. But the point is, there is no *pernicious* subjectivity here, a conclusion Putnam apparently endorses; everyone can agree that, if you use one system there are—objectively— three objects, and if you use the other convention, the answer is seven. (See Putnam 1987, 18-20.)

To put it in a nutshell, relatively speaking, low-level observation is potentially high in objectivity, in the sense that the reports of my observations can easily transcend the merely personal or subjective. My observations are open for cross-check, testing, and criticism by other inquirers, even if I use a different set of conventions from these colleagues.

Furthermore, it is important to stress that there is nothing in Hanson to suggest that people with beliefs that differ from my own are *bound* to disagree with me about such observations. Contrary to what some radical Hansonists claim, there is no evidence that people with markedly different theoretical frames—for example, Freudians and behaviorists—actually see different things at the basic or low inference level being discussed here. They might notice—or fail to notice—different things, but when these are brought to their attention, they agree about what they have seen. Of course, they might still disagree about the significance of what they have observed, but this is not a point under contention in the present context.

Even Hanson's famous claim that the astronomers Tycho Brahe and Johannes Kepler would see different things while watching the dawn (this was discussed in the previous chapter) is a claim that can be recast to support the point being made here (Hanson 1965, chap. 1, passim; but see, particularly, the concession he makes at the bottom of page 23). Both scientists would agree that the sun was moving higher in the sky relative to the horizon—a point Hanson acknowledges; but, of course, Tycho would interpret this as the sun moving, while Kepler would regard it as a case of the earth rotating away from the sun. Their disagreement is spectacular, and Hansonists get good mileage from it, but what gets obscured is the agreement of the two men at the "low inference" level. Ernest Nagel has made a similar point, using a different example:

> it is simply not true that every theory has its own observation terms, none of which is also an observation term belonging to any other theory. For example, at least some of the terms employed in recording the observations that may be made to test Newton's corpuscular theory of light (such terms as "prism," "color," and "shadow"), underwent no recognizable changes in meaning when they came to be used to describe observations made in testing Fresnel's wave theory of light. But if this is so, the observation statements used to test a theory are not necessarily biased antecedently in favor of or against a theory; and in consequence, a decision between two competing theories need not express only our "subjective wishes," but may be made in the light of the available evidence. (Nagel 1979, 93)

If, however, the results of observation are couched in abstract theoretical terms—in "high inference" terms—then there might well be disagreement or misunderstanding. Consider the following example: Most people, whether Freudians or behaviorists, Republicans or Democrats,

Americans or Australians or Koreans, deists or atheists, astrologers or astronomers, would agree upon a visit to a classroom that they saw a teacher working with a particular number of pupils. They also probably would agree with the low inference observation that at a certain stage in the lesson the teacher asked one pupil a series of questions. They might not all agree, however, with the higher inference observation that at this point the teacher was forcing the pupil to do some high-order cognitive task involving Piagetian abstract reasoning. (Here it is clear that the distinction between observation and inference or conclusion is becoming blurred.) To get all the observers to agree with *this* observation—and more to the point, to get them to be able to critically evaluate the incident (which is the heart of objectivity)—more than mere translation into a native tongue would be required. To be able to discuss, to criticize, to evaluate warrants, the observers would all have to share—at least for purposes of discussion and communication—the same theoretical framework (this is what Hanson seemed to have in mind when he wrote of "theory-laden perception"). And it is worth noting, in passing, that even if they all did have the same framework, it is not certain that they would necessarily agree—for some might judge that the Piagetian categorization of the pupil's task was erroneous. (Similarity of framework is a guarantee—at best—of communication, but not of much else.)

The moral of the example is this: Just because, on some accounts, the more abstract description is "less objective" in the sense that it is less "pure" and is more "contaminated" by theory, it does not follow that there is no hope for observers to enter into mutual and fruitful discussion, criticism, and evaluation. For at a lower level of abstraction there might well be full overlap of categories and terminology (and thus there is the possibility of a higher degree of objectivity), and this more objective low inference observation would serve both as a constraint on the nature of the abstract accounts that could be put forward and as a springboard for critical evaluation. And there is always the possibility that the observers can share, even if only on a temporary basis, each other's frameworks—as in the "three versus seven objects" example from Putnam.

Israel Scheffler seems to have had something like this in mind when he stated that though none of the statements we assert

> can be *guaranteed* to be an absolutely reliable link to reality does not mean that we are free to assert any statements at will, provided only that they cohere. That the statement "There's a horse" cannot be rendered theoretically certain does not permit me to call anything a horse. (Scheffler 1967, 119)

Scheffler points out that language offers constraints on what is to count as a horse (just as, in the earlier examples, it provided constraints on what is to count as a patch of red and what is to count as a pupil answering a question), and "such constraints generate credibility claims which enter my reckoning critically as I survey my system of beliefs" (Scheffler 1967, 119). In short, then, Hanson has pointed to a problem that ought to be in the forefront of the minds of observers, but in pointing out the theory-laden nature of high inference observations, he has not offered grounds for abandonment of the notion of objectivity.

There is a further consideration that strengthens this optimistic conclusion. In the earlier discussion the point was made that the term *objective* is used more or less as a seal of approval, marking the fact that an inquiry or conclusion meets certain quality standards. There are poor inquiries, infected with personal biases, and there are more worthy inquiries where the warrants that are offered are pertinent and have been subjected to critical scrutiny. The same situation exists with respect to observations. There are certain well-documented factors that influence observers and that can make their work less credible. (In social science terminology, they can be spoken of as *threats to the validity* of observational or qualitative work.) For example, it is known that observers are prone to misjudge frequencies of occurrence of events they are watching, unless they use some quantitative scoring; and they are prone to be over-influenced by positive instances and underinfluenced by negative instances. (The significance of these factors is discussed in Phillips 1987; see also chapter 10.) Thus, the conclusions reached by a shoddy observer who has not taken account of these factors would be properly judged by the research community as being less objective than the conclusions reached by a more careful person. Once again, objectivity is seen to be a vital notion, and its abandonment would be fatal—as Nisbet realized—for the integrity of the research endeavor.

c. The Myth of "the More the Merrier"

In an influential essay (Ernest House, for example, discusses it admiringly and in some depth; see House 1980, 86ff.), Michael Scriven points out that sometimes objectivity is thought about in terms of the number of inquirers or observers: Data that only one person has been able to collect is regarded as subjective and dubious, but there is usually a more favorable judgment when a number of people have been involved (Scriven

1972). Scriven argues, however, that quality and numbers of investigators do not always go together. Thus, he distinguishes between qualitative objectivity, where the data are of high quality (no matter how many observers or inquirers were involved), and quantitative objectivity, where more than one person has replicated the findings (which does not guarantee veracity). Scriven writes of the two types of objectivity:

> Now it would certainly be delightful if these two senses coincided, so that all reports of personal experience, for example, were less reliable than all reports of events witnessed by a large number of people. But as one thinks of the reliability of reports about felt pain or perceived size, on the one hand, and reports about the achievements of stage magicians and mentalists on the other, one would not find this coincidence impressive. (Scriven 1972, 95-96)

Scriven's points are crucial; he has shown that it is untenable to give an account of objectivity solely in terms of group consensus—qualitative objectivity is not reducible to quantitative. Thus, the audience consensus that a magician has made a woman levitate freely in the air, and the group consensus that the world is flat, are objective views in the quantitative sense only, that is, those things are what the groups concerned are agreed upon. But the consensus is *only* that; and the agreement does not mean that the views concerned are correct, or warranted, or that they have been tested adequately, or that they have been reached in a way that has avoided sources of bias and distortion. And yet the number of observers remains a crucial factor in many influential accounts of objectivity. Fred Kerlinger, for example, in his widely used textbook on behavioral research, refers to an "objective procedure" as "one in which agreement among observers is at a maximum" (Kerlinger 1973, 491). Kerlinger neglected to point out that what is crucial is how the agreement was brought about!

Something more is needed to account for the qualitative sense of "objectivity"; some account has to be given of what makes a viewpoint objective in the sense of having a respectable warrant and being free from bias. Alternatively, one could follow the lead of Elliot Eisner and many others; in effect, they deny that there is any such thing as qualitative objectivity, and thus there is *only* group consensus or quantitative objectivity. The problem here—apart from the issue of whether they are right about the null status of qualitative objectivity—is that quantitative objectivity is not worth very much. Indeed, it is not worthy of the label *objectivity* at all; a more appropriate term is simply *consensus*. And the problem, of course, is that consensus about an incorrect or untrustworthy or substandard position is hardly worth writing home about. Eisner's view has the same defect as Kerlinger's:

> What so-called objectivity means is that we believe in what we believe and that others share our beliefs as well. This process is called consensual validation. (Eisner 1979, 214)

It is important to realize, along with Scriven, that *consensual* and *validation* are uncomfortable bedfellows. Scriven makes it clear that *validity* is a term that belongs with *qualitative objectivity*, not with *quantitative* or *consensus*. Nevertheless, the concern of Kerlinger, Eisner, and others with the role of the community of believers is not entirely misplaced, as will soon be seen.

The missing ingredient, the element that is required to produce objectivity in the qualitative sense, is nothing mysterious—but it has nothing to do with consensus. Gunnar Myrdal, Karl Popper, Israel Scheffler, and others have put their fingers on it: it is acceptance of the *critical tradition*. A view that is objective is one that has been opened up to scrutiny, to vigorous examination, to challenge. It is a view that has been teased out, analyzed, criticized, debated—in general, it is a view that has been forced to face the demands of reason and of evidence. When this has happened, we have some assurance (though never absolute assurance) that the view does not reflect the whim or bias of some individual or group; it is a view that has respectable warrant. Myrdal states:

> The method of detecting biases is simple although somewhat laborious. When the unstated value premises of research are kept hidden and for the most part vague the results presented contain logical flaws. When inferences are confronted with premises, there is found to be a *non sequitur* concealed, leaving the reasoning open to invasion by uncontrolled influences. . . . This element of inconclusiveness can be established by critical analysis. (Myrdal 1969, 53–54)

Popper expresses a similar point in a manner that makes even clearer that a community of inquirers can only hope to be qualitatively objective when conditions allow them to subscribe to—and actually apply in practice—the critical spirit:

> What may be described as scientific objectivity is based solely upon a critical tradition which, despite resistance, often makes it possible to

criticize a dominant dogma. To put it another way, the objectivity of science is not a matter of the individual scientists but rather the social result of their mutual criticism, of the friendly-hostile division of labour among scientists, of their cooperation and also of their competition. For this reason, it depends in part, upon a number of social and political circumstances which make criticism possible. (Popper 1976, 95)

Sandra Harding, a philosopher who espouses "feminist standpoint epistemology," goes even further than Popper; she supports what she calls "strong objectivity"—an objectivity that exposes even deep-seated biases that often remain hidden (such as sexist or male-oriented biases and presuppositions). The key, in her view, is also the existence of a strong, critical community of inquirers—but it is a community that must allow the voice of the under-represented and the nonpowerful to have free reign, for these individuals are more likely to be aware of these hidden presuppositions (Harding 1996).

Thus, Kerlinger and the others need to do two things to strengthen their accounts. In the first place, they have to stress that the community of inquirers must be a critical community, where dissent and reasoned disputation (and sustained efforts to overthrow even the most favored of viewpoints) are welcomed as being central to the process of inquiry. Second, they must abandon their references to agreement or consensus. A critical community might never reach agreement over (say) two viable alternative views, but if both of these views have been subjected to critical scrutiny, then both would have to be regarded as objective. (Once again, the term *objective* does not mean "true.") And even if agreement is reached, it can still happen that the objective view reached within such a community will turn out to be wrong—for those of us living in the new nonfoundationalist age, this is the cross that we have to learn to bear!

d. Kuhnism

Thomas S. Kuhn popularized the notion that inquirers always work within the context of a paradigm—a framework that determines the concepts that are used but that also contains exemplars or model inquiries, and that directs attention to some problems as being key and directs attention away from other problems or issues that (from that perspective) are regarded as somewhat trivial. Many scholars have interpreted Kuhn as supporting a relativistic position whereby it does not make sense to ask which one of various competing paradigms is the correct one; such judgments can only be made from within a paradigm, so inquirers are not able to step outside to examine their paradigms "etically." In a sense, then, all inquirers are trapped within their own paradigms, and they will judge certain things as being true for them that other inquirers in other paradigms will judge as being false (for them). To those who have taken such Kuhnian relativism seriously, in the Kuhnian universe there has seemed to be little place for objectivity. (See also the discussion of multiple realities in chapter 6.)

Thus, sometimes when the possibility of achieving objectivity is being questioned, the focus of attention is the framework within which inquiry is being pursued. For example, Freudians use a particular theoretical frame—they are guided by distinctive concepts and hypotheses—and, of course, for a dedicated worker in this psychoanalytic tradition, the possibility of using some quite different framework does not arise as a practicable alternative. The same situation exists, it has been argued, even if the inquirer does not subscribe to some well-known paradigm; for even here, the inquirer must be working with *some* concepts and hypotheses that serve as bedrock for the endeavor. Thus:

> most research methodologists are now aware that all data are theory, method, and measurement-dependent. That is, "facts" are determined by the theories and methods that generate their collection; indeed, theories and methods *create* the facts. And theories, in turn, are grounded in and derived from the basic philosophical assumptions their formulators hold regarding the nature of and functional relationship between the individual, society, and science. (Ratcliffe 1983, 148)

Gunnar Myrdal, Elliot Eisner, Hilary Putnam, and the "anarchist" philosopher of science Paul Feyerabend (Feyerabend 1978) are among those who frequently make similar points.

It is a somewhat controversial point whether or not choice of a framework or paradigm can be made objectively; but it is clear that the tide of philosophical debate has been running steadily against Kuhn (and relativism) and hence in favor of the view that it is possible to judge as better or worse the considerations that are advanced in support of any particular paradigm (Newton-Smith 1981 and Siegel 1987). More to the point, the following is also very clear: *Within* any particular framework inquirers can go about their work with more or less facility. Not all Freudians are equally adept; some are bunglers, some are misogynists or suffer from homophobia, and some may even be anti-Republican or anti-Democrat in orientation, and their work as Freudians might be indelibly stamped by these predilections. So sometimes when objectivity is being discussed, the focus of interest is whether or not it is possible to escape from bias while working or making judgments inside one's framework. Myrdal seems to have had this focus when he wrote:

> Biases are thus not confined to the practical and political conclusions drawn from research. They are much more deeply seated than that. They are the unfortunate results of concealed valuations that insinuate themselves into research at all stages, from its planning to its final presentation. As a result of their concealment, they are not properly sorted out and thus can be kept undefined and vague. (Myrdal 1969, 52)

The point, of course, is that the two foci—choice between paradigms, and choices and work within a particular paradigm—must not be confused. An argument that establishes that at one of these levels objectivity is impossible to achieve (accepting, for the sake of discussion, that such an argument could be mounted) does not address the issue of whether the other type of objectivity lies out of reach. There are, however, grounds for believing that this confusion does exist. Eisner, for example, argues strongly that it is naive to believe in framework objectivity, but his published advice on methodology of qualitative research does not stress the dangers of bias in judgment within frameworks, and he does not discuss in any detail the steps that can be taken to avoid it (see the discussion in chapter 10). As was seen earlier, with one broad stroke he does away with objectivity in all its senses, and he replaces it with consensual validation.

Can objectivity of judgment within a framework or paradigm be achieved? It seems clear that the answer is in the affirmative. Consider a group of qualitative researchers who are working on similar problems, using the same intellectual framework to shape their approaches. What property must their judgments have in order to be regarded as objective? As was shown earlier, it will not suffice for these inquirers merely to *agree* in their judgments. Instead, they would have to show that their own personal biases and valuations had been exposed to critical examination, and the role that these predilections played in their investigations would need to have been rigorously examined. Furthermore, as already mentioned, qualitative research (no less than quantitative research) is subject to a variety of threats to its validity—qualitative researchers are liable to misjudge the frequency rate of certain behaviors that are of interest, they are likely to be unduly influenced by positive instances and not so sensitive to the significance of negative instances, they are likely to be unduly influenced or "anchored" by experiences undergone early in the research, and so on (Sadler 1982). To achieve objectivity within a paradigm, then, the researcher has to ensure that his or her work is free from these problems, and again the presence of a critical tradition is the best safeguard. When work is sent to blind peer review, when researchers are forced to answer their critics, when researchers are supposed to be acquainted with the methodological and substantive literature (and when others can point out when they are not), and when researchers try honestly to refute their own dearly held beliefs, then bias and the other obvious shortcomings are likely to be eliminated, and the judgment (or judgments) reached by the community of scholars should be objective in the relevant sense.

e. The Conflation of the Contexts of Discovery and Justification

The philosopher of science Hans Reichenbach drew what is now a well-known distinction between the context of discovery in science and the context of justification. In recent years it has been argued by some that the distinction between these is blurred at best, and a few seminal writers seem to have ignored the distinction altogether—though with arguably disastrous results. (See, for example, the mischief this causes in some of Piaget's work; this is discussed in Phillips 1982.) Nevertheless, for heuristic purposes Reichenbach's distinction turns out to be a very fruitful one.

The relevant point in the present context is this: Processes involved in—and even central to—the *making* of discoveries during the pursuit of a research program may not be involved—and might be counterproductive if allowed to intrude—when the discoveries are *checked* and *tested* and *critically evaluated.* Both Israel Scheffler and Karl Popper see this distinction as crucial for understanding objectivity in research. Thus, Popper, having in mind the context of discovery, writes that

> we cannot rob the scientist of his partisanship without also robbing him of his humanity, and we cannot suppress or destroy his value judgments without destroying him as a human being *and as a scientist.* Our motives and even our purely scientific ideals . . . are deeply anchored in extra-scientific and, in part, in religious valuations. Thus the "objective" or the "valuefree" scientist is hardly the ideal scientist. (Popper 1976, 97)

Objectivity in research is not, for Popper, a property of the individual researcher—"It is a mistake to assume that the objectivity of a science depends upon the objectivity of the scientist" (Popper 1976, p. 96).

Objectivity, in this view, is a property of the context of justification; and as we have seen in the earlier discussion, it is in a sense a social matter, for it depends upon communal acceptance of the critical spirit. (The topic of value-neutrality shall be taken up in chapter 13.)

CONCLUSIONS

Before bringing this discussion to a close, a penultimate point must be made. It may have been noted that, throughout, nothing very much has been made of the distinction between quantitative and qualitative inquiry. For many authors, of course, the distinction is crucial, and qualitative inquiry can only be objective in so far as it approximates to quantitative inquiry. Fred Kerlinger seems to be representative:

> Objective methods of observation are those in which anyone following the prescribed rules will assign the same numerals to objects and sets of objects as anyone else. An objective procedure is one in which agreement among observers is at a maximum. In variance terms, observer variance is at a minimum. This means that judgmental variance, the variance due to differences in judges' assignment of numerals to objects, is zero. (Kerlinger 1973, 491)

He acknowledges that all methods of observation are inferential, but the procedures that assign numbers are "more objective." From the point of view of the new nonfoundationalist philosophy of science, there is little difference between qualitative and quantitative inquiry. Bad work of either kind is equally to be deplored; and good work of either kind is still—at best—only tentative. But the good work in both cases will be objective, in the sense that it has been opened up to criticism, and the reasons and evidence offered in both cases will have withstood serious scrutiny. The works will have faced potential refutation, and in so far as they have survived, they will be regarded as worthy of further investigation.

Another way of putting this is that in all types of inquiry, in so far as they want to reach credible conclusions, there is an underlying epistemological similarity. Even in hermeneutics—a mode of qualitative inquiry that at first sight seems far from the "objective" science of physics—there is appeal to evidence, there is testing and criticism of hypotheses (Follesdal 1979; see also chapter 2).

It turns out, then, that what is crucial for the objectivity of any inquiry—whether it is qualitative or quantitative—is the critical spirit in which it has been carried out. And, of course, this suggests that there can be *degrees*; for the pursuit of criticism and refutation obviously can be carried out more or less seriously. *Objectivity* is the term—the "stamp of approval"—that is used to label inquiries or procedures that are at one end of the continuum; they are inquiries that are prized because of the great care and responsiveness to criticism with which they have been carried out. At the other end of the continuum are inquiries that are stamped as being "subjective"; these are inquiries that have not been sufficiently opened to the light of reason and criticism. Most human inquiries are probably located somewhere near the middle, but the aim should be to move in the direction that will earn a full stamp of approval.

Reprinted by permission of the publisher, and with slight changes, from Eisner, Elliot W., and Alan Peshkin, eds., *Qualitative Inquiry in Education: The Continuing Debate* (New York: Teachers College Press, © 1990 by Teachers College, Columbia University. All rights reserved.), "Subjectivity and Objectivity," by D. C. Phillips, 19-37.

8

POPPERIAN RULES FOR RESEARCH DESIGN

... empirical science should be characterized by its methods: by our manner of dealing with scientific systems: by what we do with them and what we do to them. Thus I shall try to establish the rules, or if you will the norms, by which the scientist is guided when he is engaged in research or in discovery. (Popper 1959, 50)

INTRODUCTION

Although Karl Popper penned the words quoted above in the early 1930s, in the book that was to serve as the foundation of his reputation as a philosopher of science, over the next six decades he did not actually contribute to the technical literature in what most scientists would regard as the realm of methodology—by and large, he remained a philosopher and dealt with the *logic* or *theory* of methodology, not with the "nitty-gritty" of scientific research design and practice (certainly not in the social sciences and related fields).

Nevertheless, despite this logical or philosophical emphasis in his writings, it appears that they have had a warmer reception among practicing scientists than with professional philosophers. For what Popper gave scientists was a way of thinking about their work qua scientists—an orientation or attitude that enables them to gain a "meta-level" perspective on the specific methodological, empirical, and theoretical problems that they are grappling with. This ultimately was more valuable for them—and probably more practically efficacious—than any detailed methodological insights he could have provided; as Magee puts it, Popper's work has had "a notably *practical* effect on people who are influenced by it: it changes the way they do their own work" (Magee 1985, 4). Sir Peter Medawar and

137

Sir John Eccles, both Nobelists in the medical/biological sciences, are among the distinguished researchers who have been impressed by Popper in this way. (A longer list of admirers from science, art history, and politics is given by Magee 1985, chap. 1.)

But physical, biological, and medical scientists considered as a group probably are less self-conscious about their work, and are less inclined to cite philosophers, than are social scientists and educational researchers, who—perhaps because of their concerns about their status as *scientists* and because of the well-known charge brought against those of them who subscribe to the naturalistic ideal that they suffer from "physics envy"—often are eager to discuss and try to defend their research studies in philosophical or quasi-philosophical language. And one of the authorities drawn upon in this context is Karl Popper. The following statement from a recent essay in the *Educational Researcher*, written by the prominent educational psychologist Nathaniel Gage, is not atypical; it occurs in a passage where Gage is assessing the work of the social psychologist Kenneth Gergen:

> What then demarcates scientific from nonscientific knowledge—from mere opinion, superstition, and the like? Popper's criterion is falsifiability. Theory and observation give us the basis not for scientific truth but merely for conjectures, which scientists must try to falsify. . . . In the abstract, Gergen's position is nonfalsifiable and hence not scientific. (Gage 1996, 8)

Although philosophical critics of Popper might blanch at Gage's brief excursus into difficult territory, I will argue that this usage of the principle of falsification or falsifiability is—in practice—more beneficial than not. Of course, there is much else in Popper that ought to be drawn on by social scientists and educational researchers as they carry out (as well as assess and talk about) their work, but as space is limited I shall have to confine myself here to this one aspect of Popper's work. In short, I propose to make an initial attempt to provide what Popper did not, namely an application of the idea that progress in our knowledge arises via falsification, to some of the practical methodological issues that arise in the course of social science (and especially educational) research; but I shall also try to make clear why this aspect of Popper's work has been so appealing to those members of the educational and social science research communities who have come into contact with it. The following discussion, then, is not a detailed examination of the pros and cons of the philosophical writings of Karl Popper; rather, the focus is on some practical methodological issues in research, but the issues that are selected for examination shall be ones where, I shall try to show, Popper's discussions of falsification have something to contribute. (I do not wish to claim that I am the first to have taken steps in this direction; Donald Campbell—a social scientist who also had notable philosophical skills—produced a variety of important work on research methodology that bears the stamp of Popper's influence. See, for example, Cook and Campbell 1979.)

Before getting underway with my main discussion, there is an obvious objection to my plan that needs to be dealt with.

POPPER AS TOUCHSTONE: AN OBJECTION

Despite its high standing with many scientists, Popper's work has been subjected to serious criticism by epistemologists and philosophers of science (see, for example, Newton-Smith 1981; Stove 1982; and Stokes 1998). Therefore, it might seem to be an exercise in futility to devote much time to discussing its practical influence or significance unless these criticisms can be answered. After all, would we waste any time considering the practical relevance, for scientists in the late twentieth century, of the phlogiston theory of combustion, which has long since been refuted?

While I believe that the work of Miller and others (see Miller 1994) goes some way toward defending Popper against his critics and therefore leads to a softening of the previous objection, I shall not be able to defend this opinion here (I should stress that I do not rate Miller's spirited defense of Popperian "critical rationalism" as being a complete success). Instead, I shall take two different tacks: First, the aspects of Popper's work that have drawn most critical attention are his theory of verisimilitude (approach to, or nearness to, truth) and the issue of whether or not the use by researchers of nonfalsified hypotheses involves a "whiff" of induction (i.e., whether use of these hypotheses assumes—inductively—that they are likely to hold true in the future). These issues certainly relate to Popper's ideas on falsification but do not seem to undermine the use of falsification as a significant aspect of normal research design. Second, I think it is important to note that the general objection I raised earlier assumes that a position that is subject to philosophical criticism is thereby rendered practically sterile—but this, of course, is far from being the case, for a position can have fruitful practical implications or applications while not getting matters quite straight at the theoretical or philosophical level.

An extreme example is provided by Newtonian theory; although we now see that this is far from getting the theoretical picture right, it is still a fruitful theory to use in most practical settings. (And successors to Newton's theory have to be able to account for its practical success.)

Building on this point a little, I wish to suggest (1) that Popper's philosophical writings on falsification can be translated into practical guidance in a way that other contemporary philosophies of science usually cannot, and (2) that this guidance is both benign and productive.

1. Philosophers of science often have as their focus the interests of philosophers, and they do not adopt the perspective of scientific researchers (it is notable that most examples used by philosophers of science involve cases of *past* scientific work, where problems have at least been temporarily resolved), and they often set up their discussions by taking what Thomas Nagel has called "the view from nowhere"—which is helpful, perhaps, for philosophers but not for researchers.

Consider, for example, the following passage from a recent interesting book, in which the author is discussing progress in science:

> Explanatory progress consists in improving our account of the structure of nature, an account embodied in the schemata of our practices. Improvement consists either in matching our schemata to the mind-independent ordering of phenomena (the robust realist version) or in producing schemata that are better able to meet some criterion of organization (for example, greater unification). (Kitcher 1993, 106)

To be told that in order to progress we should match our theories with "mind-independent" nature is advice that, in the abstract, probably neither Popper nor I would disagree with; the problem, however, is that in practice this advice is sterile, for mere mortals cannot tell whether or not theories actually *do* match reality (William James, of course, made a similar point in his controversial writings on truth). So this account is not of much practical use to the working researcher unless it is supplemented by an account of how we are to settle this vital issue (hence Popper's belief that we only can make "progress" by locating and then eliminating our errors). The other criterion mentioned by Kitcher—greater unification—is practically more easily decided, but, of course, also is dubious as we cannot be sure that, simply on the basis of the fact that our theories hang together, they therefore must reflect the structure of nature (coherence or unification is quite a weak epistemic criterion). Only a person standing outside nature, standing "nowhere," could determine whether or not our theories actually do "match" nature. Unfortunately, researchers do not stand "nowhere"; they are never in such a privileged position. (These remarks should not be taken as a decisive criticism of Kitcher, for his lengthy book has much of great worth in it, and I have taken an isolated quotation for illustrative purposes; nor do I wish to suggest that Popper is entirely free of similar limitations, but on the whole, much of his philosophy is fairly directly translatable into practice. On the particular issue raised in my example, Popper often stressed that ascertaining the truth of our hypotheses is a "regulative ideal" but that in practice we will never be able to determine whether or not we have attained this goal. See, for example, Popper 1965, 226.)

2. Popper's philosophy is *benign* in two senses: first, it cannot lead researchers far astray—the errors to be made by following Popper (if any) are not serious; and second, in practice even those who disagree with his philosophy can often follow him with profit and without any logical inconsistency. Popperian guidance is *productive* in the sense that it will incline those who follow it to accept criticism, state their claims with clarity, cast their research designs in fruitful ways, open their theories and hypotheses to empirical test, and so forth (good things all). But more of this in a moment.

THE MANY FACES OF FALSIFICATION

It is well-known that the central idea of Popper's philosophy of science is falsification (and the related notion of falsifiability): Science is demarcated from nonscience by the fact that its hypotheses are, in principle, *falsifiable;* and science progresses, not by the proving or confirming of hypotheses, but as it were, negatively, by way of refutation or *falsification.* For Popper, a genuine test of a hypothesis is a serious attempt to falsify it; if the hypothesis withstands this attempt, it is *corroborated* (but not confirmed or verified)—which means that it survives, temporarily, perhaps to face refutation tomorrow. Popper's ideas here were based on the simple logical insight (technically known as *modus tollens*) that although no finite body of evidence can definitively prove or establish the truth of a universal hypothesis of the form "all X are Y" (except in the rare cases where we have been able to examine every X), acceptance of one piece of negative evidence (an X that is *not* a Y) can refute or falsify the generalization.

This process was brilliantly captured in the title of his book *Conjectures and Refutations;* readers of this work sometimes fail to notice the two quotations at the front that serve to drive home the moral—one from Oscar Wilde, "Experience is the name every one gives to their mistakes," and the other from J. A. Wheeler, "Our whole problem is to make the mistakes as fast as possible. . . . " In his first great book, *The Logic of Scientific Discovery*, falsification served as the glue that bound the whole work together—his discussion of the empirical base of science, of the demarcation of science, of simplicity, of degrees of testability, and of corroboration (his replacement for the notion of confirmation). It is no wonder that this is the aspect of Popper's work that springs most readily to mind for some practicing researchers (as my earlier citation of Nathaniel Gage demonstrated).

It is important to note that Popper was not a *naive* falsificationist (see Lakatos 1970); he realized that, just as our decision that a hypothesis has not been refuted is revisable in the light of later experience, so, too, is our decision that it has been refuted; all of our knowledge-claims (whether positive or negative) are merely tentative hypotheses. Furthermore, Popper knew full well that a hypothesis can be saved from refutation by a number of stratagems—for example, by claiming that one of the auxiliary or supplemental hypotheses that we accepted in order to carry out our tests was mistaken (see Popper 1959, 42, 50). The scientific attitude, however, consists in accepting the methodological principle that one should avoid saving hypotheses in this way (unless some further warrant for so doing is available).

It is time to turn to some points about the practicalities of falsificationist methodology in educational research.

A. We do not have to look far to see why falsification is so important for educational researchers; the chief clue was given by Popper when he remarked in the early pages of *Conjectures and Refutations* that it is easy to find apparent "confirmations" of any theory if one looks for them (Popper 1965, 37)—but what counts is whether or not our conjecture survives a strenuous attempt to refute it, by our failure to find evidence that is incompatible with it. We can, for example, apparently "verify" the theory that the world is flat by citing some "confirmations" ("it looks flat," "balls placed on the flat ground do not roll away," and so forth), but nevertheless the theory is wrong. Now, the relevant point here is that the field of education is beset by conflicting theories and viewpoints, all of which were inspired by *some* observations or data and which are held by their adherents thereby to be established; therefore, carrying out studies that merely add to the stock of reasons that can be offered as to why a theory is right achieve little. For one thing, adherents of opposing theories can do the very same thing—it is a fact of life that theories (including the most fanciful) usually have *some* evidence in their favor! To researchers working in the midst of such complex social/educational situations, Popper's insight comes as a breath of fresh air—it is intuitively plausible that seeking confirming evidence is far inferior to seeking refuting evidence! (I cannot see that those who disagree with Popper over the philosophical details of his work can sensibly disagree with this practically liberating insight.)

B. Once it is realized that, in real-life research situations, falsification is an important key to progress (and possibly the only practicable one) and that attempted falsification comes about through subjecting a hypothesis or theory to a test in which there is a serious chance of it failing, the path is clear to a fruitful approach to research design. Far too much research in education (and in the "soft" social sciences) relies upon *very* weak testing; the noted psychologist and philosopher Paul Meehl has stated that much testing in "soft psychology" does not expose theories or hypotheses "to grave risk of refutation" but "only to a rather feeble danger" (Meehl 1991, 24)—a situation that he traces to over-reliance upon the use of statistics (a tradition emanating from the work of R. A. Fisher), which, "with its soothing illusion of quantitative rigor, has inhibited our search for stronger tests" (Meehl 1991, 28).

But there is more to it than reliance upon statistical testing; researchers need to re-orient themselves to think in terms of rigorous attempts to refute the hypotheses they are interested in. I can convey what I have in mind here by recounting my experience in the first doctoral oral examination I attended as a faculty member in a university in the United States, after my migration from Australia about two and a half decades ago. (The following details have been altered a little in order to protect the guilty.) The candidate had written a dissertation that he claimed was a "test" of a theory devised by one of our faculty members; the theory pertained to the relationship between elementary school students of different ethnic and cultural backgrounds, and it had originally been developed after an interesting series of studies carried out in a relatively poor and culturally diverse school district a few miles from campus. Before I read the dissertation, my mind raced: How would I test this theory? Why, by going to an ethnically diverse school district in quite a different social setting and involving students with ethnic and cultural backgrounds quite different from those in the original study—in my mind I settled on Hawaii, with Fiji and South Africa as back-ups. To my dismay, the doctoral candidate had journeyed only a few miles from campus to another local school district, with virtually an identical ethnic makeup and which was similarly impoverished and had the same kinds and degrees of social problems as the district in which the theory had been formulated! At the oral exam there was no answer to my remark that if the theory had worked in the first school setting, it was highly likely to work in the second, and thus it had not been given a genuine, searching test. As the work in the dissertation was otherwise quite competent, however, we settled on a compromise—the candidate would drop reference to "testing" the theory and would speak instead of "replicating" it. (Replication, of course, serves a purpose, but it is not as challenging to the theory as a specifically designed *test;* but there is always the chance that the replication could fail, although in this particular case the selection of the site and the subjects had maximized the theory's chances of success.)

Experience has taught me that a diagram is helpful here, although it somewhat oversimplifies matters. (See figure 8.1.) If one depicts as a circle the "universe of potential evidence or experience" that is pertinent to the theory under test, then the evidence actually used to generate the theory comes from a very small segment. If one then imagines that nature might have hidden potentially falsifying evidence somewhere else in the "universe," the task of the researcher is to design a study to locate this; it would be good to find it as soon as possible (we need, as Wheeler noted, to make our mistakes as quickly as possible, or rather, to *discover* that we have made a mistake as quickly as possible—for there is little point in prolonging our allegiance to a flawed theory). To use the figurative language of the diagram, searching in a small segment contiguous to the one where the theory worked is not likely to be efficacious. Popper has pointed out that we must use our background knowledge to find "the *most probable kinds* of places for *the most probable* kinds of counter examples—most probable in the sense that we should expect to find them in the light of our background knowledge" (Popper 1965, 240).

C. The tendency to search for "confirming" rather than disconfirming or refuting evidence is particularly strong in research that uses qualitative methods. (There are many varieties of qualitative research, and there is a remarkable range of views about how such a researcher should go about collecting evidence or data; as I do not wish to be taken as rashly generalizing my remarks here to apply to all schools of thought, I will use qualifiers throughout. Chapter 10 makes some further points about qualitative inquiry.) The situations under which much qualitative work is done fos-

Diagram 8.1 Falsification and the Universe of Evidence

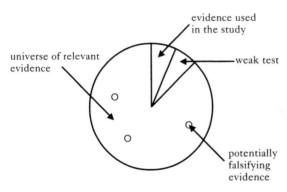

ters this attitude; either as participant or nonparticipant observers, these researchers are quite often studying complex social settings where there is an overwhelming supply of material that potentially is worth noting. A simplifying hypothesis about what is taking place in a particular setting will be eagerly embraced, for this will prevent the observers from drowning in data by providing guidance about what to note and what to ignore (Popper's often-cited point that all observation is theory-laden springs to mind here).

Some qualitative approaches make use of predetermined observation categories or checklists; others make a virtue of the fact that hypotheses are not determined in advance of the fieldwork and stress that the categories should emerge as the data are being collected (for example, the "grounded theory" approach of Glaser and Strauss 1967). In either case, however, theories or hypotheses are made use of—either before the observations commence or during the course of the study; the fact that these then have a directive influence on the study (the hypotheses or theories guide the researchers as to what is relevant and what is not, and what is not is usually not paid attention to and often fails to be recorded) is, at best, often only paid lip service. The development of a so-called "mental set" that directs the observations is known to be an important "threat to validity" of qualitative research (Sadler 1982).

Qualitative inquirers, however, have not been entirely insensitive to these issues; the literature contains a number of suggestions about how the "credibility" or "believability" of the products of qualitative inquiry can be assessed, but unfortunately, many of these can be seen to be defective when examined from a Popperian perspective (see chapter 10 for further discussion). It should be noted at the outset that many qualitative inquirers are reluctant to use the terms *true* or *truth*, even as a Popperian "regulative ideal"; this failing has reached almost epidemic proportions among those recent workers who use the so-called "narrative method" (see chapter 4). But the tendency to replace *true* or *truth* by *credibility* and so forth simply will not suffice, and for a simple reason—a study can be credible or believable but not true, just as a swindler's story is untrue but usually is quite believable. Many accounts of "exotic cultures" by early anthropologists (who often were missionaries) were judged to be highly credible by educated circles in the Europe of the day, but now are regarded as quite wrongheaded (i.e., they have been falsified). And, to complexify matters, the truth is often quite incredible: a president of the United States *was* involved in at least the cover-up of a burglary; and a fur-covered mammal that is egg laying, and that has webbed feet and the bill of a duck, actually *does* exist in the antipodes (the platypus)! The plain fact is that there is no reliable connection between believability (a subjective or historically and culturally located criterion) and truth.

The major criteria used by qualitative researchers boil down to four (a similar list is discussed in chapter 10, but the issues here are so important that a little redundancy may not be amiss):

1. Coherence or "structural corroboration." The idea here is that a qualitative study is to be believed, or is credible, if its segments "hang together." Popper put the objection to this in a nutshell:

> Thus while coherence, or consistency, is no criterion of truth, *simply because even demonstrably consistent systems may be false in fact*, incoherence or inconsistency do establish falsity; so, if we are lucky, we may discover inconsistencies and use them to establish the falsity of some of our theories. (Popper 1965, 226, emphasis added)

Of course, inconsistency within a theoretical system does not indicate that *every* item is false (although all might be), but it does indicate that there is an error somewhere.

2. Inter-researcher agreement or consensual validation. This criterion amounts to saying that a qualitative account is to be believed if several different researchers say the same thing or acknowledge that a particular account squares with their own experience. But once again, the fact that an account is agreed to by several (or even many) individuals does not mean that it is true. All of us can provide examples of theories or accounts that once were widely agreed to but that were later shown to be untrue (i.e., were refuted); wide consensus in the Middle Ages that the world is flat did not make it true that it is actually flat.

3. Cross validation, or triangulation. The criterion here is a little more complex—researcher A collects evidence that "validates" one aspect of a theory or account, while researcher B, who is taking a different approach, gets evidence "validating" some other aspect of the theory. Thus, the theory is established as credible and probably even true! Certitude supposedly increases even more if researcher C turns up another confirming line of evidence. Ignoring the Popperian point that no evidence can ever completely "validate" or "confirm" a theory, what we have here is a situation that relates to what is called in logic and philosophy of science "the inference to the best explanation" and that also directly parallels the use of circumstantial evidence in criminal trials—the "truth" of the prosecution's case is established by several different (and independent) groups of facts that all converge on the guilt of the accused. The logical situation really is this: evidence A is *compatible with* the theory under examination (X is guilty); but so is evidence B and C; therefore, the theory is true (it is true that X is guilty). Certainly, this form of argument can often establish that it is credible to believe the theory (the theory that X is guilty may be the best explanation we can think of for all these facts—at the moment), but, of course, the truth of the theory has *not* been established, and the line of argument is not logically valid (the leap from "compatible with" to "true" is an enormous one). And there is little need to point to the fact that many a person found guilty on the basis of circumstantial evidence has later been exonerated when new evidence came to light that refuted this judgment.

4. Checking with the individuals who were studied. This criterion is widely touted in the qualitative research community; the following exposition of it is from a book by two well-known educational researchers who also write quite broadly on social science methodology (the "flip-flopping" over "truth" and the use of what they seem to regard as synonyms stand out):

> The determination of credibility can be accomplished only by taking data and interpretations to the source from which they were drawn and asking directly whether they believe—find plausible—the results. This process of going to the sources—often called "member checks"—is the backbone of satisfying the truth-value criterion. (Guba and Lincoln 1982, 110)

The criterion, then, is this: After you have done some descriptive work in a social setting—and even better, if you have come up with an explanation for the events that you have observed—you then obtain validation by finding out if the people you observed find your descriptions and/or theory plausible. If so, your work satisfies the "truth-value criterion."

Taken as a general criterion by which to judge qualitative inquiry, this seems to me to be so patently implausible that I am amazed it has such broad currency. The crucial flaw is that no distinction is made here between types of problems that might be being pursued, and in particular it is cavalier with respect to the emic/etic distinction. (1) *If* the problem is the emic one of *cataloguing* the beliefs or actions of the individuals you have observed, then checking your description with them is certainly a wise step to take, but even here there can be serious complications—your native "informants" may not be telling you (and may not want to tell you) the whole truth about what they believe, and so their assent to your account is not a fool-proof indication that you have accurately described their beliefs; and, of course, their actions can be described in a variety of ways, and the way they would want to describe what they have done is not necessarily the way you or others would want to describe what had happened. I may think that I was responding to provocation by my spouse, but an observer might describe it as a case of attempted male suppression of a woman—once again, Popper's point that all observation (and related description) is theory-laden springs to mind. (2) But when it comes to the *explanation* you have crafted for the events you have seen (usually an etic endeavor if you are a social scientist and those whom you have observed are not), the criterion of "member checks" completely falls apart: Do we really think that our explanations of psychological pathologies, or of cultural practices such as female genital mutilation (or even much less horrendous practices), or of a teacher's reactions to students of different social backgrounds to her own, should be made hostage to whether or not those whose actions or practices they are actually agree with—or find credible—how we have explained these practices?

Some methodologists of qualitative research, such as Miles and Huberman (1984), do mention in passing that "looking for negative evidence" is an important tactic; the thrust of my discussion thus far has been to suggest that—in practice—it is about the only one of any substance. Finding a credible or believable theory or account is sometimes (but not always) the first step, but by itself it is an extremely halting and weak step for the reasons discussed earlier. The qualitative researcher should be disciplined enough to keep working after this step has been accomplished (if it is accomplished at all)—he or she should actively seek data that, if found, will refute the hypotheses or accounts or descriptions that have been developed. And while the qualitative researcher is engaged in this search, he or she should not be misled by spurious criteria or defective methodological rules.

D. The strong Popperian emphasis on refutation raises a set of issues familiar to educational researchers and statisticians under the guise of "Type I" and "Type II" errors, which in turn relate to the use of the so-called "null hypothesis" method in the conduct of true (i.e., randomized) experiments and the use of inferential statistics. The discussion should start with the null hypothesis.

At first blush the use of the null hypothesis method is quite Popperian, although when I once wrote to Sir Karl about this he indicated that he was not aware of any specific connection between it and his own work. Nevertheless, the logical resemblance is startling. Highly simplified, the essence is this: A randomized experiment using a control group and a treatment group is instituted to throw light on the question of whether the treatment produces an effect. But here is the trick—rather than attempting to establish that the treatment *does* have an effect, the null hypothesis method inverts the process and assumes that there is *no* difference and therefore that the treatment has had no effect; and the data are analyzed in an attempt to *refute* this null hypothesis. In short (and crudely), instead of trying to confirm the hypothesis that is of interest (the experimental hypothesis), the researchers attempt to refute—or show as highly unlikely—the null hypothesis; for if they are able to do this, they apparently have established the likely truth of the experimental hypothesis! This ingenious procedure was devised early this century by the noted statistician Sir Ronald Fisher. (It should be noted that descriptions of the logic of this method given in many elementary statistics books are quite sloppy; accounts differ in subtle but important ways from book to book. The chief variation is in the way the null hypothesis is defined; some works say it is the hypothesis that the treatment does not have an effect; others say that it is the hypothesis that the means of the scores of the control and experimental groups will be the same; and still others conflate the two of these. My own discussion, alas, is also somewhat sloppy but, it is hoped, not fatally so; precise discussion of the issues here would take a monograph, not merely a portion of a chapter in a book.)

Although the *logic* here is Popperian, there actually is a strong Popperian objection to this procedure (for a lively exposition of this point by a psychological researcher, see Meehl 1991): More is involved in the testing of a hypothesis than merely adopting the *form* of an attempted refutation. The hypothesis should be a bold conjecture, with lots of content; and we should not know beforehand either that it is untrue or that it is almost certain to hold in the context in which we are testing it—the test should be a genuine one and one from which we can learn something, whether the hypothesis survives the test or not. Early on, Popper wrote (in a passage in which I have omitted some sentences not pertinent to the issue at hand):

> According to the view that will be put forward here, the method of critically testing theories, and selecting them according to the results of tests, always proceeds on the following lines. *From a new idea, put up tentatively, and not yet justified in any way*—an anticipation, a hypothesis, a theoretical system, or what you will—conclusions are drawn by means of logical deduction. . . . And finally, there is the testing of the theory by way of empirical applications of the conclusions which can be derived from it. (Popper 1959, 32-33, emphasis added)

None of the conditions Popper mentions here are met in the "testing" of the null hypothesis. First and foremost, it is not an informative and bold hypothesis; it merely states (in one of its formulations discussed earlier) that at the conclusion of the experiment the means of the scores of the two groups (or some similar measure) will be the same. This is quite a bland conjecture. Second, not only is the null hypothesis "not justified in any way," but, according to many authorities, it is not justified at all in virtually any educational or social setting (see Morrison and Henkel 1970)—in fact, it is known with virtual certainty beforehand that the scores of the two groups will *differ*. This line of reasoning is as follows (see, for example, Meehl 1991, 24): No two human groups, even when (or perhaps especially when) selected randomly, will be *exactly* the same in their mean score on some dimension of interest—no two such groups are going to be exactly alike with respect to average weight, or height, or IQ, or ability to learn new material in math or science or whatever, or in their responses to a treatment or to some set of test items. In short, the null hypothesis is virtually certain to be false!

There are added complexities here, of course, but these do not affect the point I am making. Thus, although there will always be a difference between the control and experimental groups, there is the important issue of whether the difference has been produced by chance or has been produced by the treatment. The answer to this cannot be established with certainty; instead, statistical tests of significance are used to guide researchers in deciding between these two explanations. It is common for research-ers to say (in my view, somewhat sloppily), if it seems likely that there is only a random difference, that the null hypothesis has been supported—for what really is of interest in this whole procedure is not merely whether there is a difference between the two groups, but whether there is a dif-ference that is likely to be due to the treatment that is being tried out. But, as we have seen, *this* hypothesis has not been tested directly. A final complexity is that a researcher can *always* obtain highly statistically sig-nificant results indicating that the treatment *did* make a real difference (i.e., that the null hypothesis has been falsified), by using a large sample size. Paul Meehl sums all this up rather nicely:

> from the fact that the null hypothesis is always false in soft psychology, it follows that the probability of refuting it depends wholly on the sen-sitivity of the experiment—its logical design, the net (attenuated) con-struct validity of the measures, and, most important, the sample size, which determines where we are on the statistical power function. Put-ting it crudely, if you have enough cases and your measures are not to-tally unreliable, the null hypothesis will always be falsified, *regardless of the truth of the substantive theory.* (Meehl 1991, 25)

The basic point in all this, however, is that refuting an uninformative null hypothesis that is wrong anyway amounts to an incredibly weak "test" of the actual hypothesis that we are interested in and runs quite contrary to the spirit of Popper's work—for, according to Sir Karl, what counts is the testing of "risky predictions" (Popper 1965, 36). (Paul Meehl makes much of the fact that in sciences such as physics, statistical testing of this sort is virtually never used. The hypotheses of interest are tested *directly,* not by the inverted logic of the null hypothesis test; this is made possible by the fact that the theories or conjectures here are very precise—Popper would say they have lots of content, and so they can yield quite specific, testable predictions.)

E. The previous discussion leads neatly into the topic of types of er-rors. In carrying out a study or running an experiment, researchers run into two dangers when analyzing their data. First, they can decide that the experimental treatment produces a real effect when in fact there is no effect at all but only chance differences between the groups in the study—they can accept a theory or hypothesis when actually it is false. This is called a Type I error. Second, they can reject a hypothesis or conjecture that actually is true. This is called a Type II error. In sum, the errors are as follows:

Type I: Acceptance of a false theory or conjecture
Type II: Rejection of a true theory or conjecture

Most books on research design identify Type I errors as being of greater consequence—it is worse to accept error than it is to reject truth. (This is a practical and not a logical or epistemological point—for epistemically, *both* are actually *errors;* but the argument often made is that in real-life situations the consequences of Type I errors are usually, although not always, worse than those of Type II errors. I am dubious about this, for in both cases one's actions are being guided by faulty hypotheses.)

It is interesting to look at these errors through a Popperian lens. First, Popper would argue, I think, that the brief definitions of Type I and Type II errors given herein need to be reformulated, for he would be displeased with the terms *accept* and *reject. All* our knowledge is conjectural; and we need to revise continuously the previous decisions we have made about what has been falsified and what has not. Researchers working on a problem formulate a conjecture that they hope is true; they carry out a study that is designed as a test—the aim is to detect whether this conjecture is erroneous. If the evidence indicates that indeed it is, then the conjecture is discarded (but tentatively, for all decisions are revisable in the light of later experience). If, however, the conjecture is not falsified by the study, the researchers will maintain it; but, as Popper insists, they should not *accept it* in the sense of *trusting it fully*—for probably in some future study it will be falsified. Popper wrote:

> The fact that, as a rule, we are at any given moment taking a vast amount of traditional knowledge for granted . . . creates no difficulty for the falsificationist or fallibilist. For he does not *accept* this background knowledge; neither as established nor as fairly certain, nor yet as probable. He knows that even its tentative acceptance is risky, and stresses that every bit of it is open to criticism. (Popper 1965, 238)

Our "background knowledge," of course, includes those items we believe at present to be unrefuted, but it also includes those things that we think have been refuted. (Popper only occasionally discussed the issue that our *refutations* as well as our corroborations are only tentative; but early in *The Logic of Scientific Discovery* 1959, 50, he did state that "In point of fact, no conclusive disproof of a theory can ever be produced; for it is always possible to say that the experimental results are not reliable. . . . ") Thus, for a start, a Popperian reformulation of the types of errors would be as follows:

Type I: Tentative maintenance of a false hypothesis
Type II: Tentative rejection of a true hypothesis

The second thing that Popper might say about all this is that we can never completely insulate ourselves against either of these types of errors; *all* of our knowledge is fallible, and much of what we think to be true is, in fact, likely to be erroneous. So long as we keep an open mind about what we are taking as "background," so long as we are prepared to revise our tentative beliefs in the light of future experience, and so long as we strenuously test (try to refute) those beliefs that we are using to guide our actions, eventually we will be able to detect our current errors—we will see that we have falsely judged some conjecture to be true or some treatment to be effective, or that we have falsely rejected a conjecture or we have falsely judged some treatment to be ineffective. Of course, in the process we will make other mistakes, but that is the human condition! Popper made this point by way of a verse by Xenophanes (which he translated himself):

> But as for certain truth, no man has known it,
> Nor will he know it; neither of the gods,
> Nor yet of all the things of which I speak.
> And even if by chance he were to utter
> The final truth, he would himself not know it;
> For all is but a woven web of guesses. (Popper 1965, 26)

F. Researchers in education and the social sciences who design experimental studies often think in terms of "threats to validity," but this is a notion that is more broadly applicable to research and certainly is relevant even to nonexperimental, qualitative work. A Popperian slant can be given to this topic.

Broadly speaking, a threat to validity is a flaw either in the design or the execution of a study that weakens/threatens the validity of the conclusions that might otherwise have been drawn. Consider three common examples: (1) If extraneous influences are allowed to impinge upon the treatment group but these do not affect the control group in a randomized experiment, then the inference that the experimental treatment caused whatever differences were noted between the two groups is not valid. A key principle of the experimental method is that there should be only *a single* difference between the two groups, namely, that one group received the treatment and the other group did not; but in this example, there was more than one difference—the experimental group not only received the treatment, it also was affected by the extraneous factors (and it is these that might have produced the results that were noted). (2) After the two groups have been formed by random assignment of individuals, and the experiment has started to run, nonrandom attrition might occur that unevenly affects the control and experimental groups; this poses a serious challenge to the inference that the experimental treatment was responsible for the difference between the scores of the groups on the post-test. Thus, the experiment might involve preschool children, but during the experiment the older ones might be withdrawn by their parents (in order to start school), and this nonrandom withdrawal might be greater in one of the groups in the study than in the other—thus skewing the results by magnifying the difference between the scores of the two groups. (3) In qualitative research, the investigator might quite early on form a hypothesis about what is happening in the group that is being studied; this "mental set" poses a threat to the validity of the conclusions because subsequently the investigator is highly likely to pay attention only to factors that are compatible with this guiding conjecture—and so may not notice conflicting events.

It is regarded as good practice in educational research to anticipate the major threats to the validity of a study and, so far as is practicable, to try to neutralize these. Thus: An experiment running for a long period in a field setting can be monitored to detect any extraneous events as early as possible, and perhaps these can be deflected; attrition may not be preventable, but at least it can be monitored so that its impact on the study can be assessed; qualitative researchers can be trained to record their guiding hypotheses and to document the fact that they have searched for evidence that would be disconfirming. Now, at first sight it might seem that attempting to insulate your research from threats to validity is contrary to the spirit of Popperian philosophy and is an attempt to bolster yourself against refutation. Deeper reflection will show, however, that it is quite the reverse.

In essence, preventing the operation of a threat to the validity of a study makes interpretation of the conclusions that are reached less ambiguous. In a study where the treatment has been confounded by other factors, any gain that is found might, but just as well might not, have been caused by the treatment; or if the study shows no significant difference between the experimental group and the control, this could be because the treatment was ineffective, but it equally might result from the countervailing influence of the extraneous factors that threatened the study's validity. In neither of these possible scenarios can we decide whether or not the hypothesis that the treatment is effective has actually been refuted. Therefore, it has not faced the most challenging test that was possible. If, however, the threat to validity has been prevented from operating, any gain on the outcome measure (or lack of it) must be due solely to the effectiveness (or lack thereof) of the treatment. Thus, rather than hampering refutation, guarding against threats to validity actually greatly fosters it. This leads directly to the next (and last) point.

   G. It should be clear from the preceding discussion that, in Popper's view, ambiguity, vagueness, and obscurity or general lack of clarity are the enemies of progress in human knowledge—for these hamper the giving of pertinent criticism and the bringing to bear of severe empirical tests (criticism, of course, being a type of test or attempted refutation). For Popper, content, clarity or precision, and testability were all related; he claimed, counter-intuitively and controversially, that the bolder and clearer our hypotheses, the more *improbable* they were for they ruled out or "forbade" more:

> There are, moreover . . . *degrees of testability*: some theories expose themselves to possible refutations more boldly than others. . . . A theory which is more precise and more easily refutable than another will also be the more interesting one. Since it is the more daring one, it will be the one which is less probable. But it is better testable, for *we can make our tests more precise and more severe.* (Popper 1965, 256)

Given this strong emphasis on opening one's conjectures to criticism and potential refutation, it is no surprise that Popper was a bitter opponent of the intellectual fashion that makes a virtue of obscure, but impressive-sounding, prose. In an attack on Habermas and the members of the so-called Frankfurt School of "critical theorists," he wrote:

> Many years ago I used to warn my students against the widespread idea that one goes to university in order to learn how to talk, and to write, impressively and incomprehensively. . . . There is little hope that they will ever understand that they are mistaken. . . . that the standard of impressive incomprehensibility actually clashed with the standards of truth and rational criticism. For these standards depend on clarity. One

cannot tell truth from falsity, one cannot tell an adequate answer to a problem from an irrelevant one, one cannot tell good ideas from trite ones, one cannot evaluate ideas critically, unless they are presented with sufficient clarity. (Popper 1976, 294)

Educational researchers have as much to learn from this as have philosophers! And we all must take responsibility for fostering this lesson—the valuing of clarity, and the willingness to give and receive rational criticism, can only thrive in a professional community that takes active steps to achieve these things.

9

POSITIVISM

Nowadays, the term *positivist* is widely used as a generalized term of abuse. As a literal designator it has ceased to have any useful function—those philosophers to whom the term accurately applies have long since shuffled off this mortal coil, while any living social scientists who either bandy the term around or are the recipients of it as an abusive label are so confused about what it means that, while the word is full of sound and fury, it signifies nothing.

The antipositivist vigilantes, who realize nothing of this, still claim to see positivists everywhere. (When one is confused or suffering from delirium, it is possible to see *anything*.) Displaying what often amounts to an embarrassing degree of philosophical illiteracy, the vigilantes rarely bother to distinguish between classical (or Comtean) positivists, on the one hand, and the even more nefarious logical positivists, on the other. Furthermore, they use a number of faulty criteria, either singly or in combination, to identify their illusory foe. The general fantasy is that anyone who is impressed by the sciences as a pinnacle of achievement of human knowledge, anyone who uses statistics or numerical data, anyone who believes that hypotheses need to be substantially warranted, anyone who is a realist (another unanalyzed but clearly derogatory word) is thereby a positivist. The following discussion has as its aim the clarification of these delusions.

As a preliminary, however, it needs to be affirmed that the corpus of the sciences *does* constitute a magnificent achievement. The issue is, for those who want somehow to learn from—and to emulate—the sciences: What precisely has been the source of their success? Before those who wish to copy the sciences in their own investigations are heaped with outright condemnation, it seems a counsel of wisdom to examine the analysis of science that they give—for while some accounts may be narrow and deficient, and deserving of abuse, other accounts might be such that we are likely to profit from them! It is in this spirit that we should approach the work of the classic positivists and logical positivists.

CLASSICAL OR COMTEAN POSITIVISM

With respect to positivism, the truth is less straightforward than the fantasy. The term itself was coined by the French philosopher Auguste Comte, who published his six-volume work *Cours de Philosophie Positive* in fits and starts between 1830 and 1842. In this work Comte argued several different things. First, he held that each branch of knowledge, by an "inevitable necessity," passes through "three different theoretical states"— "the theological or fictitious state, the metaphysical or abstract state, and the scientific or positive state" (Comte 1970, 1). (It is interesting to note, in passing, that there is a similarity between this aspect of Comte's work and the views of the American pragmatist C. S. Peirce on the stages that human communities pass through with respect to the "fixation of belief"; see Peirce, in Konvitz and Kennedy 1960, 82-99.) The development of the modern discipline of biology would be a good example here; at first the behavior of living things was explained in terms of souls or spirits, then in terms of wildly metaphysical notions such as "vital forces" or "entelechies" (hardly an improvement), and then finally in terms of the biochemical mechanisms expounded in modern science. Clearly, Comte's and Peirce's belief in intellectual stages reflected the nineteenth-century conviction that intellectual progress had occurred and that "scientific" modes of explanation and description were an advance over earlier forms.

Second, Comte offered a classification of the "positive sciences" that attempted to clarify "the arrangement of the sciences in the order of their natural connection, according to their mutual dependence, so that one might be able to present them successively" (Comte 1970, 46). Comte realized that the sciences could be classified in many ways—indeed, if there were six general types of science, he pointed out there were 720 distinct classifications possible (Comte 1970, 51). But he was after a classification that reflected the way in which each successive science was "founded on a knowledge of the principal laws of the preceding one while serving as the basis of the following one" (Comte 1970, 51–52). (Why it should even be possible to produce such a classification, he really does not adequately say; a view such as Comte's requires that many thorny issues relating to reduction be resolved. Comte's younger contemporary, the British essayist Herbert Spencer, offered a dry but detailed set of other criti-

cisms; see Spencer 1949.) At any rate, Comte reached the "final result that
we have [in order] mathematics, astronomy, physics, chemistry, physiol-
ogy, and social physics" (Comte 1970, 67)—the latter being, of course,
Comte's way of referring to what we now call the social sciences (and sociology in particular).

Finally—and for our purposes most significantly—Comte advanced a
type of Humean empiricism that led in the direction of antirealism with
respect to the underlying entities of the physical sciences and that also led
in the direction of a type of instrumentalism according to which talk about
such underlying entities—atoms and the rest—is only shorthand to replace
more accurate but more cumbersome talk in terms of the data of direct
experience.

This last set of issues is complex, and the material needs to be spelled
out more fully; a good place to start is a key passage that occurs in Comte's
Introduction:

> Finally, in the positive state, the human mind, recognizing the impossi-
> bility of obtaining absolute truth, gives up the search after the origin and
> hidden causes of the universe and a knowledge of the final causes of
> phenomena. It endeavors now only to discover, by a well-combined use
> of reasoning and observation, the actual laws of phenomena—that is to
> say, their inevitable relations of succession and likeness. (Comte 1970, 2)

In these two sentences Comte dispels, for the careful reader, a number of the myths about positivism: he eschews the pursuit of "absolute
truth," and he disavows the quest for unobservable ("hidden") scientific
entities and resolves to stick to the realm of observable phenomena.
Whether his arguments are powerful enough to sustain these positions is
a different matter—the point is, the fantasy about positivists is that they
were/are realists, who believe in absolute truth—and who regard scientific
investigation as being the "royal road" to attaining it. To reinforce this
important point, it is appropriate to quote from Popper:

> For the commonsense theory of knowledge is liable to lead to a kind of
> anti-realism. If knowledge results from sensations, then sensations are
> the only *certain* elements of knowledge, and we can have no good rea-
> son to believe that anything but sensation exists. (Popper 1985, 106)

To say a little more about Comte's empiricism and the difficulties it
entails for him and his successors: The classical empiricists regarded

knowledge (knowledge about the physical universe, but not necessarily knowledge of mathematics and logic) as being based in sense experience—there is nothing that we know about the world that did not "enter" the "understanding" except through the senses. The seventeenth- and eighteenth-century figures John Locke and David Hume argued this position in great detail. Hume, consistently with this basic orientation, raised important problems about causation and induction: What do we experience, when we experience two events, that entitles us to identify one as the "cause" of the other? For what we see is the two events, and the temporal and spatial relations between them, but we experience nothing more, no necessary connection or link that establishes that the one *produces* the other. So, on this skeptical line of thought, the Humean empiricist has to abandon (or recast as mere constant correlation) the notion of causation. Similarly, when we see that one event follows another, what do we experience that allows us to make the induction that the one will *always* follow the other or will follow the other on some particular future occasion? For our experience is limited to what we *can* experience; we cannot experience "necessity," or the future, so we cannot say (on the basis of experience) that one event will always and necessarily follow the other! This line of thought throws into question the warrant for our belief that the laws and theories of science will hold true in the future (or in those parts of the universe where we have not yet had experience).

This empirically based skepticism is far-reaching. The entities postulated in scientific theories—including atoms, quarks, social forces, psychological drives, and cognitive structures, to mention only a few—are not experienceable in any direct form that would be acknowledged by Hume or Comte, and so their status as *things*, as "furniture of the world," becomes dubious. Perhaps, at best, they can be regarded as convenient fictions, as shorthand ways of referring to what *can* be experienced (readings on measuring instruments, or performance on psychological tests, and so forth).

It is hard to live as a skeptic, and few folk manage to do so consistently. It is not clear that Comte was such a one. In the passage cited previously, for example, he clearly departed from the "straight and narrow" when he stated that the positivist endeavors to discover "the actual laws of phenomena," that is, their "invariable relations of succession"—for, according to the empiricist argument cited earlier, *no* experience can establish "invariable relations." Similarly, Comte was critical of those who wished to determine what weight and gravitational attraction "are in themselves, or what their causes are" (Comte 1970, 9), for such matters lie beyond experience; and yet, in virtually the same breath, he is admiring of "the Newtonian law of gravitation" (Comte 1970, 8), which—because of its universal pretensions—clearly takes us beyond the experiential realm. There is thus some justice in John Stuart Mill's judgment, a few years later, that Comte "had not lived up sufficiently to his positivist principles" (Keat and Urry 1982, 75). Neither did Comte find it necessary to discuss in detail what, precisely, we *can* experience—some later writers (including psychologists as well as philosophers) would claim that we experience *things* and not mere "sense data" such as patches of color. (John Dewey and William James, for example, claimed that experience was much more richly populated than the classic positivists would allow—James even called his own position "radical empiricism," and Dewey explicitly stated "that direct experience contains, as a highly important direct ingredient of itself, a wealth of *possible* objects." See Dewey 1941, 539.) This is a nontrivial matter for contemporary social scientists; do we experience, for example, social phenomena or do we only experience individual people acting in certain ways (which leaves "social phenomena" as empirically illegitimate inferences or "constructions")? And, for that matter, do we actually experience people, or are these also "constructions" from our data of raw sense experience?

Comte's legacy, therefore, was a complex one. He bequeathed to subsequent generations the conviction that religious or metaphysical modes of explanation were not satisfactory when applied to empirical phenomena, for their key concepts were not adequately warranted by empirical data; and together with this he passed on his great admiration for the procedures that he believed were followed in science (or, in successful instances of science). But, clearly, his empiricism left a difficult skeptical legacy and (arguably) an impoverished account of experience and of the nature of science.

Although many of Comte's specific arguments have become less apposite with the march of time, it remains difficult not to sympathize with his main concerns (and with Peirce's concerns in his essay "The Fixation of Belief"). Belief systems that do not incorporate some form of observational testing or empirical constraint give rise to "chimerical hopes" and "exaggerated ideas of man's importance in the universe" (Comte 1970, 6), and they make use of metaphysical concepts that become "so empty through oversubtle qualification that all right-minded persons considered them to be only abstract names of the phenomena in question" (Comte 1970, 8). Neither can Comte be blamed for being interested in determining the intellectual method that has made science so successful, although we might not be so confident as he was regarding the outcome of the deliberations:

> The first great direct result of the positive philosophy is then the manifestation by experience of the laws that our intellectual functions follow in their operations and, consequently, a precise knowledge of the general rules that are suitable for our guidance in the investigation of truth. (Comte 1970, 24)

LOGICAL POSITIVISM

Somewhat similar motivations seemed to have been at work in the logical positivists of the 1920s and '30s. Centered around Vienna, and therefore also called "the Vienna Circle," the group was made up of people with a range of interesting backgrounds: Schlick and Frank from physics, Carnap and Waissman from mathematics and philosophy, Neurath from sociology, Godel and Hahn from mathematics, and Kraft from history. Later Reichenbach, Hempel, Ayer, and others were associated with the circle. As a group they exerted a powerful influence over the image of science that was held by many physical and social scientists of the following decades. Their influence was particularly marked in the English-speaking world, due to their being scattered there when they escaped from Nazi persecution. The physicist Percy Bridgman (Bridgman 1927) developed his ideas on operational definitions under this influence (it was an interesting twist of fate that his operationism survived, and even flourished, in the social sciences long after it had been passed by in the physical sciences); and B. F. Skinner met logical positivism while in graduate school, and his behaviorism can be interpreted as an application of this philosophy to the realms of psychology (John B. Watson's behaviorism pre-dated the work of the logical positivists, although it might have been indirectly influenced by C. S. Peirce).

The logical positivists are notorious for their development of the "verifiability principle or criterion of meaning." Their idea, of course, was to rule out of serious consideration (by means of defining them as meaningless) any statements the method of verification of which cannot be specified in terms of sense experience. (Clearly, this was an extension of the skeptical empiricism inherent in Hume and Comte.) Attempts to state this principle became very complex, but a simple form read as follows: "A statement is held to be literally meaningful if and only if it is either analytic or empirically verifiable" (Ayer 1960, 9). Or, more colloquially, "If it can't be seen or measured, it is not meaningful to talk about."

Here again, the American pragmatists were close to the logical positivists in spirit. Peirce, too, wanted to find a way of settling "metaphysical disputes that might otherwise be interminable" (see Peirce, "How to Make Our Ideas Clear," in Konvitz and Kennedy 1960); the nice phrase here is actually taken from William James, in Konvitz and Kennedy 1960, 29). And so Peirce—anticipating the logical positivists by half a century—devised the pragmatic maxim of meaning that was, in thrust, very similar to the verifiability principle of meaning. Peirce illustrated how such a principle or maxim could wreak havoc with fanciful metaphysical problems—for example, he argued that the theory that a diamond is soft until it is actually scratched, whereupon it becomes hard, is identical in meaning with the theory that diamonds are always hard, because there are no circumstances whatever when the two theories would lead to different testable consequences. To cite another example: John B. Watson may well have known of Peirce's pragmatic maxim of meaning, as he studied under Dewey at the University of Chicago, and Dewey certainly knew of it and had been influenced by it. But whatever the source, Watson's classic paper of 1913, which founded the behavioristic movement in psychology, contained a major thread of ideas that would have delighted Peirce, Comte, and the (later) logical positivists. Watson urged psychologists to abandon the notion of "consciousness" because there were no clear-cut observational criteria for using it; he wrote that so far as making observations was concerned, it mattered neither "jot nor tittle" whether one supposed consciousness was present or not. Only behavior is observable, and only by focusing on this could psychology become scientific. The opening lines of Watson's revolutionary paper of 1913 are notorious:

> Psychology as the behaviorist views it is a purely objective experimental branch of natural science. Its theoretical goal is the prediction and control of behavior. (Watson 1948, 457)

The philosopher and social scientist Michael Scriven summarized the positivists' use of the verifiability criterion of meaning as follows:

> The Vienna Circle or *Wiener Kreis* was a band of cutthroats that went after the fat burghers of Continental metaphysics who had become intolerably inbred and pompously verbose. The kris is a Malaysian knife, and the *Wiener Kreis* employed a kind of Occam's Razor called the Verifiabil-

ity Principle. It performed a tracheotomy that made it possible for philosophy to breathe again. (Scriven 1969, 195)

Scriven illustrates that it is possible for a nonpositivist to be sympathetic with at least part of the logical positivist program. Karl Popper, too,
has been extremely critical of the verbal excesses of Continental philosophers, and, using prose that the logical positivists would have admired, he
has accused the leader of the Frankfurt School, Jürgen Habermas, of fostering a cult of "un-understandability" (Popper 1976). Popper also wanted
to clearly demarcate metaphysics from science, and his early work was
driven by the so-called criterion of demarcation, which, to a careless reader,
looks like a close variant of the logical positivists' criterion of meaning.
Popper argued that science and metaphysics were demarcated by the principle of testability: If a proposition could not be tested, then it was not
scientific, and therefore it was metaphysical (for Popper only recognized
the two categories). However—and this is a crucial difference—Popper did
not regard metaphysics as *meaningless;* it simply was not science. The logical positivists, on the other hand, not only demarcated science and metaphysics, but labeled the latter category as containing—literally—non-
sense! Popper, in contrast, insisted that metaphysics was an important
field, and he suggested that in fact many scientific ideas start life as metaphysical. Not only, then, is Popper not a positivist, he also claims to have
been the person who destroyed logical positivism (Popper 1974, esp. 69)!
But the rumor persists that he was a fellow-traveler, fueled probably by
the fact that he lived in Vienna in his youth and had contact with the
Circle, and even had his first book published by them (an act of intellectual charity that both parties probably lived to regret).

The verifiability criterion of meaning raises, in a particularly virulent
way, the dilemma about laws and the theoretical entities of science that
we saw Comte did not deal with in a fully consistent manner. The first
set of problems that arose here for the logical positivists concerned the
issue of what will count as a satisfactory verification procedure in any given
case. Their answers usually involved reference to a class of elementary
"observation statements"; that is, in discussing how a given term or proposition could be "verified" and hence given meaning, the logical positivists usually claimed that the verification had to be in terms of simple, "rock
bottom," direct, and indubitable descriptions of sense experience. (There
is a temptation, of course, to allow *indirect* observation, such as observations via instruments, but this only opens the floodgates.) This doctrine

had a checkered history, and the logical positivists were not always in full agreement about it. Rudolf Carnap's formulation was as follows:

> (w)e have to proceed from what is epistemically primary, that is to say, from the "given," i.e., from experiences themselves in their totality and undivided unity. . . . The elementary experiences are to be the basic elements of our constructional system. From this basis we wish to construct all other objects of prescientific and scientific knowledge. (Carnap 1969, 108-109)

This doctrine was eventually undermined by the realization (found in the work of Wittgenstein, Dewey, Popper, and Hanson; see Hanson 1958, chap. 1) that perception is theory-laden. Sense experience, in other words, is not a secure, theory-neutral foundation of our knowledge, for our theories and our knowledge influence both what we see and how we see it. (It is another interesting twist of fate that Comte shared this realization, at least in elementary form, but evidently did not realize its key significance. Thus he wrote, almost as a throw-away remark: "For if, on the one hand, every positive theory must necessarily be founded upon observations, it is, on the other hand, no less true that, in order to observe, our mind has need of some theory or other." See Comte 1970, 4-5.) The logical positivists—less prescient than Comte—would these days be classified as holding a version of foundationalist epistemology (knowledge is built upon a foundation of theory-free, or "neutral" sense experience), whereas it presently seems that nonfoundationalism is the only position that is viable (see the discussion in chapter 6).

Now, given the way the logical positivists typically treated verification, it is no surprise that, on the whole, they took the skeptical path opened by Hume and Comte and were not realists with respect to the status of the entities referred to in scientific theories. (Of course, they might not have seen this position as skeptical!) Consider the entities postulated in subatomic theory; these are not directly observable, and even indirect confirmation is a complex business. So, rigorous use of the verifiability principle of meaning poses a problem here—what do we mean when we speak of protons, electrons, or quarks? Can they be regarded as real entities if there is a problem with respect to their verification in terms of direct sensory experience? Alternatively, should they be interpreted as theoretical fictions? There is a parallel problem about the laws of nature, for, as we saw in regard to Comte, universal generalizations of the form "all *X* are *Y*" cannot be verified (for usually we cannot observe all members of the class *X*).

So, to repeat, many of the logical positivists were led to take a non-realist or antirealist stand. Even as late as 1956 Rudolf Carnap was still grappling with this issue, and he wrote that a major concern was still

> the problem of a criterion of significance for the theoretical language, i.e. exact conditions which terms and sentences of the theoretical language must fulfill in order to have a positive function for the explanation and prediction of observable events and thus to be acceptable as empirically meaningful. (Carnap 1956, 38)

Carnap was still confident, at this late stage in the history of logical positivism, that he would be able to draw the line "which demarcates the scientifically meaningful from the meaningless" (Carnap 1956, 40). Six short years later Grover Maxwell was scathing about this position:

> that anyone today should seriously contend that the entities referred to by scientific theories are only convenient fictions, or that talk about such entities is translatable without remainder into talk about sense contents or everyday physical objects . . . strike(s) me as so incongruous with the scientific and rational attitude and practice that I feel this paper should turn out to be a demolition of straw men. (Maxwell 1962, 3)

Thus, there is little comfort here for the antipositivistic vigilantes with whom the present discussion opened. Typically, these folk have themselves accepted the antirealism, relativism, and even subjectivism that is not uncommon today across the pure and applied social sciences and that is traceable, at least in large part, back to the influence (and/or misinterpretations) of the work of Thomas S. Kuhn. But whatever the source, their beliefs place them much closer to the spirit of the logical positivists than they suppose in even their wildest dreams! For the logical positivists, as we have seen, were also antirealist, they did not have much time for the notion of absolute truth, and they wanted to remain close to the raw phenomena of experience. Thus, it is clear that the vigilantes are fundamentally confused—logical positivism may be indefensible, but it is not for the reasons that the vigilantes suppose; rather, it is indefensible for much the same reasons as is the position of many of the vigilantes themselves. In turning on the logical positivists, the vigilantes are turning on their own kind.

RESPECT FOR SCIENTIFIC METHOD

A little more needs to be said, however, about the respect for scientific method that was part, at least, of the positivists' credo. This is often what offends the vigilantes—they see the slavish imitation of science as being detrimental to the progress of the social sciences. And so it is—if the view of science that is held is an indefensible one! (The discussion of naturalistic strategies in chapter 5 is also pertinent to this issue.)

Here the vigilantes are both right and wrong. They are right to be critical of the positivists' analysis of science; but they are wrong to set up a "straw man" and to act as if all admiration of science is beyond the pale simply because the positivists turned out to have admired something of a monster. As indicated earlier, Comte and his successors regarded the key method of science as being the primacy given to sense experience, to which Comte added the quest to find the (observable) laws of phenomena. By the light of our contemporary understanding this is a considerable oversimplification, if not worse.

There has been no dearth of others who have admired science, and who have given analyses of it that differ markedly from the one provided by the positivists and logical positivists. This is not the place to recount the Popperian analysis or the Deweyan (to pick two that are particularly interesting and compatible with my own predilections). But it can be said that there are substantial reasons for believing that *all* effective thinkers, across a very broad range of disciplines—including the humanities—use similar intellectual methods. Whether these are collectively called the "scientific method" or the method of "effective thinking" is a matter of personal preference. Both Dewey and Popper give strikingly similar analyses of this "method"; which, of course, is not a *method* in the sense that an algorithm is put forward, the slavish following of which is guaranteed to lead always to a happy outcome—their "method" is much more open-ended than that. (See the comparison of these in chapter 6 of the first edition of this book.) Basically, effective thinking, in science and elsewhere, involves the identification and clarification of problems, the formulation of tentative solutions, and the practical (or theoretical) testing of these and the elimination of those that are not successful in resolving the original problem. For all intents and purposes this "method" is a "soft" extension of what has come to be labeled as the hypothetico-deductive method in science.

The antipositivistic vigilantes, if indeed they are seriously interested in thinking effectively about the empirical realm, have nothing to fear from such an account of "scientific method"—it is quite unpositivistic (although it is, one supposes, compatible with Comte's desire to commandeer scientific method for wider use among those who study human affairs). Furthermore, as philosophers like Dagfinn Follesdal have pointed out, this method is used even in areas such as hermeneutics, which are typically regarded as being far removed from the field of science (Follesdal 1979).

Perhaps it is fitting, by way of conclusion, to recall that among all the defects, the positivists and logical positivists were interested in serious questions, and they gave an interesting (but flawed) series of answers. R. W. Ashby has reminded us that the

> logical positivists contributed a great deal toward the understanding of the nature of philosophical questions, and in their approach to philosophy they set an example from which many have still to learn. They brought to philosophy an interest in cooperation. . . . They adopted high standards of rigor. . . . And they tried to formulate methods of inquiry that would lead to commonly accepted results. (Ashby 1964, 508)

10

QUALITATIVE RESEARCH AND ITS WARRANT

It is generally held that William Topaz McGonagall (d. 1902) was the worst poet ever to have been published in the English language. One commentator has written:

> He was so giftedly bad that he backed unwittingly into genius. Combining a minimum feel for the English language with a total lack of self-awareness and nil powers of observation, he became a poet. (Pile 1980, 123)

We can thank our lucky stars that he did not become a naturalistic qualitative researcher—another profession for which he would have been singularly unqualified.

Unlike McGonagall, but like genuine poets, qualitative researchers are supposed to have keen powers of observation, heightened self-awareness and realization of how their own personalities can shape their work, and a sensitive command of the language in which they will report their observations. There is, however, one important respect in which poets and qualitative researchers differ—the works produced by poets may be intended to be enjoyable, insightful, and stimulating, but usually it is not necessary that they be *accepted as true*. "Half a league, half a league, half a league onward . . . , " and the rest, is a poetic rendering of the charge of the Light Brigade, but only the innocent (or the Hollywood scriptwriter) would take it to be a factual description of what actually happened on that fateful day in the Crimea. Indeed, in many cases the notion of "truth" does not seem applicable to poetry at all; consider the lines of John Keats: "Thou still unravish'd bride of quietness. Thou fosterchild of Silence and slow Time." These words are magical—they are evocative and communicate a great deal; to ask whether they are true or not is to make a serious "category mistake."

On the other hand, qualitative researchers generally *do* intend for their findings to be taken as veridical. To say that a description of a classroom, life in an urban gang, or village life in some exotic culture is evocative but is not meant to be true or false is merely another category mistake—it is to identify qualitative research as being poetry or something similar (although, as I argued in chapter 4, even narratives must sometimes be true, especially when they are produced by researchers). Moreover, it is a mistake that is fatal for qualitative research; if a qualitative description or analysis is not true or false (i.e., if in principle these terms are not applicable to it), then the issue of whether that description or analysis is to be believed or acted upon cannot arise—it is not sensible to say that one believes the lines by Keats, just as it is not sensible to say that one believes Mozart's clarinet concerto and is prepared to base policy or social intervention upon it.

Thus, in order to be believed (or disbelieved), and in order to be (or not to be) the basis for intervention or for policy, it is absolutely necessary to have the property of being true or false; and to have one or other of these properties the statement, finding, theory, or whatever must make some claim about some state of affairs. (This is not to say that we can always, or even often, determine whether the item under consideration is *actually* true or false.) All of this seems to have been acknowledged by Miles and Huberman, authors of what has become one of the standard volumes on naturalistic qualitative methodology; in an earlier paper they wrote:

> The results (of qualitative research, especially the "connoisseurship" approach) are expected to be taken seriously, to be accepted as plausible, even valid, beyond the corps of people using the critical perspective. Otherwise, no one beyond the observer would be illuminated, and no serious claims of connoisseurship could be made that other publics could acknowledge. (Miles and Huberman 1984, 21)

The foregoing argument establishes that truth is necessary for certain societal functions to be carried out; but it is also necessary to point out that people have surprising "hang-ups" about it. Today truth has a similar status to that occupied by the topic of sex in the bygone Victorian era—it is not a topic that refined folk like to discuss, at least in public. (In private, of course, both topics have been the focus of much attention and have been the butt not only of words but of deeds.) In both cases euphemisms have been used, as if the embarrassing topics would vanish if they were not referred to in a direct and forthright manner. Thus, expressions like "X is true" and "X is the truth" are often avoided by qualitative researchers and get replaced by "X is to be believed" or "X can be assented to"—a harmless enough verbal ploy, because most folk realize that, in general, to *believe* X *is* to *accept* X *as being true.* The practice only becomes pernicious when some qualitative researchers claim that there is no "truth" but still want their account of X to be believed! (I have confused a number of graduate students who hold this general position by asking them whether or not "it is true that it did not snow at Stanford today" and then by following up and asking if they were claiming this question did not make sense. It is difficult really *not* to believe in truth; even Rorty, who is often cited in such discussions, does not completely do away with truth, but he insists on the stylistic point that the "t" be printed lower case—he only objects to "Truth.") It is worth stressing that not *all* qualitative researchers are guilty of the sin that I am pointing to; and not all qualitative researchers are the butt of criticism in the following discussion. In general, the negative points to be made do not apply to those who work in the well-established anthropological or ethnographic tradition, but rather it is some of the newer modes of qualitative work that are the targets here.

Other euphemisms are common as well; questions about truth are often stated in terms of validity or justification. "Is this conclusion valid?"; "Is it justified?"; "Can this result be trusted?" are questions posed by researchers from different poles of the "newer" qualitative continuum. This word game is somewhat more dangerous, for, if it is not played carefully, it can very easily lead to pernicious results. Before pursuing this discussion, however, some clearing of the terrain needs to take place.

SOME TRUTHS ABOUT TRUTH

1. There is one euphemism that has a great deal to be said in its favor. John Dewey was reluctant to use the term *truth*, and he decided to replace the term by *warranted assertibility*. The reasoning is complex (it is to be found scattered through the pages of *Logic: The Theory of Inquiry*), but it is clear Dewey recognized that when truth claims are made, to be taken seriously they must be supported with appropriate arguments or evidence. It is, indeed, the strength of the warranting argument or evidence that *allows* a truth to be recognized and labeled as such. This approach, too,

can easily accommodate those cases where what was formerly regarded as truth is reidentified as nontruth—what has happened here is that the warrant for assertion has been withdrawn, it has been found to be in error. The great merit of Dewey's language, then, is that it highlights the necessity to have an *adequate warrant*—which in his view can come only from "competent inquiries" (Dewey 1966, 8; see also the discussion in Phillips and Burbules 2000). What should count as the criteria of adequacy and competency is, of course, a sticky question.

2. It is held by many—including some in the qualitative camp who have been eager to latch onto this, and including also some who have been infected by postmodernist doubt—that recent developments in philosophy of science have made the notion of truth otiose. (The argument here is that if philosophers have shown that the notion of truth has to be abandoned in the physical sciences, then qualitative researchers should have no concerns about it at all.) This is a misinterpretation of the contemporary scene. Certainly, there has been a great freeing up with respect to what counts as evidence for and against the truth of a scientific hypothesis; it can no longer be held that any single test result can be definitive one way or the other. The role of theories in influencing observations, the relation between theory and evidence, the role of auxiliary and *ad hoc* assumptions—all of these have been elucidated in the recent literature (see Phillips 1987 and also chapter 6 of the present volume). It is now recognized more clearly than ever before that our human judgments about what is true are fallible and subject to constant revision. And it is recognized that we cannot even be sure that our constant revisions are bringing us nearer to the truth; Popper's great attempt to produce a theory of verisimilitude is acknowledged as being a failure, even by his closest admirers.

But nowhere in the mainstream of philosophy (anything can happen, of course, in the "lunatic fringe") is it held that we are free to believe whatever we want, that there are no constraints on belief. Even Kuhn, who has been seen by some as the apostle of rampant relativism, does not believe in intellectual anarchy. (He sees most investigators in any particular field of natural science, at most times in history, as being in one paradigm, but during revolutionary periods they are spread over two. Kuhn certainly does not see every investigator being in his or her *own* paradigm. In other words, he does not do away with truth but sees judgments about what is true as being made internally to a paradigm.) And, as noted previously, Richard Rorty, who wants to do away with Truth, does not want to abandon truth, nor does he throw out the need for standards or warrants for belief; toward the end of his influential *Philosophy and the Mirror of Nature* he writes of "knowing" as being "*a right, by current standards, to believe*" (his acknowledged debt to Dewey is quite evident here), and he goes on to say that more attention should be given

> to the relation between alternative standards of justification, and from there to the actual change in those standards which make up intellectual history. (Rorty 1979, 389–390)

To say that standards change or evolve is not to say that there are no standards or that there should not be any!

3. The Kuhnian-inspired notion that there may be rival paradigms, with their own views of what is true, has led to the development of a more extreme position—there are *multiple realities,* so there are multiple sets of truths, all of which are true at the same time (see the discussion in chapter 6). Several of the newer apologists for qualitative methods of research have held this; William Filstead, for example, claims that this view is related to the philosophical position of idealism, and he states:

> The qualitative paradigm does not conceive of the world as an external force, objectively identifiable and independent of man. Rather, there are multiple realities. (Filstead 1979, 35–36)

A similar statement is to be found in Guba and Lincoln:

> Naturalistic inquirers [their name for qualitative researchers] make virtually the opposite assumptions [to positivistic, scientific inquirers]. They focus upon the multiple realities that, like the layers of an onion, nest within or complement one another. Each layer provides a different perspective of reality, and none can be considered more "true" than any other. Phenomena do not converge into a single form, a single "truth," but diverge into many forms, multiple "truths." (Guba and Lincoln 1982, 57)

On one interpretation, Guba and Lincoln and the others who hold similar positions are saying something rather trite, and they are mistaken in thinking that there is a conflict here with what "traditional" or "non-naturalistic" scientists believe. Of course, a phenomenon can be examined from different perspectives; a motor accident can be approached in terms of the physics of the collision, in terms of economics, in terms of the psychological states of the drivers, in medical terms, and so on. Such accounts may all be true; they are complementary or orthogonal, not conflicting. But it seems as if Filstead, and Guba and Lincoln, have something else in mind—possibly they envision multiple but conflicting truths that can, nevertheless, all be true. The discussion here can best progress in terms of an analogy: Consider rival religions, which give quite incompatible accounts of the nature of the Deity (one says He or She has property P, and the other holds the opposite). Each religion has its devotees who regard it as true, but it is hard to conceive that *all* accounts are true at the same time. (Of course, *which* account is true is not the issue here.) Even a Deity would be hard-pressed to both have, and not have, property P, at the one instant. There is a strong tradition in the philosophy of religion that even a Deity must conform to the laws of logic; it is sobering that according to Filstead, and Guba and Lincoln, the physical realm outstrips the power of a Deity here (for according to them, it can have opposing properties)! Certainly, they owe their readers further discussion on this extraordinary point. (This issue is pursued further in chapter 6.)

Whatever these various writers mean, they cannot coherently hold that any view that anyone cares to assert must be accepted as being true. They do not want to eradicate the need to put forward warrants for belief (indeed, this and other books by Guba and Lincoln deal with how to produce effective warrants in social program evaluation settings). They seem to realize that not everyone who postulates an alternative reality is right—it is possible for such a person to be paranoid, deluded, or simply in error. So, then, there must be criteria for judging the warrants that are advanced on behalf of claims to have detected new realities. Guba and Lincoln raise this issue in the following terms, using quotation marks around the word *"truth"* to warn their readers that they are unhappy with it and intend to replace it by *"credibility"*; nevertheless, the concern with warrant is still apparent:

> How can one establish confidence in the "truth" of the findings of a particular inquiry for the subjects with which—and the context within which—the inquiry was carried out? (Guba and Lincoln 1982, 103)

This, then, is the moral of the discussion so far: The worry about what will count as a satisfactory qualitative warrant for beliefs or truth claims will not wane. On all but the most exotic (and incomprehensible) views of the nature of truth and knowledge, there arises the issue of why the account of some phenomenon that is given by a qualitative researcher (or, for that matter, any researcher) should be believed.

IS QUALITATIVE WORK MORE SUSPECT THAN QUANTITATIVE OR EXPERIMENTAL?

The points made so far apply to *all* research. All truth claims, in all areas, need to have warrants; and all truth claims, in all areas except perhaps logic and mathematics, are never absolutely established—they may be strongly supported by warrants, but they never reach the stage where they are immune from revision in the light of the results of further inquiry. So why, then, should qualitative research be singled out for special attention?

A number of methodological problems, while not entirely confined to the province of qualitative research, are especially serious here. They are somewhat interrelated, so the following listing is not exhaustive or precise; the categories could easily be collapsed or expanded:

a. As N. R. Hanson and many others have shown, observation is theory-laden. It is somewhat easier to correct for (or control) the biasing effects of prior knowledge and beliefs when one is observing inanimate nature than it is when observing human or social phenomena. For we ourselves are human, and our beliefs about humankind are strongly held and are bound up with our feelings and our valuations.

b. It is unlikely that an observer will enter into social relationships with any inanimate or subhuman entities that are under study; this is quite likely to occur in the human or social domains. The point, of course, is that in social relationships the behaviors, beliefs, and perceptions of the parties concerned are likely to be affected; people do and say things partly with the likely reactions of the other actors in mind; and emotional bonds start to form. It is hard to know what to make of observations that are made under these conditions, unless the observer has been especially sensitive and has taken careful precautions.

c. An observer does not have to make especial efforts to understand or empathize with inanimate objects, but there are good grounds to believe that if observation of human and social phenomena is to be sensible, then it is often unavoidable that the reasons held by the people being observed must be comprehended (see the discussion in chapter 2). But attainment of this understanding of the reasons and beliefs held by other people often results in some fellow feeling with them—it is difficult to be distant and unconcerned; in short, it is difficult to be objective.

These problems are widely understood by qualitative methodologists; and Miles and Huberman, and, of course, many writers in the ethnographic tradition, offer positive suggestions. Others take these problems as indications that the study of human or social affairs can never be "scientific" or argue that objectivity is an unattainable—and perhaps even a misplaced—ideal.

   d. Insofar as qualitative researchers rely on nonformal or "intuitive" modes of data processing, they have to face squarely the fact that "whatever its other strengths, the mind is apt to make errors of judgment and inference" (Sadler 1982, 199). For example, human observers are quite prone to be unduly influenced or "anchored" by their first impressions of a situation, they are overinfluenced by positive instances supporting a hypothesis or bias but undervalue negative instances, they incorrectly estimate "base rate" frequencies of behaviors they are studying, they do not allow properly for missing data even when they know it is missing, and so forth. Again, some—but by no means all—qualitative methodologists are sensitive to the problems here, and they take care to minimize the threats to the validity of their studies (while others call such precautions the illicit remnant of positivism) (see Bryman 1984, esp. 85).

   e. There is an especially difficult problem that can arise in some—but not all—qualitative research. It does not arise if the aim of the research is to catalogue the beliefs that are held by the people who are being studied, and it also does not arise if the purpose is entirely descriptive. But it does arise when qualitative research aims to uncover causes—and this is not uncommon, especially in research that hopes to result in advice on how to improve performance (e.g., how to improve effectiveness of teaching or how to combat juvenile delinquency) or in research that is related to evaluation of programs or settings. Causal links are rarely accessible to unaided observation; in most settings there are many interacting factors at work, and to tease out those that are causally responsible for effects is no easy task. Usually, a degree of control will have to be exercised—some factors will have to be held constant, while others are varied. The classic statement of this is in the work of John Stuart Mill:

> In every instance which comes under our observation, there are many antecedents and many consequents. If those antecedents could not be severed from one another except in thought or if those consequents never were found apart, it would be impossible for us to distinguish (a posteriori, at least) the real laws, or to assign to any cause its effect, or to any effect its cause. To do so, we must be able to meet with some of the antecedents apart from the rest and observe what follows from them,

or some of the consequents and observe by what they are preceded. We must, in short, follow the Baconian rule of *varying the circumstances*. (Mill 1950, 210)

The qualitative researcher who seeks causes thus has to become an experimenter (even if the experiments are not true, randomized ones)—a matter that those in the anthropological tradition have long recognized. In short, naked observation is generally a poor device for warranting causal claims or for warranting advice on intervention or on future policy (for such advice itself is dependent upon having causal knowledge of situations). Many of the newer qualitative methodologists have not seriously grappled with the difficult problems here.

By way of summary of this section of the discussion, it seems appropriate to cite the assessment given by Martin Hammersley of the work of the influential Chicago qualitative sociologist Herbert Blumer. Hammersley writes that nowhere is

> Blumer clear about the nature of the process of testing that he claims is involved in naturalistic (i.e., his form of qualitative) research. He seems to place faith in the idea that by "going directly to the social world" and examining it we will discover its nature. I think he sees any fixed procedure as a barrier to such discovery because it impairs the flexibility of the researcher. The latter must be free to adapt to, to be moulded by, the world. In my view, though, while exploration, flexibility, and creativity are necessary, the idea that if one adopts a flexible attitude towards the world in one's interactions with it, one will come to discover its nature amounts to a naive form of realism. It underestimates the potential for bias and error. (Hammersley 1989, 189)

Hammersley could have added that observation, or even "flexible" interaction with the world, is not sufficient to sort out the causal chains that operate in the social world. The point, simply, is this: the social world can be given *many* descriptions, and the issue arises as to why we should accept the description that a particular researcher happens to favor. The fact that the researcher happens to favor it is not a sufficient warrant.

In the light of all these complexities, the issue again arises as to how well the warrants that are suggested in the literature fare—will the warrants favored by qualitative researchers (when, indeed, they explicitly favor a warrant) stand up to scrutiny?

WILL THE SUGGESTED WARRANTS WORK?

Qualitative methodology has won a foothold in many branches of the "pure" and "applied" social sciences; it has, of course, long been a feature of some branches, such as anthropology. But the foothold was not always won easily in the other branches. In sociology, for example, several journals ran symposia in the late 1970s (see Bryman 1984, 76); and there was an attendant amount of name-calling and labeling:

> In some cases writers have chosen not to use the quantitative/qualitative distinction and have instead used terms which have been used as synonyms. The terms "positivist" and "empiricist" often denote the same fundamental approach as "quantitative," while "naturalistic" field research, "ethnographic," "interpretivist," and "constructivist" are sometimes used instead of "qualitative." (Bryman 1984, 77)

A strikingly similar debate raged in the field of educational research during the 1980s and early '90s, chiefly in North America; some of the contributors here (including Miles and Huberman, and Guba and Lincoln) have been influential more broadly across the applied social sciences. To make the following discussion manageable, it is this more recent debate that shall be the focus of attention—the points are applicable across the social sciences. (Some of the issues to be discussed here were also touched upon in chapter 8, in the context of Popperian research methodology.)

The literature on qualitative methodology in the educational research domain contains a variety of suggested warrants and a host of ways of conceptualizing warrants—ways that are generally notable for their avoidance of the embarrassing term *truth*. Some writers admit that there is a problem here—that is, they acknowledge that the warrants that have been suggested are not adequate for the task in hand. In the work of Miles and Huberman referred to earlier, this concern about qualitative methodology has been raised, and they have written that "As we have said often, qualitative analyses can be evocative, illuminating, masterful, and downright *wrong*" (Miles and Huberman 1985, 230). In the discussion that follows, their own suggestions concerning warrants will be examined, as will the views of the Stanford researcher Elliot Eisner, and Egon Guba and Yvonna Lincoln. (These three sets of authors are considered because between them, they seem to cover the whole spectrum of the newer qualitative methodologies. At one pole, Eisner is a self-declared eclecticist, relativist, and instrumentalist [Eisner 1983, 14], and a connoisseur to boot; Miles and Huberman are at the other pole—they call themselves "right-wing" qualitative researchers, or "soft-nosed positivists" [Miles and Huberman 1985, 23]; and Guba and Lincoln are—perhaps—somewhere in between.) For want of a better criterion, the discussion will proceed alphabetically.

1. Elliot Eisner. Eisner sees the issue of the truth of qualitatively generated findings in terms of "validity" and "trustworthiness." He asks, "How can we know if educational criticism (his version of qualitative investigation) can be trusted?" (Eisner 1979, 213). He goes on to provide three criteria—structural corroboration, referential adequacy, and multiplicative replication.

The first of these, structural corroboration, is easily dealt with. Eisner himself admits—after advocating its use—that it is not a reliable yardstick. For structural corroboration is the process in which various parts of the account or description or explanation give each other mutual support; it is a process of "gathering data or information and using it to establish links that eventually create a whole that is supported by the bits of evidence that constitute it" (Eisner 1979, 215). Possession of this type of corroboration, of course, shows that the account is coherent, but coherence is not correlated with truth. As Eisner notes, a swindler's story is coherent and convincing!

Turning to the second criterion: A work (for example, a description of a classroom) has referential adequacy, when it enables us to see features that it refers to but that we may not ourselves have noticed:

> When the critic's work is referentially adequate we will be able to find in the object, event, or situation what the cues point to. (Eisner 1979, 216)

The problem here, of course, is that seeing what the critic or qualitative researcher is talking about does not mean that the account is *true.* Thus, I can read Hitler's description of (among other things) the post–World War I Germany in *Mein Kampf,* and had I been alive at the time I might—with a little effort—have been able to see the world through his eyes, but this does not mean that his account would have been veridical. Or, to take a less loaded example, it is possible to look at an autistic child after having studied the Freudian theory about this condition; one can see what the Freudians are talking about. (One can do the same with the behaviorist theory.) The fact that this can be done does not establish the *truth* of the theory.

An argument drawn from contemporary philosophy of science can be used to bolster this conclusion. For any data set, no matter how large, an infinite number of theoretical explanations can be given—a phenomenon that has come to be called "the underdetermination of the theory of nature." So the fact that we may all see the same things does not speak to the truth of any one theoretical account. But it must be stressed again that there are problems for Eisner's criterion at less lofty levels than the realms of theory—the actual *description* of the situation that is observed may be challengeable. Just because I can see what the Freudian is referring to, does not mean that I thereby endorse that his or her description is the correct one. (After all, I can also see what the rival behaviorist is referring to.) Another way to put this is that observations do not come with the appropriate descriptive or explanatory language pre-attached by nature; multiple descriptions seem always to be possible.

So Eisner is down to one last criterion, which involves other people having seen the same things; he calls this "multiplicative replication," and he himself does not place much weight on it. For consensual validation (which is what the criterion amounts to) is a two-edged sword; all sorts of cults and fads have been "corroborated" in this way, but one would be hard-pressed to say this was a sign of their truth. (On occasion Eisner bravely bites the bullet and suggests that there is no such thing as truth, it is *only* a matter of what a community believes. This, of course, has the consequence that it is true that the earth is both spherical and flat, because there are communities who believe either thing. On the positive side, it must be acknowledged that this nicely solves the problem with which this chapter began—there is no problem about the truth of qualitative research findings, because *each one* of them is true, providing that a community can be found that will subscribe to it!)

In case, however, there are some readers who do not find this satisfactory, the discussion will turn to the work of Guba and Lincoln.

2. Guba and Lincoln. These writers argue that the question of "truth value" can be reduced to the question of "credibility" (Guba and Lincoln 1982, 104–105). They suggest various techniques, such as reducing involvement with the human subjects the field-worker is interacting with; they also build upon Eisner's notion of structural corroboration. However, after a detailed discussion of techniques that are useful here, they make a significant remark:

> the techniques discussed above do not themselves establish credibility—at best they simply increase the probability that data and interpretations will be found credible.

What then is their answer?

> The determination of credibility can be accomplished only by taking
> data and interpretations to the sources from which they were drawn and
> asking directly whether they believe—find plausible—the results. This
> process of going to the sources—often called "member checks"—is the
> backbone of satisfying the truth value criterion. (Guba and Lincoln 1982,
> 110)

It is worth noting that this same procedure is standardly used by ethnographers working within the anthropological tradition.

In one sense this is no advance, indeed it is a retrograde suggestion;
but in another sense it is sound. The heart of the matter here is the precise nature of the findings or account the "credibility" of which is being
probed. If the account that the qualitative researcher is dealing with is an
account *of the beliefs* held by an individual or by a group of subjects—and
this is the central focus in ethnographic work—then the appropriate criterion may well be whether or not these subjects agree that the researcher
has indeed accurately recorded their beliefs. But this is not central in most
of the work done by qualitative researchers of an Eisnerian or Guberian
stamp. When the account produced by the qualitative researcher is an
account of a classroom, or of the effects of some educational or social program, or the like, then it is clear that the endorsement of the participants
in the classroom or program in question has little or nothing to do with
the truth of the account. A qualitative researcher's account of an interaction between a therapist and an autistic child might be true or false quite
independently of the assent or dissent of the two participants; similarly,
an account of a classroom might be true even though the teacher (or the
pupils) disagree with it.

This is such a major point that it is worth stating in another way. If
the purpose of a piece of qualitative work is *emic*, that is, if the intent is
to give an account of how the participants in a situation see it, then checking the account with the participants (or with a selected "informant") is a
vital step. On the other hand, if the intent is *etic*, that is, if the purpose *is
not* to describe a situation from a participant's viewpoint but from, say, an
Eisnerian connoisseur's outside perspective, then getting the imprimatur
of the participants is beside the point—their judgments about "credibility" are irrelevant.

Guba and Lincoln are paying the price, here, of misidentifying truth
with credibility. Credibility is a scandalously weak and inappropriate

surrogate for truth or veracity—under appropriate circumstances any non-sense at all can be judged as "credible." It is time, then, to turn to the next set of authors to see if they fare any better.

3. Miles and Huberman. These writers start in a promising way by noting that qualitative analyses can be illuminating, masterful, and evocative, but also *wrong* (Miles and Huberman 1984, 27 and 230). They also use the expression "truth space." But then they start to drift off target by identifying the attainment of truth with the possession of certain data-processing methods:

> The problem is that there is an insufficient corpus of reliable, valid, or even minimally agreed upon working analysis procedures for qualitative data. (Miles and Huberman 1984, 22; see also 1985, 230)

Of course, a lot depends upon what procedures they have in mind to recommend, and as will be seen shortly they undoubtedly have some important ideas. But in general it must be recognized that there are *no* procedures that will regularly (or always) yield either sound data or true conclusions. If there were such procedures, then steady progress in human understanding would be guaranteed—indeed, it would probably become a matter of following routines, and eventually knowledge generation could be taken over by computers. The words of philosopher of science Paul Feyerabend are worth quoting in this context:

> The idea of a method that contains firm, unchanging, and absolutely binding principles for conducting the business of science gets into considerable difficulty when confronted with the results of historical research. We find, then, that there is not a single rule, however plausible, and however firmly grounded in epistemology, that is not violated at some time or another. It becomes evident that such violations are not isolated events. . . . On the contrary, we see they are necessary for progress. . . . More specifically, the following can be shown: considering any rule, however "fundamental," there are always circumstances when it is advisable not only to ignore the rule, but to adopt its opposite. (Feyerabend 1970, 21–22)

Feyerabend states that, in fact, there is one rule: "Anything goes."

The point of this is not to strengthen the skepticism (or Feyerabendian "anarchism") that is already rampant in the modern academic world. The point is merely to issue a caution to those who read Miles and

Huberman as saying that the formulation of true belief is simply *a matter of finding, and following, certain analytic procedures.* They themselves recognize this danger, and they warn against "overpreoccupation with method rather than substance and the development of a crippling, mechanical orthodoxy" (Miles and Huberman 1984, 28).

Miles and Huberman suggest a dozen "verification tactics," many of which have already been alluded to—they draw liberally on Eisnerian and Guberian ideas. Mostly, their suggested procedures, if followed, would produce consensus among investigators (i.e., multiplicative replication) rather than research findings that are true. This direction in their work is clearly revealed in the preamble to their list of tactics:

> How do we know whether a conclusion is surreal or real? By "real" we mean another competent researcher, working independently at the same site, would not come up with wholly contradictory findings. (Miles and Huberman 1984, 27)

It must be stressed that no objection is being made here to having researchers, as far as possible, independently check each other's work. On the contrary, this is a counsel of wisdom. But the point is that this is a relatively weak guarantee of "reality" or "truth" (as the history of anthropology and of physics bear witness). It may be the best that we can hope for, but it should be recognized for what it is, warts and all.

In fact, Miles and Huberman succeed in doing a little better. One of their twelve tactics is "looking for negative evidence," and while this is not absolutely foolproof and cannot establish that a finding or conclusion is right, it can help in what Popper has called "error elimination" (see the discussion of falsification in chapter 8). Indeed, this tactic is worthy of elaboration and deserves a much more central place than they have given it—it is buried as number eleven in their list and does not seem to play a role at all in the methodology recommended by Eisner or Guba and Lincoln (Miles and Huberman 1984, 28). Popper, in various places, makes the telling point that any fool can find confirmations for an hypothesis, but what is crucial is whether or not refuting evidence can be found. (Of course, it has to be actively sought.) Again, this does not *guarantee* truth, but if believability is important—and all the qualitative methodologists considered in this chapter regard it as such—then surviving a serious attempt at refutation provides the strongest basis that probably can be attained for belief. Dewey, too, regarded the testing of hypotheses as a vital step in effective inquiry resulting in the warranting of belief; and like Popper he saw that conclusions cannot be proven as true, but they can be eliminated as false (he should have said: probably false):

> Denial of the consequent grounds [i.e., warrants], however, denial of the antecedent. When, therefore, operations yield data which contradict a deduced consequence, elimination of one alternative possibility is effected. . . . Elimination of other possibilities progressively reduces the likelihood of fallacious inference. (Dewey 1966, 318–319)

Those readers who do not find Dewey and Popper convincing about the relationship between refutation and growth of knowledge (warranted belief), may find the following statement authoritative—in Proverbs 12:1, it is written that "Whoso loveth correction loveth knowledge, but he that hateth reproof is brutish."

UNSATISFYING CONCLUSION

The worry about the warrant for conclusions drawn from a qualitative inquiry will not wane, largely because the worry about the warrant for conclusions drawn from *any* inquiry will not wane. But we should not be fobbed off by *purported* resolutions to this worry that really do not address the relevant issues. Believability, credibility, consensus, coherence—all these things are no doubt important, and a piece of research would be the better for possessing them; but these things do not guarantee the truth of the research conclusion, indeed, they might not even be indicators of truth. Nevertheless, truth is a *regulative ideal;* it is much better to strive for it, even though it is akin to the impossible dream of the Man from La Mancha, than it is to strive for something less worthy.

Qualitative research is hard work, and, as indicated, it is work that is not always destined to meet with success. But it may not be as hard as writing poetry. McGonagall immortalized the pain and effort that is involved in the terrible lines he penned in tribute to his physician, Dr. Murison:

> He told me at once what was ailing me;
> He said I had been writing too much poetry,
> And from writing poetry I would have to refrain,
> Because I was suffering from inflammation on the brain.
> (McGonagall 1980, 45)

Qualitative researchers need to have a much clearer understanding of their own limitations than McGonagall had.

D. C. Phillips, "Validity in Qualitative Research," *Education and Urban Society*, 20 (1), November 1987. © 1987 by Sage Publications, Inc. Some minor changes have been introduced. Reprinted by permission of Sage Publications, Inc.

11

SOCIAL CONSTRUCTION OF KNOWLEDGE

As intimated in chapter 1, if an unsuspecting researcher was to carry out a computer search for articles across the fields of education, sociology, psychology, and epistemology that used the term *constructivism*, the results would be overwhelming. And also quite bemusing—for it would turn out that the term is used almost without rhyme or reason. The situation has become so confusing that to be told that a particular individual is a "constructivist" is to acquire no useful information whatsoever.

In my discussion in chapter 1, I tried to bring some order to this troubling situation by delineating two very broad constructivist "camps," each of which had substantial "within group" differences; I labeled these (1) "psychological constructivists" (Piaget, von Glasersfeld, and even Vygotsky would be included here, and the empiricist philosopher John Locke would be a borderline figure), and (2) "social constructivists." Members of the first group have, as the focus of their interest, the "constructions" or "cognitive and memory structures" or "understandings" in the mind of the individual learner or knower, and how these are built up. Members of the second group are concerned with the public bodies of knowledge—the disciplines—and how these are constructed over time; they downplay the role played by "external reality" in shaping our beliefs, and instead they stress (to varying degrees) the role played by social processes within knowledge-producing communities. Most of my efforts in the earlier chapter went into clarifying certain features of the first group, the psychological constructivists, so here I propose to focus upon the second. But before we can grapple with any of the interesting theses put forward by one or other of the social constructivists (actually, I will only have space to deal with one such thesis, albeit a centrally important one), there is a great deal of preliminary work to be done.

187

CLEARING THE GROUND

1. It is notable that the quite remarkable spread of social construct-ivism over the past two decades has not taken place quietly—the debates between constructivists and their critics have been pursued with vigor and with growing heat. Exchanges were lively, but relatively polite, in the early 1980s; for example, there was a notable lengthy debate in the pages of the journal *Philosophy of the Social Sciences* between the philosopher of science Larry Laudan, whose contribution had the provocative title "The Pseudo-Science of Science?" and David Bloor—a central member of the "Strong Program in the Sociology of Knowledge," also known as the "Edinburgh School"—whose lively response had the misleadingly meek title "The Strengths of the Strong Program" (see Laudan 1981; Bloor 1981). However, the follow-up debates spawned by these papers quickly became, in the words of one commentator, "acrimonious" (Fuller 1993, 12; many of the relevant papers were collected in Brown 1984).

By a little more than a decade later the emotional temperature had risen even further. A variety of interesting events occurred in the first half of the '90s, ranging from vituperative exchanges at conferences to publi-cation of fiery books and reviews. At the annual meeting of the British Association for the Advancement of Science in 1994, the presentation by embryologist Lewis Wolpert was disrupted by loud shouts of "rubbish" as he attacked the claims of strong sociologists of knowledge who saw sci-ence as a "social construct"; their "results are either trivial, obvious, or wrong," Wolpert is reported to have said (*Times Higher Education Supple-ment,* September 16, 1994, 44). The book by the two scientists Gross and Levitt, which appeared in the same year (Gross and Levitt 1994), referred to the constructivist view of science as "a species of muddleheadedness" that was prominent among a large segment of the American academic com-munity that "dislikes science" (Gross and Levitt 1994, 1–2)—an attitude that they labeled "medieval." A more moderately toned book that also offered a critique of social constructivism—*Making Science,* by sociologist Stephen Cole (Cole 1992)—was in turn attacked by one constructivist reviewer as "high-flown Monty Pythonery" that "ontologically gerryman-ders so blatantly" on behalf of the traditional view of science (Lovie 1995, 612). In another cause célèbre, the philosopher Martha Nussbaum wrote a review in which she lambasted those feminist philosophers who hold the view that logic—in particular, the fundamental mode of argumentation known as *modus ponens*—is a "male patriarchal creation oppressive of women" (Nussbaum 1994, 59). The response to Nussbaum was immediate and predictably hostile (see these replies, and Nussbaum's retort, in *New York Review of Books* 1995). But perhaps the most famous event has been the publication of—and reaction to—a "spoof" article giving a constructivist and postmodernist reading of the field of research known as quantum gravity; the article was taken as serious, and was published before the hoax became known (Sokal 1996). (I discuss these and other cases in a little more detail elsewhere; see Phillips 1997.) Before leaving this litany of cases of high drama, however, it should be noted that even Thomas S. Kuhn, whom many regard as one of the great ancestral figures of contemporary social constructivism, entered the fray and stated in a public lecture at Harvard that the claims of the Edinburgh School are "absurd: an example of deconstruction gone mad" (Kuhn 1992, 9).

The previous discussion must not be taken as suggesting that there are no books and essays, on either side of the constructivist divide, where name-calling and epithets are kept to a minimum; but as one reads in this general field, it is difficult to avoid reaching the conclusion that strong feelings are bubbling just beneath the surface. And the reason for this is not difficult to discern: *There is a lot at stake.* For it can be argued that if the more radical of the sociologists of scientific knowledge (not to mention a variety of postmodernists and some feminist epistemologists) are right, then the validity of the traditional philosophic/epistemological enterprise is effectively undermined, and so indeed is the pursuit of science itself. In the most radical scenario, epistemology has all the validity and relevance to the modern world as medieval alchemy; in more moderate scenarios epistemology at least has to be reconceptualized as part of—but not a special or authoritative part of—what Rorty called the "conversation of mankind" (Rorty 1979). The picture is even bleaker for science, which, according to many of the social constructivist and postmodernist accounts, becomes little more than an exercise in ideology building (in the pejorative sense of this expression). As Cleo Cherryholmes summarized the case, scientific research is a species of practice, and "human interests, myths, ideologies, values, and commitments shape what researcher-theorists claim to know . . ." (Cherryholmes 1988, 111); it is noteworthy that he does not list nature itself as playing any role in shaping or constraining what scientists believe about it! Or as Latour and Woolgar put it, in their famous constructivist study *Laboratory Life*,

> there is little to be gained by maintaining the distinction between the
> "politics" of science and its "truth." . . . the same "political" qualities are

necessary both to make a point and to out-manoeuvre a competitor. (Latour and Woolgar 1986, 237)

Evelyn Fox Keller offers another diagnosis of why the exchange has been so heated, particularly on the part of those who favor a traditional ("modernist" or "Enlightenment") view of science: In these times when research is incredibly expensive,

> the basic fact is that science—especially big science—is in a position of utter and absolute dependency. Without the continuing support of the nonscientific public, the institution of science as we have come to know it, and as working scientists have come to take for granted, will end. It is hardly surprising that scientists would want the public to perceive their ventures in the best possible light. . . . From the anxious perspective of scientists alarmed by recent trends in funding, science studies comes to look like the enemy within. (Keller 1995, 15)

I have pointed out, in my earlier chapter on constructivism, another factor that might explain the intensity of the debates: The constructivists generally have strongly held sociopolitical motives (for example, the need to make scientific research communities more inclusionary) that undergird their work and seem to be related to—if not to drive—their analyses of the production of knowledge.

2. I mentioned earlier the speciation and formation of sects that has taken place within the broad social constructivist camp; the "within group" variation here should not be underrated. Thus, the social constructivists form a truly Wittgensteinian family, with few if any common threads linking the intellectually widely dispersed members. Marx presumably must be credited with being one of the family's distant ancestors, for he held the view that the ruling ideas/beliefs in a society are those of the ruling class and serve its (economic) interests. That is, beliefs or ideas are tools or weapons in the warfare between the classes in society. The constructivist picture here is somewhat muddied by the fact that Marx traced the causal chain back to the material/economic base of society, and he also allowed for the fact that acting upon ideas can reflexively produce changes in that material and economic base.

But if Marx is the base drummer in the social constructivist orchestra, there are many other instrumentalists: Emile Durkheim, Mary Douglas, Thomas Kuhn, Richard Rorty, Michael Mulkay, Barry Barnes, David Bloor, Harry Collins, Stanley Fish, Bruno Latour, Michel Foucault, the three Steves—Fuller, Woolgar, and Shapin—and a diverse group of feminist thinkers, including Sandra Harding, Helen Longino, Lynn Hankinson Nelson, and Evelyn Fox Keller. These folk surely constitute a strange ensemble, for they are not playing the same tune, nor are they following the beat of the same conductor. Some (such as Kuhn) even have tried to resign from the orchestra (see Kuhn 1992); and a few marginal figures can be discerned (such as Goldman and Kornblith) who keep one foot firmly planted on traditional epistemological ground while they gingerly test moderate constructivist waters with the toes on the other foot.

For those who like more order than is apparent in this list, a number of rough groupings of social constructivists can be identified, ranging from those whom Latour (in an interesting paper 1992, 276) called "radical," through "progressive," and all the way to a "marsh" of "wishy-washy" scholars; Latour used as his categorizing principle the degree to which it was insisted that "external nature" played an important role in shaping the "knowledge" that was produced. In more conventional terms, there are (roughly) the members of the strong program, the scholars in the field known as social studies of science (sometimes also called "science and technology studies"), the postmodernists and an overlapping group of feminist epistemologists, and finally the group of moderate and even "conservative" constructivist philosophers (see Kornblith 1994) who work in the domain of "naturalized epistemology." But even within these groupings, there is a great deal of individual variation. In a recent book Sergio Sismondo separates out six distinct uses of the "construction metaphor" (although he recognizes that there are more), and he writes that

> Even though social constructivism and constructivism are popular as approaches to science, it is sometimes unclear exactly what is claimed is constructed and how. . . . "social construction" and "construction" do not generally mean the same thing from one author to another and, even within the same work the terms are meant to draw our attention to several quite different types of phenomena. (Sismondo 1996, 49)

As most of these groups and individuals—however we characterize them—focus their discussions on the social construction of *scientific* knowledge, I shall follow their example in the present discussion.

3. There is an issue that seems to me to be so clear-cut that I am reluctant to raise it; but, as I have occasionally been questioned about this, it is as well to state my position explicitly. The question can be asked: "Of what relevance to education are the debates over social constructivism?" My reply is set out in the following paragraphs.

Teachers of the natural sciences, math, psychology, history, economics, and so forth—both in high schools and in universities—often want
their students to acquire more than just an understanding of the *findings*
in these fields; they also want students to appreciate the nature of these
fields, in the sense that they want students to be acquainted with *how
knowledge is built up or acquired* in these fields, how it is established or tested
or how it attains its status as knowledge; and, certainly, textbooks often
give some account (usually a truncated and half-hearted one) of these
matters. To make the point in the terminology made famous in the 1960s
by Paul Hirst and Joseph Schwab, educators often expect students to understand not only the substance or "substantive structure" but also the
tests against experience and the techniques—together, the "syntactical
structure"—of the subjects they are studying. (For a discussion of Hirst
and Schwab, see Phillips 1987, chap. 11.)

Now, if the views of the social constructivists are correct, we need to
revise thoroughly the account we give to students of the syntax of the disciplines they are studying. Physics—to take an example where the issue
emerges rather starkly—should no longer be depicted as being the quest
for a true account of the objectively determinable properties and forces
in the preexisting natural realm, which has reality independent of what
humans happen to believe about it at any particular time, this quest being loosely guided by a rationally defensible "scientific method."

The precise story to be told in place of this traditional account will
differ according to which social constructivist you listen to but might well
be along the following lines, which, among other things, problematizes the
notion of an independently existing "nature" (this crude "thumbnail
sketch" will be rounded out more carefully in the subsequent discussion,
where some at least of the philosophical issues will be laid out more
clearly): The natural realm is not preexisting but rather is constituted
by our inquiries, and rather than being driven by a rational "scientific
method" our inquiries take the form that they do because of various social factors and processes; and it follows from this that "the [preexisting]
natural world has a small or non-existent role in the construction of scientific knowledge" (Collins 1981, 3). As Woolgar puts it, there is "an inver-
sion of the relationship between objects in the world and their representation. It was suggested [in his earlier discussion] that representational
practices *constituted* the objects of the world, rather than being a *reflection*
of (arising from) them" (Woolgar 1993, 67, emphasis added).

Some at least of the social constructivists would not hesitate to draw
some philosophical "morals" from this, which in all likelihood also would

become part of the "meta-narrative" that they would substitute for the traditional account of the nature of disciplines such as physics. Steve Fuller writes (concerning the beliefs of another noted radical social constructivist, David Bloor): "Echoing the later Wittgenstein, Bloor holds that science can be explained as a form of life without importing conceptions of truth, rationality, and reality that require special philosophical grounding." Indeed, Bloor and his allies "argue that the appeal to philosophical concepts has largely had political, not scientific, import—to consolidate allies and to exclude rivals" (Fuller 1993, 12). Rorty is even blunter: We should "see knowledge as a matter of conversation and of social practice, rather than as an attempt to mirror nature . . ." (Rorty 1979, 171).

In short, if one or other of the more radical social constructivist accounts was to be accepted, physics would no longer be depicted in our textbooks and classrooms as an enterprise that seeks true accounts of external reality; physics instead would be depicted as a political enterprise or as a realm of Rortyean conversation—a conversation that, explicitly, is *not* shaped to any significant degree by external nature and by warranting reasons. Later I shall discuss the flawed view of how humans act and settle upon beliefs that undergirds the social constructivist position here.

4. In his book *The Rationality of Science* (1981), the British philosopher W. H. Newton-Smith has a detailed discussion of Thomas S. Kuhn's work on scientific revolutions. He noted that Kuhn starts by making claims that are strong, exciting, but false; however, when under pressure, Kuhn backs off and softens them so that they become more credible, but weak and boring. I claim that the same phenomenon can be noticed at crucial places in the work of many social constructivists. In the terminology used by the social constructivist Bruno Latour in 1992, there is a tendency for those who initially hold a radical social constructivist position to move toward progressivist or even "wishy-washy" positions. (Forman 1995 argues a similar point in detail.)

In a volume with the revealing title *Rethinking Objectivity* (Megill 1994), one of Bloor's colleagues at the center of the "strong program," Barry Barnes, writes that sociologists of knowledge

> should now beware of overshooting the mark. Several of the most significant current difficulties and weaknesses in the field are over-reactions to the individualism, rationalism, and realism typical of so much epistemology. (Barnes 1994, 27)

At first blush, it seems as if Barnes has significantly softened his earlier relativistic social constructivism: The weaknesses in the position are due to overreacting to realism and so forth. On the assumption that one is either a realist (of some form or another) or one isn't, the only way an antirealist can stop "overreacting" is by *becoming* a realist! But, in this case, social constructivism is on the road to becoming a boring position, for the door has been opened to allowing that reality or "nature" plays *some* role in shaping the beliefs that are held about it. This latter view is one that—in my estimation—is both true and boring. (It is boring in the following sense: If members of the strong program had said this in the first place, their works would have generated little if any controversy, the arguments would not have taken place, and the heat would not have been generated. Furthermore, the present chapter would hardly have needed to be written!)

But there is a further point to be made here: Barnes was attempting to have his cake, and eat it, too. For, immediately preceding the passage just quoted, in which he called for the abandonment of "*overreaction,*" Barnes suggested that "sociology of knowledge was correct in its *uncompromising rejection* of [preexisting] epistemology" (Barnes 1994, 27, emphasis added). So we have the following position being canvassed, one in which the exciting element is first reaffirmed, then denied and modified in a boring direction that—if taken seriously—completely undermines what has just been reaffirmed: Traditional "individualistic" and "realist" epistemology should be uncompromisingly rejected, and yet it is a mistake for social constructivism to "overshoot" the mark and "overreact" to this epistemology about which, nevertheless, we are urged to be uncompromising!

If I may be forgiven for making a sociological point in the midst of a philosophically oriented discussion, one very important function *is* served by Barnes's shilly-shallying here—he has given himself a route by which to escape from serious criticism. For if one were to attack his rejection of realism and so forth, he can say this is beside the point as he himself has pointed out that such rejection is an overreaction; and yet if one were to criticize his new flirtation with realism, he can also argue that this is beside the point as he has reaffirmed that it is correct to be "uncompromising" about it. In effect, Barnes is illustrating that a position that is internally inconsistent has some significant advantages in social settings that do not put much emphasis on the importance of logical consistency.

In an essay in 1981 another strong sociologist of knowledge, Harry Collins, whether wittingly or not, adopted a variant of the same strategy—he made a very strong claim in one paragraph and on the very next page softened it to such an extent that it became innocuous. Collins was writing an introduction to a collection of work in a special issue of a journal (which included, inter alia, one of his own papers); all of this work had been carried out in what he labeled "the empirical program of relativism," and he described it in these terms:

> One school, however, inspired in particular by Wittgenstein and more lately by the phenomenologists and ethnomethodologists, embraces an explicit relativism in which *the natural world has a small or non-existent role* in the construction of scientific knowledge. One set of such analyses is gathered in this issue of *Social Studies of Science*. (Collins 1981, 3, emphasis added)

However, Collins went on to state that "All the papers confirm the potential local interpretative flexibility of science which prevents experimentation, *by itself*, from being decisive" (Collins 1981, 4). The words I have emphasized here mark a significant shift; to say that experimental results, by themselves, do not decisively shape the nature of scientific belief (which is in my view a true but unexciting moderate position) is a far cry from the exciting (but ultimately incredible) claim that *no* experimentation, *no* input from nature, plays a role in shaping scientific belief. (I should note that the notion of "nature" is held by some constructivists to be itself socially constructed; this is true, in a sense, but it does not seem to allow constructivists to extricate themselves from the problems here—for one thing, it still begs the question of what role external reality plays in influencing what we construct about it.)

The issue that arises here is a critical one for the remainder of my discussion: Which theses—the exciting but incredible ones, or the moderate, wishy-washy, and boring—should be the focus of attention when evaluating the positions held by various social constructivists? My strategy in the final section of this chapter will be to opt for excitement, on the ground that it is the exciting versions of social constructivism (rather than the dull ones) that have been of widespread influence over the past two decades.

Before turning to a more detailed examination of one of these exciting ideas held by the more radical of the social constructivists, however, there is one last preliminary issue to be discussed. This will necessitate returning to the issue of having one's cake and eating it, too.

5. In his book *Science: The Very Idea*, the social constructivist Steve Woolgar noted that, to most minds, there is an "apparent absurdity" to the radical social constructivist position (Woolgar 1993, 67); he put this down

to the strong hold that the traditional account of science has upon most of us. The point is, however, that the radical social constructivist position *is* absurd and does not suffer merely from *apparent* absurdity.

But here, of course, another interesting issue arises: How is it that intelligent people, like Bloor and Woolgar and the rest, can accept a general position that is so absurdly counter-intuitive? My own hypothesis about this is as follows: Bloor (to stick with him as a major foundational figure) overstates his case in the early pages of his book and then later modifies his claims in a moderate direction, without recognizing that he has thereby shot himself in the foot! When attacked, as for example in the exchange with Laudan in 1981, his defense makes use of his moderate statements; but when speaking at a very general level he reverts to using the earlier absurdities. The point is, he cannot let these defective claims go, for what would a "strong program" be without its strong claims? In short, Bloor attempts to keep his radical cake, but when pushed he starts to eat it in wishy-washy company.

a. Consider first the radical claims he makes in the opening pages of the first chapter of his famous book. I have strung together here a few short excerpts, together with my comments; you will need to read the chapter for yourself to see that I have not misrepresented him by using the method of selective quotation. (All the passages are from Bloor 1976; I shall just cite page numbers. In my comments I shall stick with the example of physics.)

Quote: "Can the sociology of knowledge investigate and explain the very content and nature of scientific knowledge?" (1).

Comment: This is a rhetorical question, for Bloor goes on to say that those sociologists who answer the question in the negative are guilty of "betrayal of their disciplinary standpoint." Why does Bloor's position strike many of us as absurd? Because we think that the content of the science of physics is explainable (at least to a significant degree) by physical considerations—by the theories, experimental and observational evidence, mathematical derivations, and so forth that give physicists grounds for believing that acceptance of the current content of their field is warranted. Note that this is not to say that other factors are not part of the story; but to suggest that physics-type reasons (what some writers refer to as the "internal reasons") are *no* part of the story (Bloor, after all, does not mention them here) is to suggest that we could replace physicists by sociologists— the physics of quantum mechanics is replaceable by the sociology of quantum physicists.

Quotation: "The cause of the hesitation to bring science within the scope of thorough-going sociological scrutiny is lack of nerve and will" (2).

Comment: On the contrary, it is the result of good sense; for what Bloor means by "thorough-going scrutiny" is outrageous. There *is*, of course, an important place for the sociological study of physics and physicists, but sensible sociologists should resist the temptation to explain the *content* of physics without looking at—among other things—the scientific/physical evidence adduced by physicists.

Quotation: "Similarly, the sociologist seeks theories which explain the beliefs which are in fact found [in science], regardless of how the investigator evaluates them" (3).

Comment: This merely repeats the previous mistake. In physics (as indeed in most rational human endeavors), an important part of the story accounting for why beliefs are accepted is the fact that the people involved hold that there is warranting evidence in favor of those beliefs. (Physicists, as well as other mere mortals, may, of course, be mistaken in the evaluation of the warrants for their beliefs; but to pursue this issue, the warrants themselves need to be examined.)

Quotation: "The sociology of scientific knowledge should adhere to the following four tenets. . . . These are: 1. It would be causal, that is, concerned with the conditions which bring about belief or states of knowledge. Naturally there will be other types of causes apart from social ones which will co-operate in bringing about belief" (4–5).

Comment: At first sight this looks hopeful, for Bloor acknowledges "other types of causes." However, nowhere in these strongly worded pages does he mention that the "internal" or scientific reasons or evidence must be included among these "other causes." It is worth noting that postmodernists fill out Bloor's list by adding political, economic, ideological, and perhaps psychological causes to his "sociological" ones; also, as is well-known, Lyotard is "incredulous" about the justificatory metanarratives—in terms of truth, evidence, and so forth—that are told in an attempt to warrant belief in the universal claims of science (see Lyotard 1984). Bloor is not alone.

Bloor continues on with his list of "tenets"; the second one reinforces the view that he is *not* concerned with the reasons or evidence that might be adduced within physics in support of the beliefs of physicists—for the truth or falsity of beliefs is not to be taken into consideration.

Quotation: "It [sociology of science] would be impartial with respect to truth or falsity, rationality or irrationality, success or failure" (5).

Comment: Case made—Bloor's position, as stated here in the opening pages of his first chapter, does have more than an *appearance* of absurdity. His position is absurdly "strong."

b. We now need to move a few pages further into Bloor's book, where—despite his strong earlier claims—he becomes moderate and wishy-washy. For, suddenly, he allows that *experience* plays a role in science! In one powerful passage he writes:

> No consistent sociology could ever present knowledge as a fantasy unconnected with men's experiences of the material world around him [sic]. Men cannot live in a dream world. (29)

Worse still for his earlier position, within a few lines he acknowledges "the reliability of perception and the ability to detect, retain, and act upon perceived regularities and discriminations" (29). But why, then, did he not allow that reliable perceptions and discriminations are part of the evidentiary material that convinces physicists to accept the things (the content of physics) that they do?

A hint about the answer to this question can be found in the closing pages of Bloor's first chapter. Here he makes a not unreasonable point (one amply endorsed in mainstream philosophy of science):

> But theories and theoretical knowledge are not things which are given in our experience. They are what give meaning to experience by offering a story about what underlies, connects, accounts for it. This does not mean that theory is unresponsive to experience. . . . [But] *Another agency apart from the physical world is required to guide and support this component of knowledge.* (12–13, emphasis added)

On a straightforward reading, to admit that "another agency apart from the physical world is required" is to allow that "the physical world" is *part* of the story that must be told to account for the beliefs of physicists. In the rest of this passage, Bloor is quite right: theory is *underdetermined* by experience/nature (see Phillips 1987, part A, and chapter 6 of this volume). This means that it is possible to erect alternative theories to account for our experience, our scientific data. But Bloor has made a monumental error in supposing, then, that because alternative theories can be produced, it somehow follows that experience/nature can be *left out of the account* of why physicists believe the things they do.

A simple thought experiment can illustrate this: Suppose that the experience of physicists had been quite different (than it actually was) when they were experimenting with magnets or with electric currents; or suppose that balls rolling down inclined planes did not (and do not) act in the manner that Galileo and countless subsequent physicists have observed. Clearly, the nature of the contents of the discipline of physics would now be quite different from what it is—for, because the balls (or whatever) would have behaved differently, the beliefs we arrived at would have been different. One of the causal factors helping to shape the contents of physics is the evidence or experience that physicists obtain when experimenting or observing, even though this evidence alone does not fully determine the nature of the theories that can be developed to explain it.

The moral is that external nature cannot be conceptualized in *any way that we please*—as Bloor seems to acknowledge. (This point is argued strongly by Israel Scheffler 1967.) If Bloor is serious about the points he is making in these later passages, he cannot consistently leave untouched the absurd remarks he made in describing the essence of the strong program in the opening pages of his book. The strong program has to become a wishy-washy program (to borrow Latour's expression) in order to be credible.

There is an even deeper fault underlying Bloor's work: He seems to have an unacceptable model of what it is to be human, of what factors cause humans to act and to adopt beliefs. For his strong words do not acknowledge that humans are rational beings. I will turn to this central point in the discussion further on.

EXPLAINING BELIEF

There is a (wishy-washy) sense in which it is entirely uncontroversial to claim that knowledge is socially constructed: A scientist will be working on a problem that is describable in a public language (even if this is a technical language), and it will have emerged *as* a problem in the context of a shared conceptual/theoretical framework. Furthermore, he or she will be using a set of communally endorsed practices and tools—concepts, apparatus, research designs, data analysis techniques, forms of inference, and the like—that are familiar to (and that probably have been developed by) others in the same professional specialization. The evidence that is collected either will be of a type that is accepted as relevant to the issues at hand by specialist colleagues (who themselves constitute a socially defined group), or else it will be evidence that the inquirer can argue is relevant and worthy of acceptance. The knowledge-claims that result from this work will be expounded in papers that are examined by journal referees, conference organizers, respondents at meetings, and so on, and attempts at replication will most likely occur. A claim that survives this scrutiny, and that is judged as important or that is widely used by others in the specialty as a basis for their own work, might eventually be written up in textbooks and become part of the curriculum in schools and universities. In these important senses, then, knowledge is a social product; an inquirer working *entirely* on his or her own, using no social resources *whatsoever*, is a ludicrous fiction.

Because knowledge production is a social phenomenon in the sense previously mentioned, it follows that sociologists, anthropologists, and psychologists are right to stress that it can be studied in the manner in which other social phenomena can be studied—namely, empirically, using the methods of the social sciences in an attempt (perhaps) to delineate at least some of the causal processes involved. To put it bluntly, the production of scientific knowledge can itself become the subject of scientific scrutiny—a statement that has the air of paradox although in fact there is nothing paradoxical about it at all. Insofar as they are saying this, Bloor, Woolgar, and others are on firm ground. Indeed, Bloor expressed this so-called "causal principle" in his early formulation of the "strong program," and in the following passage there is nothing at all that I would want to disagree with: The sociology of knowledge

> would be causal, that is, concerned with the conditions which would bring about belief or states of knowledge. Naturally there would be other types of causes apart from social ones which will cooperate in bringing about belief. (Bloor 1976, 4–5)

There are three crucial issues, however, that arise concerning this social-scientific program: (a) What are these *"other types of causes"* that can be (or, should be?) invoked to explain the social construction of knowledge?; (b) What *aspect* of the construction of knowledge can be explained in sociological terms?; and (c) Are knowledge-claims that are *true* (or judged to be true) explained in different terms from those that are *false?*

a. Types of causal factors. Bloor himself noted that the causes that could be invoked to explain the construction of knowledge, in addition to sociological ones, were psychological, political, or historical; and many postmodernists would agree with him. We saw earlier that Cherryholmes gave a comparable list, and Latour and Woolgar were approaching close to Bloor when they argued that the study of scientific truth should not be distinguished from politics. Presumably, the point here is that a scientist's tenacious pursuit of a particular problem (to take a simple example) might be explainable in sociological terms (the scientist might be displaying the behavior or interests typical of a member of a particular socioeconomic class), or in political terms (the scientist might be under pressure from some powerful figure such as the head of the laboratory), or in economic terms (he or she stands to make a handsome profit), or in psychological ones (there might be Freudian undertones in the scientist's behavior). And, of course, these are not mutually exclusive, for many phenomena are overdetermined or multiply caused. But it is notable that what is excluded by the radical social constructivists (or at least, what is not explicitly mentioned) is the *content* of the science that is being wrestled with and the status of the warrants or supporting arguments or evidence for the beliefs that are being taken seriously by those scientists; in the earlier discussion Bloor's shilly-shallying over this issue was discussed at some length (it will be recalled that different portions of his classic book take contradictory stands on the role of a scientist's experience).

The position held by Latour and Woolgar is also revealing. In the early pages of *Laboratory Life* they discussed what their approach should be to studying the construction of knowledge in the scientific laboratory in which Latour's data were collected, and they ended up *rejecting* an "emic" orientation wherein they would have to try to understand the meaning (for the participants or subjects they were studying) of the terms and ideas that these individuals were using in their knowledge-producing activities. Latour and Woolgar took this decision on grounds that are difficult to comprehend and that have something of the flavor of "gobbledy-gook": They say they were aware of the dangers of "going native" (which apparently would have been an issue if they had adopted the emic approach and had attempted to understand their scientists, although Latour and Woolgar are far from clear on this vital point), and so they decided to treat the concepts of the participants "as a social phenomenon" (Latour and Woolgar 1986, 39). The point is, that by whatever strange logic, Latour and Woolgar ended up studying how knowledge is produced, by adopting the perspective of outsiders—that is, *without* taking into account the *meaning* of the conceptual/theoretical material the scientists in the laboratory were discussing, questioning, and taking as their framework, and in terms of which these individuals were expressing the very knowledge they were constructing!

The enormity of the position adopted here by Latour and Woolgar cannot be underscored sufficiently; and clearly, their stance is quite at variance with the one that is adopted by mainstream ethnographers who "bend over backward" to understanding the point of view of the groups they are studying. One consequence of the strange methodological decision of Latour and Woolgar is this: Having decided *not* to take into account the *content* of the discussions, arguments, and papers that occupied much of the laboratory scientists' time, and by narrowing their attention to only the observable sociopolitical interactions (and suchlike) in the laboratory, Latour and Woolgar were ensuring that they would "discover" that knowledge construction is "political" in nature and that issues of "truth" are irrelevant and play no causal role. In the "Postscript" to their book's second edition they even tried to pass off as an advantage the fact that when Latour started the fieldwork, all of which he carried out without Woolgar's assistance, his "knowledge of science was non-existent; his mastery of English was very poor; and he was completely unaware of the existence of the social studies of science" (Latour and Woolgar 1986, 273). Given that field-workers usually are expected to be aware of the ways in which their own backgrounds can bias their "findings"—a point that social constructivists, postmodernists, and feminist epistemologists often wisely are sensitive to—this is an astounding admission. Peter Slezak had a similar reaction to the one I have just expressed:

> On the face of it, the authors' own description of their project in Laboratory Life reads more like a parody than a serious inquiry. . . . the idea that the inability to understand one's human subjects is a positive methodological virtue is surely a bizarre conception even for anthropology. For Latour and Woolgar, however, it is intimately connected with their doctrine of "inscriptions." The meaninglessness of the "traces, spots, points" and other recordings is a direct consequence of Latour's admitted scientific illiteracy. (Slezak 1994, part 2, 336)

Slezak points out that Latour and Woolgar, among other failings, do not appreciate the difference between understanding the people they are studying and believing them; their approach thus turns "incomprehension into a methodology" (Slezak 1994, part 2, 336; see also Slezak 2000).

b. What aspects of knowledge construction are being explained? It is a principle widely accepted in the social sciences that the appropriateness of the methods adopted by researchers should always be evaluated in the context of the questions that they are attempting to answer. In light of this principle, I am not suggesting that it is always necessary for investigators to understand what those they are studying are saying or believing. It all depends upon what it is that the researchers concerned are trying to elucidate. The "methodology of incomprehension" adopted by Latour might be appropriate for *some* sorts of inquiries. An example of a research tradition that was fruitful, and where there was a conscious effort *not* to pay attention to the meanings and understandings of the people being studied, is the work done on the interaction patterns that occur during conversations; researchers here concentrated not on the content of the conversations they were studying, but rather focused (for example) on the timing of remarks, the length of pauses, and the other nonverbal signals by which individuals in the conversations established their respective turns to speak.

However, Latour and Woolgar were not chiefly interested in matters such as this; together with others involved in the social studies of knowledge (including, of course, the members of the Edinburgh School) they were concerned to account for the production of the actual *content* of science and other domains of knowledge. Writing in a later book, Woolgar stated:

> It should be clear from these tenets [of the strong program, of which he is supportive] that mathematical statements such as "2 + 2 = 4" are as much a legitimate target of sociological questioning as any other item of knowledge. . . . What kinds of historical conditions gave this expression currency and, in particular, what established (and now sustains) it as a belief? This kind of question is posed without regard for the (actual) truth status of the statement. (Woolgar 1993, 43)

But surely it was strange for him to *exclude* the "truth status" or the theoretical arguments within mathematics from being elements giving "2 + 2 = 4" its "currency"! (Certainly, during the course of history, views of mathematicians have changed about the way statements like "2 + 2 = 4" should be analyzed; but to discuss and assess these views, and their changes, the *content of mathematics* has to be explored—mathematics as a discipline cannot be replaced by sociology of knowledge.)

Woolgar revealingly concluded, a few pages later, that "a central achievement of the sociology of scientific knowledge is its scepticism about the role of logic and reason especially in mathematics and science" (Woolgar 1993, 50)—an "achievement" that depended entirely upon Woolgar and his fellow-travelers *legislating* or *assuming* at the outset that these factors played no causal role. Many years ago Bertrand Russell, looking at different research traditions to those that concern us here, noticed this same phenomenon:

> One may say broadly that all the animals that have been carefully observed have behaved so as to confirm the philosophy in which the observer believed before his observations began. Nay, more, they have all displayed the national characteristics of the observer. Animals studied by Americans rush about frantically, with an increasing display of hustle and pep, and at last achieve the desired result by chance. Animals studied by Germans sit still and think. . . . To the plain man, such as the present writer, this situation is discouraging. (Russell 1948, 32–33)

To which one can add: Scientists studied by sociologists from Edinburgh or France spend their days in laboratories manipulating meaningless symbols and making meaningless inscriptions.

c. Should the knowledge claims that are regarded as true be explained differently from the ones that are false? It is clear that the radical social constructivists I have paid most attention to in this chapter don't wish to allow the distinction between "true" and "false" to have any purchase— for if they did allow that this distinction was causally relevant, they would be forced to consider, and assess, the grounds upon which judgments of truth and falsity were made. Latour, for one, would have been sorely at a disadvantage if his investigations had needed to move in this direction— his behavioristically oriented methodology was not able to deal with *reasons*. But it is not only Latour who dismissed this distinction; Bloor had included as the third of his four central tenets of the strong program a principle of "symmetry": work done within the program "would be symmetrical in its style of explanation. The same types of cause would explain, say, true and false beliefs" (Bloor 1976, 5).

Some background here might make the position of the social constructivists somewhat more understandable. They were reacting against a view, advocated by a number of philosophers, to the effect that the acceptance of true propositions by scientists called for no (further) explanation, but what was needed was an account of why researchers accepted false ideas. Imre Lakatos argued particularly strongly for this position (Lakatos 1978).

Lakatos drew a distinction between internal and external accounts of science; and he argued that since science is an intellectual, knowledge-producing endeavor, internal accounts must take precedence over external ones. The general idea seems to be this: Internal accounts focus upon the intellectual problems that scientists were struggling with, the evidence that was available, the theories that were held at the time, the standards of evaluation that were judged to be warranted and appropriate to the situation, and so forth. Now, if a scientist was to accept an idea that, by these internal standards and so forth, was judged to be true, the scientist would be behaving rationally (given the context) and no further explanation would be required (for to say that a person was acting rationally in a given situation is to say that the person was acting appropriately). If, however, given the preponderance of the internal evidence and so forth, the scientist was to accept an idea that was false (judged by these standards), then his or her behavior was in need of further explanation—for now the scientist was not doing what seemed to be required of a rational person. On these sorts of occasions, Lakatos argued, explanations should be sought externally; perhaps the scientist had been swayed by political or religious factors, or was guilty of sexist or racist bias, or so forth.

Here, I think, the social constructivists were guilty of misinterpreting the position of Lakatos and others (whether this was fueled by incautious wording of the philosophers' theses is another issue). The constructivists took it that what was being claimed by the philosophers was that true belief needs no causal explanation, whereas their own position was that all belief should be subject to causal explanation. Hence, Bloor formulated his "principle of symmetry"; and Woolgar commented favorably on "the insistence of sociologists that both truth and error are equally amenable to sociological analysis" (Woolgar 1993, 42).

In what way were the social constructivists misinterpreting the philosophers? Simply this: Lakatos and the others were not claiming that belief in true ideas is uncaused. Rather, they were suggesting (perhaps in too subtle a way for the social constructivists to comprehend) that true beliefs are explained (given the *ceteris paribus* background assumption that the scientists concerned have normal neural mechanisms and so forth) by the fact that there are reasons, warrants, evidence, and so forth available that indicate that the ideas *are indeed true*. In other words, the *content* of ideas, and the *content* of the justificatory arguments that support acceptance of these ideas as being true, *are part of the causal story* that needs to be told (and this is an *internal* story)! The philosopher Larry Laudan put this quite powerfully when he wrote a critique of Bloor's foundational book:

> If Bloor's caricatures were to be accepted, we should believe that most
> philosophers . . . have maintained that there is literally nothing that

causes us to believe what is true and that nothing is causally responsible for rational action and rational belief. But Bloor's analysis of the philosophical tradition will not stand up to scrutiny. For as long as we know anything about the history of philosophy, epistemologists have been concerned to explain how to discover the true and the rational. The suggestion that most philosophers have believed that true beliefs just happen, that rational behavior is uncaused, that only "aberrant" belief is part of nature's causal nexus, is hard to take seriously. (Laudan 1981, 178)

I should note in passing that social constructivists (not only the radicals, but the moderates as well) also make the point that the internal/external distinction breaks down once we recognize that the work of scientists goes on in a sociocultural setting that influences it; but it should be clear (although it is not clear to many constructivists) that it does not follow from this that the point made by Lakatos and others can be disregarded. For even if the distinction cannot be maintained (my own view is that it is a rough or permeable distinction rather than a watertight one), what were previously called "internal reasons" still do not go away—these epistemic or nonsocial factors (as Kornblith calls them) remain part of the total amalgam of internal/external factors, whatever language we use to describe this. But, for the radical social constructivists, these internal/nonsocial factors disappear from the account altogether, as we have seen in passages from Bloor, Woolgar, and Latour. Hilary Kornblith (among others—see for example, Elgin 1997, chap. 10, and Hacking 1999) has described a moderate position that recognizes the role played by both internal and external factors (however they are grouped together or interact):

On any account, then, belief acquisition and retention must be seen as a product of both social and non-social factors, and both kinds of factors will come in for investigation in the course of epistemic evaluation. Moreover, on any reasonable account, both kind of factors will play a role in explaining individual differences in belief. There is still room for a great deal of disagreement about the relative weight of these two kinds of factors. (Kornblith 1994, 102)

Harold Kincaid puts the point even more succinctly:

Surely science is a social process and scientific belief does have social causes. Yet that fact does not *entail* that evidence, reasons, scientific method, and rationality do not ground science. (Kincaid 1996, 38)

It is time to bring this over-long discussion to an end. But in concluding, it is worth highlighting what, according to my analysis, is the central
issue at stake in considering the "causes of belief" and the position of
many of the social constructivists on this matter—a position that has important implications for education, as Slezak has noted (Slezak 1994, part
1; Slezak 2000): The adherents of the strong program, and many of those
engaged in the social studies of knowledge together with fellow-travelers
from the postmodernist camp, have a deficient model of what it is to be
human (although I think that many of them would be surprised to learn
this). They see humans as *behaving*, as being objects that are caused to do
certain things because of the publicly observable "external" forces (sociological, political, economic, and so forth) that bear down upon them, and
perhaps because of psychological drives (or "internal forces") such as the
lust for power or fame. As Slezak has noted in an important discussion,

> the externalist conception of theories as caused by features of the social
> milieu is a form of stimulus control theory akin to Skinnerian
> behaviourism. On this conception, beliefs are the causal consequence of
> external environmental, social factors rather than internal, cognitive, in-
> tellectual ones. (Slezak 1994, part 1, 267)

Philosophers of science and epistemologists generally hold what I
would argue is a more defensible model, one that has been widely canvassed by recent philosophers of social science in the English-speaking
world and for over a century by hermeneuticists and philosophers from the
Continent: Humans do not merely behave as a result of external or internal forces (e.g., physiological), although undeniably these are of importance, but they also engage in *voluntary actions* as a result of the ideas,
beliefs, meanings, motives, and knowledge that they possess. (See the
discussion in chapter 2.) This is not to say that there is no interaction between the two domains of external and internal forces, on the one hand,
and voluntary action, on the other; clearly, this is often quite substantial.
But to treat knowledge construction as a behavior rather than as an action
is, in a sense, to dehumanize it and to refuse to take it seriously *as* knowledge (that is, as something that is believed because of good although not
unassailable reasons, even if these reasons are not—and could never be—
immune from social influences).

D. C. Phillips, "Coming to Grips with Radical Social Constructivisms," *Science &
Education*, vol. 6, nos. 1–2, January 1997, 85–104. © 1997 Kluwer Academic Publishers. Reprinted with kind permission from Kluwer Academic Publishers.

12

THEORIES AND LAWS

QUESTIONER: As a social scientist I try to produce theories in my areas of interest. But it has occurred to me that I don't know what characteristics a set of statements must possess in order to count as a theory—I guess up to now I have just gone on intuition. That is, if it felt as if something was a theory, I called it a theory (not that I have had overmuch success in satisfying my ambitions, I must admit). At any rate, my opening question is this: What is a theory?

RESPONDENT: My response is to quote a contributor to the periodical *New Scientist*, who wrote that "I have yet to see any problem however complicated which, when you look at it in the right way, did not become still more complicated" (cited in Matthew 1991, 112). Let's take first things first in this enormously complex issue—there is a kind of "chicken and egg" problem that can get us derailed right at the start. Arthur Caplan recently put the point this way: he said that

> the domain of examples governing philosophical reflection about science is highly determinative of how the conceptual evolution and change is understood and explained. . . . the extent to which theories can be axiomatized, and the deductive or nondeductive nature of relationships between theoretical statements are closely tied to the examples of scientific theories that are selected for analysis. (Caplan 1990, 25)

Let me enlarge on what I take his point to be: You could, as one strategy, define a theory as anything that has a set of characteristics C (you, and certainly many philosophers, have lots of presuppositions about what a theory should be like); this strategy would allow you to exclude anything that does not have these features—in other words, no matter how interesting it might be, it couldn't possibly be a theory. (This, of course, would always allow you to maintain your account of the nature of theory, because no counterexample could be found—at least, none that was allowable!) On the other hand, you could collect (without any censorship) a reasonable number of things that folk across the social sciences have at one time or another called theories, and you could then do an analytic job to find, as it were, the lowest common factor, and this would become your set of defining features. (In philosophical terminology, the two strategies boil down to giving either a stipulative or a reportive definition.)

Q: It doesn't seem unfair to say that one of these strategies guards against what statisticians call the "Type I" error, and the other defends against the "Type II" error, in the sense that one strategy is quite conservative about what will be allowed to count as a theory and might exclude some genuine cases, while the other is quite liberal and might allow a few impostors to slip in! I am drawn more to the second strategy, but it occurs to me that a melange of things have been called theories in the social sciences—some of my colleagues talk about theories of why Hitler or Napoleon acted in certain ways on specific occasions, or of theories of social mobility, or of theories of the labor market, or theories about such things as the origin of World War I or of causes of the Great Depression, or theories about Bill Clinton's presidential election victory over George Bush, or theories of the causes of the enormous high school dropout rate among minority students. The lowest common factor here indeed would be very low—does it make any sense to think that one might find any significant commonalities from such a diverse group?

R: I share your concern. Perhaps we should remember that the word "theory" is not a technical word in the vocabulary of the social sciences (unlike "free market" or "intelligence quotient"). The term does not label what philosophers would call a "natural kind." It is simply a general term that is used rather loosely, and can cover anything from a hypothesis about something ("my theory about who committed the murder is . . . ") to a highly abstract thing such as Einstein's special theory of relativity. There is no divinely ordained correct usage, but we can strive to use the word consistently and to mark distinctions that we feel are important. But this, of course, brings us back to square one again.

Q: Perhaps we could take a completely different tack, at least to get us going. I have noticed that some of my fellow social scientists have a strange fondness for, of all things, the Kinetic Theory of Gases. Robert Merton is one case in point; he sees this theory as an admirable model for what he calls "theories of the middle range" in the social sciences (see Merton 1967, esp. 39–40). Another and more recent example is the sociologist Arthur Stinchcombe; in a paper that appears to be of great philosophical interest, and that investigates the types of mechanisms to be found in social science theories, he constantly makes comparisons with Kinetic Theory (Stinchcombe 1991). Not having done any physics or chemistry since high school, I must admit to being a bit rusty. Why is this so attractive, and what features does it illustrate about theories?

R: I warn you that this is not going to be a short answer; and I stress that I will be simplifying matters out of deference to your acknowledged lack of background. That understood, here goes; I'm about to launch into an exposition of what some philosophers have called "the received view" of the nature of theories. (See Suppe 1974 and later editions, for the standard discussion of these matters.)

Q: I'm sorry to interrupt when you were hardly started, but the fact that it is labeled as the "received view" suggests to my suspicious mind that not everyone actually does receive it!

R: You're absolutely right. But almost everyone would accept much of the account I'm about to give, at least so far as Kinetic

Theory goes. We can get to the dissenters later. So, back to the main theme: The field of gas behavior illustrates a number of important points. First, the field is nowadays one that is quite well-understood, in the sense that we have a number of empirical laws and various theories that have stood the test of time. So, textbooks tend to present a picture of the field, a picture of the relations between these elements, which is of necessity somewhat static and which represents what might be called the logical state of the field now that the tumult and the shouting have died. The naïve reader sometimes goes away with the impression that the neat account that is given is also an accurate account of the history of the field—in other words, that it represents the order in which or the manner in which advances were made.

Q: Could you clarify this a little?

R: Let me start with a quotation from the philosopher R. B. Braithwaite:

> an advanced science like physics is not content only with establishing lowest-level generalizations covering physical events: it aims at, and has been largely successful in, subsuming its lowest-level generalisations under higher-level hypotheses, and thus organising its hypotheses into a hierarchical deductive system—a scientific theory—in which a hypothesis at a lower level is shown to be deducible from a set of hypotheses at a higher level. (Braithwaite 1973, 47)

The situation Braithwaite was describing can be captured in the form of a diagram depicting the "structure" of the field of gas behavior (see Diagram 12.1).

Now, both Braithwaite's words (if read incautiously) and this diagram (if it is read from the bottom up) might leave the impression that a scientist first identifies some phenomena that are of interest, then he or she makes observations and measurements of such things as pressure, volume, and temperature (to do which, one needs to have constructed operational definitions of these variables), then the relationships between these variables are found (or, in social science terms, the researcher does

Diagram 12.1 The Explanation of Gas Behavior

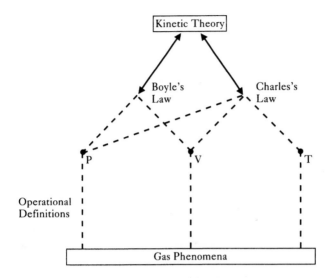

a series of correlational studies), and finally, when enough results are in hand, the scientist "puts on the theoretical hat" and
produces the theory that accounts for whatever relationships
(laws or correlations) have been found. I guess this is the picture Merton gives when he cautions that one should not theorize until enough data (in the form of correlations and generalizations) are in hand (although, to be fair, when he gave this
advice he had "grand theory" in mind—see Merton 1967, 46,
and chapter 5 in this present volume); and this is close to what
Glaser and Strauss advocate in their work on "grounded
theory" in the social sciences: "Generating a theory from data
means that most hypotheses and concepts not only come from
the data, but are systematically worked out in relation to data
during the course of the research" (Glaser and Strauss 1967, 6).

Q: And I suppose the point you are making is that this is not
the historical line of development at all?

R: Indeed—and there is absolutely no reason to suggest that
this ought to be adopted as a normative account either, that is,
as an account of how scientific work should proceed. After all,

unless scientists constantly theorize (even in a loose, speculative way) about what they are doing and what they are finding (or not finding), then their work is, at best, mechanical and is the epitome of mindlessness; it is not clear how you can decide what concepts to use when collecting data if you have no theory (however crude or incipient) in mind. (In a sense, concepts and theories make the data.) If you think this is harsh, you should see what Dewey and Popper, among others, have to say on this topic! Basically, what actually happened in the case of Kinetic Theory was that work went ahead on all fronts more or less simultaneously. Scientists were trying to work out what variables to measure and how to measure them; but they also were trying to find regularities in gas behavior, while continually speculating about what deeper or underlying mechanisms might be at work in gases. In other words, in terms of our diagram, work was progressing all over the picture but it was only very late in the history of the field that this picture emerged as a static representation of (as it were) the final "logic." (It must be said as well that in this case the precise theory did not emerge until long after the empirical laws had been found; but the point is that the attempt to find a theory did not just start then.)

Q: I guess there is no reason to think that other examples from the natural sciences would suggest anything different. Certainly, in at least some cases in the social sciences there are analogous situations—we don't know what to measure (or how to measure the things that might be of interest), we haven't been able to find reliable generalizations or correlations, and we don't know the relevant theoretical story (assuming that there is one to be had).

R: This view of the way in which science develops ought to shock many of your colleagues who set up operational definitions and then collect data and run statistical analyses to find "relationships" in a starkly a-theoretical way (and, of course, they overlook the fact that data are theory-laden anyway, so that they are somewhat deluded); I recall years ago the sociologist C. Wright Mills making the accusation that the social sciences were rife with "dust bowl empiricism" of this kind (Mills 1959).

Why don't we drop this and return to more cheerful topics—we have hardly scratched the surface of what the example of Kinetic Theory has to offer. Again with the caution that this is a somewhat "potted" history (or, as Lakatos might say, it is a "rational reconstruction" of the history; see Lakatos 1978), let us return to the times when Boyle and Charles and Gay-Lussac and others had made their empirical breakthroughs.

Q: Fine. But what were those breakthroughs?

R: To start with, Boyle found that for any given mass of gas at constant temperature (i.e., for a sample of gas where both the mass and temperature were not allowed to change), the pressure and volume were related in such a way that if the pressure were to be increased, the volume would decrease—in other words, they were inversely proportional to each other, or, in symbolic form, $P = k/V$ or $PV = k$, where k is a constant that depends on the particular gas under consideration and PV is to be read as P multiplied by V. This is regarded as an empirical law, although it only holds true under limited conditions (if it is true at all, rather than just a convenient approximation).

Q: This law appears to be equivalent, as we mentioned earlier, to generalized correlational findings that we discover in the social sciences—I suppose the finding that IQ and success at school are positively related might be an example. I wonder why we don't call this a law?

R: Maybe it is because there are problems with the relationship you cited. First, it doesn't hold, even approximately, for a fair number of individuals (that is, not all students with high IQ do well at school); it is, at best, a relation that holds if we take a large number of individual cases and average the results. Boyle's Law holds, at least approximately, for all gases. Is this a significant difference or not? Second, it is not clear that the relation between IQ and schooling is necessary—it seems that it could change quite easily, for example, if the nature of schooling were to change. (One can imagine schools in which high IQ is not necessary for success, as in the recent "accelerated schools" movement in the United States, which aims to help all students achieve success, especially those who normally would be placed in a low-achieving stream.) But, for a "genuine" law, do we believe that nature could change in such a way that it would cease to hold? Some philosophers (but not all) would argue that there is some sort of necessity about Boyle's Law—it has to hold. (Philosophers interested in this issue move off into strange realms, such as whether or not laws would hold in any "possible worlds.")

Q: I imagine that it is Kinetic Theory that accounts for this feeling of "necessity"; unless I'm mistaken, it shows why Boyle's Law has to be what it is.

R: That's certainly one way of looking at the matter—some people would be tempted to say (oversimply, of course) that laws explain phenomena, and theories explain laws! The philosopher Carl Hempel has something to say on the point you just made:

> Theories are usually introduced when previous study of a class of phenomena has revealed a system of uniformities that can be expressed in the form of empirical laws. Theories then seek to explain those regularities and, generally, to afford a deeper and more accurate understanding of the phenomena in question. To this end, a theory construes those phenomena as manifestations of entities and processes that lie behind or beneath them, as it were. These are assumed to be governed by characteristic theoretical laws, or theoretical principles. (Hempel 1966, 70)

Q: Well, this gets us back to the issue of the mechanisms that Kinetic Theory postulates. But before you go on to this, you never had an opportunity to remind me what Charles's Law was about.

R: That's easily taken care of. Boyle investigated the relation between volume and pressure where the mass and the temperature were held constant; Charles (and Gay-Lussac) found the relationship between volume, pressure, and temperature for a fixed mass of gas. The law states that the product of the pressure and volume at time one, divided by the temperature at that time, is equal to (a constant times) the product of the pressure and volume divided by the temperature at time two. Or, in symbols,

$$P1\ V1/\ T1 = (k)\ P2\ V2/\ T2$$

Q: That is a simple and elegant relationship. Now, how does Kinetic Theory explain why gases are constituted in such a way that Boyle's and Charles's Laws have to hold?

R: Not only does Kinetic Theory do that, but it also enables us to see that these laws are genuine laws (if I can be so bold as to use this terminology, which might offend some of my philosophical colleagues).

Q: I'm not clear what the point is here; what is the alternative?

R: Well, assuming for the sake of argument that the relationships found by Boyle and Charles are true of the gases they actually investigated, it might be the case that, instead of being laws that hold true (and in a sense must hold true) of all gases, they are "accidental generalizations." (See Lambert and Brittan 1970, chap. 3.) They might just happen to hold true at the moment of some gases (or even, I suppose, of all gases), but at some later date they might not happen to apply.

Q: Let me give some social science examples to see if I understand this distinction. I suppose the relation between IQ and schooling is one case. Second, we might find that, in all economically developed societies, those people in the highest socioeconomic rank tend to support the conservative political party (and the tendency is a strong one); the issue you raise is whether or not this is a law and must necessarily (in some sense of this term) be true, or whether it is just a sociotemporal "accident" and that, given certain social developments, we could easily find this not to be the case in some societies in the near future. A third example might be the finding that in all countries, more males than females are enrolled in engineering

courses—it would seem to me this is likely just to be an artifact of history and might well change.

R: That's right. It would be my guess that the middle example
is more likely to be a "genuine" law than the other two, although probably none of them warrant this label! They are
most likely to be "accidental generalizations." I caution you
that the point is not simply one about terminology; we use laws
to make predictions, to engage in engineering (and in the social sciences, social engineering is more or less the formation
and execution of policies) and so on, and we run into great
danger if what we thought were laws turn out only to be "accidentally" true. In other words, we use laws because we are
guaranteed (more or less) that they will hold in the future and
we can rely upon them, whereas generalizations that just happen to be true today may very well happen not to be true tomorrow, so any plans we had that relied upon them would be
headed for disaster. In short, "accidental generalizations" provide no basis for prediction, whereas laws do.

But let us get back to Kinetic Theory and look at how it
accounts for the two laws in terms of what Hempel called the
"underlying processes." (Actually, to shorten my discussion, I
shall just deal with one, namely Boyle's Law.) It is evident that
what scientists were after was a theoretical story that could be
stated precisely and that would have as a consequence the fact
that these empirical laws would hold true. The breakthrough
came in the form of "the dynamical theory of matter," which
one old textbook outlines as follows:

> According to modern ideas, the particles of matter in all
> states of aggregation are in a violent state of agitation. In
> gases the molecules move rapidly in all directions. They are,
> however, so small that they spend most of their time at dis-
> tances from their nearest neighbours which are large in com-
> parison with their own dimensions, and in most of their
> flight they are almost free from the influence of other mol-
> ecules. It seems justifiable to assume that the path of a typi-
> cal molecule consists of a series of straight portions, chang-
> ing direction at "collisions" with other molecules. (Starling
> and Woodall 1955, 194)

Now, this is the kernel of the theoretical story that needs to be worked out more carefully: From the story that a gas is a large collection of rapidly moving particles, can we get to Boyle's and Charles's Laws? The trick here is to conceive of the pressure that a gas exerts as being caused by the collisions of the molecules with the walls of the container. And it is known that the pressure of a gas rises as the temperature increases, which in terms of the theoretical story must mean that more molecules are colliding with the walls—which in turn suggests that temperature is a measure of how fast the molecules are moving.

What do we know about movement?

Having come this far, it is a short step to making a further breakthrough; molecules in motion can be treated as particles obeying Newton's laws of motion. It is possible, therefore, to do some simple mathematics, using Newtonian principles. But let me try to give you the flavor using words rather than math wherever possible: The force exerted by one molecule striking a wall is equivalent to the change in momentum as the molecule hits and "bounces" back. If the molecules of the gas under consideration each have mass m, and if the average velocity in the direction of the wall that was struck was u, then (from Newton) the change in momentum is 2mu for one molecule for one strike. But if the type of gas is not changed, and if temperature is held constant, 2mu will be a constant (for the mass of the individual particles and the average velocity will not change). If n is the number of molecules in one unit of volume, the total force on the wall—which will be the pressure on that unit of wall—would be 2nmu if all the molecules were striking the wall in a given unit of time; but in fact, only some fixed proportion of these will be striking the wall at any given moment, producing the pressure on that unit of wall (the proportion is a constant because the average velocities of the particles are not changing because the temperature is being held constant). So the total pressure P on the wall of a cube of unit volume (and this pressure is the same throughout the whole container, assuming the molecules are more or less evenly distributed) will be determined by some fixed proportion of 2nmu. But, for a fixed mass of gas at an unchanging temperature, 2nmu (or a fixed proportion of that) will be a constant (for n, m, and u will not change). In other words, P = fn(2nmu), where fn indicates that some proportion or function of the constant 2nmu is involved. (The same holds for the other walls.)

Now, if we take our crude equation and multiply both sides by the total volume of the gas, V, we get the new equation PV = V X fn(2nmu), or fn(2Vnmu). And eureka!, we are nearing the end, for Vn (the total volume of the gas multiplied by the number of molecules per unit volume) is N, the total number of molecules in the whole fixed sample of gas. So, PV = fn(2Nmu). But—given the conditions that were stipulated, namely, that the mass of gas is fixed and the temperature is not changing—it follows that the right hand side of the equation is still a constant. Thus, PV = constant, which is Boyle's Law.

Q: That's really impressive; I begin to appreciate why some physicists fall in love with theory.

R: Let me make one final point that will get you really enthusiastic! With the use of Kinetic Theory, scientists were able to make predictions—ones that could not have been made on the basis of the empirical generalizations alone.

Q: This must certainly have increased their confidence that they were on to something.

R: Unfortunately, philosophers are not entirely agreed about why scientists ought to have their confidence increased by successful predictions, but in fact they do! (There are technical issues in the theory of confirmation and relating to the link between theories and evidence.) But let me give merely one example of the fruitfulness of Kinetic Theory: If temperature is seen to be a measure of the velocity of the molecules, then as the temperature increases the molecules will speed up. What will happen as the temperature is lowered?

Q: I suppose it follows that the molecules will slow down. Ah— I see the implication of this; it seems to be a consequence that if the temperature is lowered far enough, the molecular motion will cease. Does this mean that there could not possibly be a lower temperature?

R: Correct; you would have reached "absolute zero." Subsequent work confirmed that this lowest temperature is close to $-273\,^{\circ}$C. And so our theory has produced a startling new insight.

Q: Let me give a verbal gloss, just to make sure that I followed what happened in this now complex case (I acknowledge that you were simplifying the deductive chains involved, so I won't take the details of your derivation very seriously).

R: That's good, because I did oversimplify; please chase up the derivation in a basic textbook if you are interested. But I'm glad that this crude account gave you something of the flavor.

Q: What happened here was that scientists had found some regularities—empirical laws—that related variables that were empirically measurable (pressure, volume, temperature). Eventually, a "theoretical story" was constructed—it was invented by creative people, I should say, and was not mechanically "generated." At any rate, this story was not in terms of P, V, or T, but in terms of unobservable mechanisms or processes (involving unobservable particles in very rapid motion), which it was hoped would account for the empirical laws. The story had embedded within it some precise rules, or "theoretical laws" as Hempel called them, that allowed specific derivations to be made from the theoretical story—in this case, these theoretical rules were Newton's laws of motion.

R: That's not a bad account; but I would add a couple of extra points of some significance. The first is that these days philosophers have problems talking about "unobservables"; there is no clear boundary in nature marking off what is observable from what is indirectly observable and from what is unobservable. And, of course, the theory/observation distinction has been abandoned. (See the discussion of this in chapter 6.) Second, it should be noted that because the theoretical story was not told in terms of P, V, and T, it needed to somehow be linked

or connected to the realm of empirically observable regularities—otherwise, it would have remained a nice story but with
no relevance to the work of Boyle or Charles. After all, their
discoveries were about P, V, and T, not about invisible particles
in motion! Philosophers have given a variety of names to these
links—correspondence rules, bridge principles, or the dictionary (see Hempel 1966, chap. 6; Nagel 1961; Campbell 1973);
while I'm on terminology, I could mention that there are also
a number of expressions for the rules or "laws" inside the
theory—internal principles, theoretical laws, the hypothesis of
the theory, or the calculus.

Q: Clearly, in the case of Kinetic Theory the links were provided by equating the pressure (which is observable and measurable) with the force of the molecules striking the walls of
the container, and by the insight that temperature (also measurable) could be conceived as indicating the velocity of the
molecules. But you had another supplementary point?

R: It is important to note the number of assumptions that had
to be made by the theorists. It was assumed that the molecules
were evenly distributed in space, that they did not lose energy
(and slow down) as a result of striking the walls, and that although they "collided" with each other, the velocities and en-
ergies were not affected (i.e., it was assumed that the particles
were perfectly "elastic"). It was even assumed that molecules
could be treated as Newtonian particles. (Some, at least, of
these are quite reasonable assumptions, but they are assumptions nevertheless.) In fact, so many assumptions are made
about the gas that it is probably not like a real gas but is what
physicists have called a perfect gas, one that real gases only
approximate in their behavior.

Q: That reminds me of the social scientist Max Weber's advo-
cacy of what he called "ideal types"; he felt that we could investigate social phenomena by building models that postulated
entities that acted in idealized or "perfect" ways—another victory for the influence of Kinetic Theory (Weber 1978, chap. 1)?
Also, I suppose, the theories of economists are similar, for they
assume that consumers are fully rational and that competition

in the marketplace is completely free—the issue here is whether the real economic life of society even comes close to what the "perfect" theory predicts.

R: These examples strike me as close parallels to the situation we have been discussing in physics. But the sociologist Arthur Stinchcombe reminds us that even if some of the assumptions about the underlying mechanisms or entities in the theory are oversimple, or even wrong, the theory might still work well enough to be very useful:

> "Assumption mongering," showing that the theories of the mechanisms are not true, is therefore seldom a useful strategy in scientific theorizing at an aggregate level. Just as statistical mechanics is still useful even if molecules of gases are not little round elastic balls, so assumptions that all people can calculate at a level two standard deviations above the mean may not be far enough wrong in *relevant ways* to undermine assumptions of rationality in economics. (Stinchcombe 1991, 384)

Q: That point is well-taken; but on the other hand, it occurs to me that the fact that there are so many assumptions and so many "boundary conditions" (such as the conditions that the temperature or the mass of gas must not change) that the theory becomes difficult if not impossible to test. And the same is true, I guess, for the empirical laws. It seems that if negative evidence was found, it would always be possible to claim that one of the important conditions or assumptions had been violated, so that the evidence does not constitute a fair test.

R: That line of thought gets us into the heart of much recent philosophy of science. Nancy Cartwright (who now occupies Popper's former chair) wrote a book called *Why the Laws of Physics Lie* (Cartwright 1983), in which she argued that the deeper or theoretical laws of physics have always been defended in the manner you suggest; there is always understood to be a ceteris paribus clause ("other things being equal") associated with scientific theories, and a scientist can always claim that other things are not equal! And the work of Lakatos and others (see Lakatos 1970) can be regarded as attempting to find criteria by which we could judge when defenses of science such as by deflecting refutation have become suspicious. (For a case study in the social sciences, see Phillips 1987, chap. 14.)

Q: I'd like us to change direction a little and explore some of the implications of this very rich example for my own work, now that you feel I understand it well enough. And I must say at the outset I now see why Merton and others were so impressed by Kinetic Theory.

One thing that immediately comes to mind is that attempts to theorize in the social sciences are often highly deficient from the perspective we have been discussing. Some researchers merely generalize the findings from one setting to all similar settings and call that a theory. I think that Glaser and Strauss foster this in their highly influential book; they constantly talk of "generating" theory from data, and they give the impression that if data are classified and compared properly, the theory will automatically emerge! (Glaser and Strauss 1967.) Another example would be the work of the sociologists Dornbush and Scott (Dornbush and Scott 1975), who studied the evaluation of workers in two types of organizations, and then produced a theory simply by generalizing these results to cover all similarly structured organizations. An example of one of their "theoretical propositions" is the following: "To the extent that performers believe that effort effects evaluations, they exert more effort to affect evaluations they consider important" (Dornbush and Scott 1975, 340).

R: I agree with you that this would not count as a theory in the physical sciences. The theory must embody different concepts—make use of different mechanisms—other than the ones that were observed. As Hempel argued, the theory should show why those observed regularities can be expected to hold, and to do this the theory cannot just contain "more of the same." Of course, to say this is not to say that the work of these social scientists is not important—to find regularities is important. I could remind you that we remember Boyle's name, but not many folk know the names of those who devised the final form of Kinetic Theory!

Q: I agree, but I presume that Dornbush and Scott and other social scientists are anxious to produce theories not only because it is prestigious, but because it also gives the feeling that we really understand the relevant phenomena. But now I start to have doubts about using Kinetic Theory as the "standard," as it were; for as we discussed at the outset, many things are called "theory" in the social sciences that bear little resemblance to it. Examples would be "dependency theory" in political science and economics (Third World countries, on the periphery of the world system, are held to be dependent on the major powers in various ways); and the theories of Marx and Freud. Now that I think of it, I'm not even sure that something so clearly a theory as evolutionary theory fits the physical science model.

R: In general terms I concur with the point you are making, but I want to quibble a bit with one of these examples. I don't have much time for Freud, but it could be argued, I think, that his theory of psychoanalysis can actually be illuminated if it is compared with Kinetic Theory. For we are then able to see what parts of Freud need to be worked upon if the whole thing is to become a solid theory. More operational definitions of key concepts need to be provided; and the bridge principles and internal principles of the theory itself are very vaguely formulated, hindering the making of derivations and predictions. But if you diagrammed Freudian psychology, you might get something that looked like a preliminary stage on the way to the final diagram we had of Kinetic Theory; some authorities regard Freudianism as a proto-science that is on its way to becoming a well-formed science—and recall that we acknowledged that Kinetic Theory took a long time to emerge.

But your point really goes deeper than whether or not Freud's and these other theories are on their way to possessing the same type of logical and deductive structure as Kinetic Theory. The issue is whether or not Kinetic Theory should be a model for all theories. In his book *Fact and Method* the philosopher Richard Miller writes that "evolutionary theory turns out to be incapable of the successes that are the job of a theory, on the deductivist account. . . . Small wonder, then, that deductivists are driven to deny that evolutionary theory is really a theory" (Miller 1987, 137). But Miller suggests that the correct conclusion is to doubt this "deductivist" account of the nature of theory. His view is that a theory should provide a causal account of the relevant phenomena, but that "many actual theories are not sufficiently well-connected with our knowledge of background conditions to be accepted as tools in the deductive style" (Miller 1987, 136). In short, Miller is prepared to accept as a theory an explanatory, causal story even though it might not be as precise as we would like; in fact, he says that few if any theories have lived up to the ideal (Miller 1987, 140).

Q: I find his view attractive, and it certainly seems odd to be forced into a position to deny that evolutionary theory is a theory. But we also have to realize that Miller's somewhat liberal position, especially about the deductive structure of theories, runs counter to what—for several decades—was the prevailing view in the social sciences. One of the classic methodology books was Blalock's text *Theory Construction*; here the ideal was espoused of achieving a "completely closed deductive theoretical system in which there would be a minimal set of propositions taken as axioms, from which all other propositions could be deduced by purely mathematical or logical reasoning" (Blalock 1969, 2). It is worth noting in passing that Dornbush and Scott set out their "theory" in the form of axioms and deductions, the axioms being generalized empirical findings—in other words, although their axioms did not resemble those of Kinetic Theory (where the elements of the theory are not ones that can be formed merely by generalizing the empirical findings), they nevertheless were trying to structure their theory in the same general deductive way that Blalock (presumably influenced by the physical sciences) was advocating.

But we need to move on. Are there any other matters on which philosophers disagree?

R: Of course, for disagreement is the spice of philosophical life. One issue about which there is a great deal of debate concerns the precise logical form in which a theory's "internal principles" or "calculus" should be expressible. (This takes the form of a debate about the syntactic versus the semantic conception of theories, which essentially revolves around the respective merits of logic versus set theory; see Thompson 1989, for an exposition of this dispute in the context of theories in biology.) There is one other area worthy of mention; I'm surprised you didn't mention it yourself as it raises quite fundamental issues about the explanation of human behavior (or action, as I would prefer to call it).

Q: With that clue, I can raise it myself! I suppose you are referring to the debate over whether or not it is entirely mistaken to base theoretical explanations of human rational action on a physical science model. The hermeneuticists, of course, are the school that most powerfully attacks the physical science model here. (See the discussion of hermeneutics in chapter 2.) The argument is that humans act for reasons; people hold beliefs and intentions that we need to know in order to explain why they acted the ways they did. It is a mistake to think that laws can be found here; the proper mode of explanation is more like what is found in literature—or in other branches of the humanities—than it is like the deductive explanation of gas behavior using Kinetic Theory.

R: This is, indeed, the debate I had in mind. Not only philosophers who are part of the hermeneutics camp challenge the appropriateness of the physical science model; the Berkeley "analytical" philosopher John Searle has been quite outspoken here. Perhaps the conclusion of one of his papers will give you an inkling of his position:

> If social explanation has logical features different from explanation in the natural sciences, then it must be because social phenomena have factual features that are logically different from the facts of the natural sciences. I believe that such is indeed the case and I have tried to identify two sorts of facts involved: first, that the form of causation is

essentially intentional causation and, second that social facts
have a logical structure different from natural facts. (Searle
1991, 344)

Q: This suggests a closely related point to me—one that ties
this present discussion in with what we were saying earlier
about the gas laws and Kinetic Theory. Scientists like Boyle
and Charles find empirical regularities in nature, and some of
these eventually get labeled as laws of nature. At some stage
the mechanism in nature that is "responsible" for producing
these regularities is discovered—and so we get a theory. Kinetic
Theory describes the mechanism of particles of matter in motion that underlies the regularities now known as Boyle's Law
and Charles's Law. However, turning to human behavior (and
especially to voluntary action), there certainly may be regularities, but it is dubious whether these should be formulated as
laws—for the point is, humans act because of reasons, values,
ideals, social customs and norms, and so forth (see chapter 2),
and these can change over time. Thus, a regularity that might
be found by studying citizens in the United States at the end
of the twentieth century might not hold true at the end of the
twenty-first, nor might it have held true at the end of the nineteenth. We might still search for the "mechanism" underlying
the regularity that has been found, but it is likely to be some
psychological or cultural "mechanism" that could change over
time. Thus, there are no laws of human action!

R: You have phrased this point in a very telling way. However,
I am not sure that you have completely made your case. It
seems to me that it is entirely possible that there might be
enduring cross-cultural regularities in the way humans act (it
may depend upon the level of abstraction to which we are prepared to go—i.e., we might have to delve to deep "structural"
levels in order to find such things). But it is also conceivable,
I must admit, that we will not find any. Yet even generalizations that are specific to the way that individuals act in particular cultures in given eras are not entirely useless—these can be
very helpful in "social engineering" and in our attempts to
understand why people act the ways that they do. In other
words, I would not want to say that these "narrower" regulari-

ties are merely "accidental generalizations" of the sort we discussed earlier. (Furthermore, we have been talking about laws of human action, but there might well be laws applicable at the "social" or "institutional" level—your objection might not be relevant to these. See the discussion in chapter 2.)

Q: Limited generalizations about human action might not be "accidental generalizations," but it doesn't seem appropriate to call them laws, either!

R: I'm not so sure—after all, the category of "law" is made by humans, and it is not a clearly demarcated category or natural kind. There are many philosophers who regard "law" as merely an honorific term that is applied to generalizations that are especially useful in a particular field of inquiry. But again I would stress that if we were able to produce a theory to explain why the particular regularity exists, we would be in a better position to decide if it was "lawlike" enough to be useful for making predictions and for giving explanations. And so we come back again to the importance of theory.

Q: Where does all this leave us? Can anything at all count as a theory?

R: I don't think that's the proper lesson to draw from our discussion. Theories do important work in the social sciences, no less than in the physical sciences, and some of the same ideals apply; but clearly the view that theories in the social sciences should resemble the structure of theories in the natural sciences (and especially in physics) may be too strong an assumption—and how could we defend it? The fact that we have to settle for a more liberal view of the nature of theories should not drive us to despair. Speaking for myself, I must admit that the "neutral" description of theory given by Miller is very appealing: "A theory is whatever explains empirical facts (often, regularities or patterns) of relatively observational kinds, through the description of less directly observable phenomena" (Miller 1987, 135). But whatever way we jump on this complex issue, we should use the term "theory" with care, and we should take pains to be clear about what we have in mind.

13

VALUES AND SOCIAL INQUIRY

In the late twentieth century there were a number of fascinating intellectual developments that are directly pertinent to the work of social scientists. The most notorious, perhaps, has been the rise of interest in relativism—a development fostered in part by the work of Thomas S. Kuhn—which, from the time of its first appearance, won a status among social scientists that it never quite attained in other domains. Another development—fostered by the apparent demise of what has been popularly labeled "positivism"—has been the rise in the numbers of those who criticize the doctrine of the value neutrality of the sciences and in particular of the social sciences. Not only has it been pointed out that, in fact, many pieces of science are heavily value-laden, but—more radically—the actual *ideal* of neutrality has come under attack. (See the closely related discussion of the attacks on objectivity in chapter 7.) In effect, these attacks on neutrality and objectivity are part of the questioning of the naturalistic ideal for the social sciences (see chapter 5).

Whether or not there is a direct logical link between the rise of relativism and the demise of positivism, on one hand, and on the other, the abandonment of value neutrality (and whether or not this "logic" is acerbated by postmodernist modes of thought and argument), there certainly is a link by way of the rhetorical style that is used—many of the adherents of both positions are cavalier with respect to careful argumentation, and leap to grand conclusions from premises that are not well-adapted to serve as such major launching places. The purpose of the present discussion is to subject the arguments against value neutrality to critical scrutiny, even if this means prolonging a debate that, according to Richard Rudner long ago, had reached "The Mystical Moment of Dullness" (Rudner 1953, 231).

The discussion, then, will proceed cautiously by way of a number of steps in which various arguments against neutrality are discussed, and necessary distinctions drawn; the excitement will gradually build from this slow and unpromising beginning.

THE ISSUE AT STAKE

As a first step it is appropriate to clarify—as far as is possible at this early stage—what is at stake here. (For a somewhat different analysis, see Miller 1987.) But unfortunately, there is no simple way to delineate the opposing schools of thought, which each set-up the issues differently. With a degree of poetic license, therefore, it can be said that the situation is roughly as follows:

1. There are some folk (these days members of an endangered species) who hold that, following the lead of the natural sciences (or, more accurately, what they *believe* to be the lead of the natural sciences), the social sciences must expunge any trace of values. Those who hold this view regard it as so holy a quest that they do not always see that it is necessary to be precise about what *aspects* of science it is necessary to expunge values from—from the day-to-day work of researchers, from the theories that are produced, from the empirical data gathering that takes place, or from the criteria by which they judge the merit of justificatory or supporting arguments and evidence. At any rate, it is held by those in this camp that the stakes are high—if we allow any chink through which values can enter, then objectivity will escape through the very same crack. As a consequence, the integrity of the social sciences will be undermined, and subjectivity and/or relativism will dominate—a nasty fate indeed.

2. Another group argues that, of course, values do, and should, play a role in the social sciences (and, indeed, in research in the natural sciences as well), but these are not ethical or political values—which *would* be destructive if allowed to influence the internal workings of science. Those who hold this position, then, are committed to the view that there are different *types* of values and value judgments, some of which have a role to play in the sciences, and some of which do not. This position will be discussed in more detail later, where it will become clearer—it is, after all, the position that I favor!

3. Others, like Michael Scriven, hold that what is puzzling is how scientists could have come to hold a view of the nature of science—the value-neutral view—"which is so patently unsound" (Scriven 1974, 290). Scriven

argues that in a variety of ways, values inevitably are involved in the sciences; to cite merely one example, the sciences are riddled with the need to evaluate (e.g., the evaluation of data and research designs and hypotheses), and evaluation requires the making of value judgments. But Scriven takes away from the relativists what he seemingly has just conceded to them, for he also insists that value judgments are not subjective but can be supported and given rational warrant in a number of ways. (See Scriven 1972, for another exposition of his views.) Richard Rudner holds a similar position to Scriven, and for similar reasons (scientists must evaluate and must accept or reject hypotheses); and he stresses that the nature of objectivity needs to be re-thought—in his view the key to objectivity "lies at least in becoming precise about what value judgments are being and might have been made in a given inquiry." (Rudner 1953, 236).

4. Finally, there are a number of scholars who agree that values must inevitably play an important role in the sciences and especially in the social sciences, but who give a different set of reasons for this belief—their point is that in the social sciences investigators are dealing with people and institutions, about whom it is not humanly possible (or desirable) to remain neutral; and because the social sciences deal with people, issues of power and influence are ever-present. The issue is not so much that values are inevitably present, but rather it becomes: *Whose* values shall dominate in the social sciences? Feminist scholars, as we shall see, are likely to argue that the values of one class of persons—namely, white males—have been unduly influential. But they are not alone in attacking value neutrality; Islamic scholars are likely to hold that this position is a "pretext" that "reflects either hypocrisy or self-delusion" (Moten 1990, 169):

> To be sure, Western political science is not value-free. Maintaining a demeanor of rigorous value-neutrality, most Western political scientists affirm the sanctity of Western liberal democracy, with its sole concern for profits and profit-maximization. To put it mildly, "they confuse a vaguely stated conventional democraticism with scientific objectivity." (Moten 1990, 170)

The same author states that while Western political science "confuses or conceals normative considerations, Islam states its values explicitly" (Moten 1990, 170). Marxist writers often advance rather similar propositions, making rather strange bedfellows.

The chief focus of the following discussion will be variants of arguments in the third and fourth of these categories—arguments that in diverse ways oppose value-neutrality and support the value-laden nature of social science; but some of what will transpire will also be relevant to the first two, which support (again in different ways) the view that at least some form of neutrality is both desirable and attainable.

AN EVALUATION OF THE ARGUMENTS

A. There is an argument against the possibility of neutrality, and for the value-ladenness of social science, that runs as follows: Because social scientists themselves are human, and because humans hold values and often act in accordance with them, then social science—being a product of humans—must embody the values of its human architects. This argument seems an obvious non sequitur; the problem lies in the failure to recognize both that not all of an individual's values are displayed in every activity he or she engages in and that not every artifact produced by a person reflects all the values that the individual holds. The fact of the matter is that the characteristics an individual displays vary according to the social contexts in which that person is located. Thus, a person might display several characteristics (and might act upon certain values) in one setting but display quite different characteristics (and act upon different values) in other settings. Indeed, it often happens that a particular setting or social activity might force an individual to *suppress* certain of his or her characteristics or values or tastes. To cite a trivial example, I recently attended a traditional French wedding, and although I have a strong dislike of—in fact, an aversion to—liver, it seemed appropriate to suppress this negative value (in this case, a "taste") and consume vast quantities of paté in order not to commit a breach of hospitality or to provoke an international incident. It is clear, then, that an argument is needed to establish why it is necessarily the case that the values a person holds must be reflected in the social science activities in which he or she engages—for the pursuit of social science might well be an activity that requires that participants suppress some of their native values and instincts.

It is worth emphasizing that those who advance this first argument with respect to values in social science are, in essence, overlooking the crucial fact that social activities are shaped not just by the characteristics of the people who engage in them, but also by the *rules or conventions* that apply to each particular activity (and that have evolved over perhaps long periods of time). And, as indicated previously, sometimes the rules of an activity require that the normal propensities of individuals be kept under tight rein. Thus, a person who in day-to-day life is the most cooperative and kindly of souls might also occasionally play tennis for the purpose of exercise and may, on the courts, suppress these humane instincts and take on an entirely different (and uncharacteristic) demeanor—but one that is entirely in keeping with the point of this competitive sporting activity. In other words, when playing tennis you adopt the rules and attitudes and values that are part-and-parcel of this game. For present purposes, the general point amounts to this: Under *some* conditions, people do have a propensity to make ethical or political or ideological value judgments, but it is not necessarily the case that they display this propensity under *all* conditions—and engaging in science may be one such exception.

Popper has an interesting variant of this general point: Referring implicitly to what is sometimes called the "context of discovery," he says that we cannot expect the scientist to shed all of his or her values "without destroying him as a human being *and as a scientist*" (Popper 1976, 97); but—especially in the "context of justification"—we can have rules and mechanisms (such as the mechanisms related to the free expression of opinions and the delivery of criticism) that "achieve the elimination of extra-scientific values from scientific activity" (emphasis added). In other words, according to Popper science is a social endeavor that proceeds according to certain rules or conventions, one of which is the excision of "extra-scientific" values, especially at the stage of testing of hypotheses; it is up to "the committee of the whole," as it were, to enforce the rules.

There is much to be said for Popper's view on this matter. Although (as Popper predicted) individual scientists might sometimes have a difficult time following the convention of value-freedom, it is clear that it is almost universally prized as an ideal or as a regulative principle for science—for example, it would be difficult to imagine the scientific community commending a scientist for allowing the interests of a manufacturing company to sway her professional judgment on an issue, and it would be impossible to get strong support for the proposition that a scientist who had falsified data had done a commendable thing (witness the horror displayed in the scientific community when it was discovered that the late Sir Cyril Burt had falsified much of his data on the intelligence of twins; see Hearnshaw 1979). It would seem that Popper is right: it is communal enforcement of the norms of science that forces scientists to monitor that their own values are not intruding where the rules of the game do not permit this to happen (and that ensures they will be called on it—even posthumously—if a breach of the rules is detected).

B. There is a much more subtle and powerful argument for value-ladenness that at first sight might seem more difficult to counter: It has been claimed that some value-orientations are so embedded in our modes of thought as to be unconsciously held by virtually all scientists. This situation has arisen—so it is argued—because all inquiries have to make use of categories and concepts, principles, rules of evidence, and so forth; and these things will of necessity reflect the interests of the most powerful groups in society. Over time these particular ways of conceptualizing the world, and inquiry, will become embedded. Thus, as was seen earlier, Islamic scholars or those in the Marxist tradition may hold that the categories of Western capitalism have permeated the social sciences; and feminist critics of science such as Sandra Harding argue that "the most fundamental categories of scientific thought are male biased" (Harding 1987, 290), a consequence of male power and the resultant domination over modes of inquiry for long periods of time—a phenomenon that had not been noticed until recently.

It is important to note that a two-pronged supporting argument is required from those who espouse such a view (who usually overlook this requirement): First, it needs to be established, by some sort of historical data, that males (or Western capitalists) have in fact been dominant in the requisite way—a fairly easy case to make, it would seem; but, second, it needs to be established—this time by a much more difficult argument—that the "male categories" (or "Western capitalist categories"), including such things as the principle of objectivity and the quest for truth as a regulative ideal, are in fact *biased*. And the charge of bias is coherent only if we can imagine some *unbiased* principles. In other words, in order to be able to make the charge of bias, the ideal of a value-neutral social science (or of objective truth) has to be accepted. Harding attempts to escape from this difficulty by means of an interesting stratagem—she wants to replace the male-oriented approach to science with a "feminist successor science" because women's "different kinds of interactions with nature and social life . . . provide women with distinctive and privileged scientific and epistemological standpoints" (Harding 1987, 295). Harding's position is more sophisticated than the exposition thus far has made it appear; in her later work she actually endorses a notion of *strong objectivity*, wherein even very deep-seated and hidden values will be exposed and eradicated—but to do this, we need the help of those who do not share such strongly embedded values and who thus will be in a better position to detect and criticize them. (See chapter 7.) Hence, to achieve objectivity our knowledge-producing communities need to empower the formerly unempowered and the excluded (Harding 1996).

At this point an example might be helpful. Over the past few years, when I have tried out some of the ideas contained in this present chapter in my classes, often they have been given a cool reception. "You have not made sufficient efforts to understand the points that critics of value-neutrality are making," I have been told. My interlocutors have gone on to say that all scientists of the past were biased—for example, Darwin was biased, and so was Broca. Darwin was biased because he used ideas taken from the reigning politicoeconomic ideology and applied these to biology; thus, the struggle for existence and the survival of the fittest, which were implicit parts of his theory of evolution, were taken over (as more than one authority has noted) from the laissez faire political and economic thought dominant among middle-class British males of his times. On the other hand, Broca, the nineteenth-century French medical researcher, had measured the cranial capacity of skulls of men and women of different races; he believed that brain size was related to intelligence and that because white men were superior in intelligence they would have larger brains than women and males of other ethnic groups (Gould 1981, chap. 3; see also House 1990, for a social scientist who makes use of this example). When Broca came across cases of white males whose brain size was too small, he corrected for such factors as body size and age; but he did not make such corrections for data coming from women or men of other ethnicities. Now, it seems clear that Broca *was* biased, in a straightforward sense of this term: He allowed his convictions to interfere with his research procedures, so that he was able obtain a result that supported his predilections. And as a result, his work was *not only* biased, it also was *poor science* (as work that allows values to intrude illegitimately is prone to be)—a point that will be pursued later in the chapter. But in what sense was Charles Darwin biased? His work—in common with *all* scientific work—was based upon assumptions, but he supported his ideas with massive and detailed data, and his theory was dissected and used to such great effect by subsequent biologists that it has now become widely acclaimed (by scientists of many races and of both genders) as a pivotal piece of modern biology. Unlike Broca's work, Darwin's has even survived Stephen Gould's critical scrutiny! Those who persist in labeling Darwin "biased" have to provide evidence (or "warrant") to support such a charge, and to make clear what they mean by this term in this context. The fact that Darwin was a male, or that he was a product of Victorian culture and was stimulated by some of the ideas of his times, does not establish that his work was value-laden in such a way that it was *biased*. (The discussion of social constructivism is pertinent here; see chapter 11.) In short, there is a confusion here between having presuppositions or the making of assumptions, on the one hand, and on the other, the presence of value-bias. The first often leads to the second, but it *does not have to*, and those who argue that in any particular case the first has led to the second have an obligation to support this charge with pertinent evidence.

To return to Sandra Harding: Whether or not her position with respect to deep-seated male bias in the fundamental categories of science is sound, the fact is that nowadays (as opposed, perhaps, to the situation in the past) Harding is free to express her views and to have them published and discussed—so that the scientific and broader academic community is forced to grapple with the issues she raises. If she and her colleagues can substantiate the charges they have brought forward, then an important source of value-bias will have been exposed, showing that it is not *necessarily* the case that social science has to be value-laden in this way (a conclusion with which I hope Harding agrees, given her desire to achieve strong objectivity); and there can be debate about the fruitfulness or validity of other perspectives on science.

C. There is a third argument about the place of values in social science that runs as follows: Whereas physical scientists study inanimate nature, social scientists study humans and social arrangements, and these are things about which it is impossible to remain neutral—a social scientist must surely notice that either the social arrangements or the people (or both) that he or she is studying are just or unjust, moral or immoral, and so forth. And, of course, this may well be the case—but it still does not follow, as those who hold this position assume, that the social science that is produced *necessarily* must embody these kinds of value judgments.

Even the fact that *some* social science that has been produced over the years has embodied such value judgments cannot be taken as establishing that all social science either *must*, or *should*, follow this path. The early work of anthropologists is a good example of this—the nascent profession was in the beginning dominated by missionaries and colonial officials who allowed their own morality to color their (usually derogatory) reports of the exotic cultures in which they found themselves, but this was not taken, in later years when the discipline reached maturity, as a model that ought to be followed.

There is a stronger variant of this third argument: Investigators have to select terminology with which to describe and explain the social phe-

nomena that they are studying. If they are faced with phenomena that
affront their own value systems, they will tend to use negatively laden
terms, and, of course, they would use positive terms for those phenomena about which they have a more favorable attitude. In this way, values
enter the social sciences. Naturally, examples abound: homosexuality may
be categorized as a form of deviant behavior; studies of family structure
may refer to "father absence" but also—more pejoratively—to "maternal
deprivation"; the psychological characteristics or abilities of white males
may be taken as the norm, in which case women and ethnic minorities may
be seen as below standard and requiring remedial treatment (rather than
the boot being on the other foot); and people who attempt suicide may
be labeled as psychologically unstable. (A host of documented examples
may be found in Campbell 1989.)

This problem is serious, and minority scholars and women are justifiably angry when they come across examples like these. But two points
need to be made. First, it is significant that these scholars *do* get angry;
they do not merely shrug their shoulders and adopt the attitude that it is
acceptable for values to shape social science in these ways. On the contrary, they wish to *remedy* the situation by pointing to the illicit role of values. Once again, this reaction only makes sense on the assumption that
values *can* be excised from social science. (In Popper's terminology, and
Kant's, value-neutrality is a "regulative ideal.") Second, the fact that such
bias *does* occur does not establish that it *must necessarily* or *ought to* occur.
As Francis Schrag points out, value-laden descriptions can easily be reformulated to avoid the problem; his example concerns two investigators with
quite different value systems studying schoolroom discipline—they both
see students throwing spitballs in one class, but they label this behavior
differently, and in a nearby school they see "well-behaved" students but
they also label this behavior with different terms:

> Suppose you deny that throwing spitballs, talking while the teacher is
> talking, and so on, constitute discourtesy, and I insist the characteriza-
> tion is apt. We still agree, however, that the students in the one school
> throw spitballs and the like, and in the other school they do not. If we
> are interested in the causes of the differential student behavior in the
> two schools we can, therefore, easily reformulate the question in this way:
> Why do the students in one school throw spitballs, and so on, while those
> in the other school do not? (Schrag 1989, 174)

It should be noted that not everyone is likely to endorse Schrag's
simple procedure. David Papineau, for example, believes that replacing a

value term by a "neutral" description is not "a workable suggestion" because the *attitudes* that people have will not change—they will merely carry over and infect the new terminology (Papineau 1978, 163–167). He is right, of course, about attitudes, but as Popper has pointed out, we should not try to strip scientists of their values—the point is that they should not allow these to poison their work. So forcing a change of terminology, and then communally policing the neutral language to ensure that there is no drift, might well be a sensible—and workable—strategy. At the very least the change in terminology is likely to sensitize members of the relevant research community to the dangers of value-laden terminology.

D. There is a different line of approach to the issue of the influence of values on science that runs like this: There are infinitely many problems that a scientist can decide to pursue, and from this plenitude he or she manages to select a small number upon which to work. So clearly the scientist has some "decision criteria," and these often—if not always—reflect that scientist's judgment about what is valuable or socially important. Such value decisions are reinforced by governmental or other funding agencies, which have clear-cut value priorities—projects that are regarded as trivial, socially frivolous, or socially dangerous are not regularly funded (and if, by mistake, they do happen to receive a grant, they are likely to be held up for public ridicule as in the famous "Golden Fleece Awards" awarded by Senator Proxmire in the United States).

Ernest Nagel put forward an answer to this line of argument that, as it stands, is not quite incisive enough but that holds the germ of an important distinction:

> In short, there is no difference between any of the sciences with respect to the fact that the interests of the scientist determine what he (sic) selects for investigation. *But this fact, by itself, represents no obstacle to the successful pursuit of objectively controlled inquiry in any branch of study.* (Nagel 1961, 486–487)

Nagel is distinguishing, implicitly, between two ways in which values can influence a science: internally and externally. Those who argue that social science is value-laden need to take care to specify which of these claims they have in mind—for the evidence that supports one of them will do nothing to support the other. A science may be externally influenced (as the Nagel extract suggests) without succumbing internally. It is also worth noting that Nagel's distinction is similar to the one that was present in an implicit form in the work of Karl Popper—for the latter's reference to "extra-scientific" values implies that in his view there also are "intra-scientific" values.

The following preliminary clarification can be offered: In most, if not all, human activities, there are decisions to be made and priorities to be sorted out. In tennis, should one serve to the forehand or backhand of an opponent? In philosophy, should one accept Bertrand Russell's or John Dewey's views on the nature of truth? In physics, which of several rival views on the nature of quasars should be tentatively accepted? In all these cases, the decisions of members of the appropriate "community of discourse" are guided by criteria and values that are part and parcel of the relevant field or activity—and if, perchance, an individual makes decisions on such matters using different and extraneous criteria, then other members of the field are likely to be very critical, and/or the decision will turn out to have been a poor one as judged by the standards inherent in the field. (David Papineau makes a similar point here: it is "self-defeating" for scientists to accept views for which the relevant evidence either is lacking or is deficient. See Papineau 1978, 172–173.) To return for sake of illustration to the philosophical example: The choice between the positions of Russell and Dewey should be made by the philosophical community on philosophical grounds—which case has stronger arguments in its favor, which philosopher best answers the points made by his opponent, which view is most compatible with other well-established philosophical positions. In short, the decision should be made using criteria and values that are internal to the discipline of philosophy, in which case the decision will be philosophically defensible. (For sake of reference, these will be called internal or disciplinary values; some writers refer to them as *epistemic values*.) If, however, the decision is made in terms of a philosopher's political values (Russell may have political views that are more conducive than those of Dewey), or in terms of the value that is placed on their social origins (Russell had an aristocratic British background and Dewey came from an American middle-class family), or in terms of some ethical criterion (one or other of these luminaries may have acted in a manner that meets with disapproval), then external values are coming into play, and the decision reached might not be philosophically defensible.

And so—to return to the more general discussion—the issue under consideration can be recast more accurately as this: To what extent do, and should, external values play a role in social science? Put in these terms, there is a lot to be said in favor of the traditional value-free position: the role of external values should be minimized. It should be stressed that there is not an issue about whether internal values should be influential (there is, of course, an issue about what precisely these internal values are)—for it is entirely appropriate, and indeed it is necessary, for the values and criteria inherent in a field or discipline to influence the inner workings of that field. Put more strongly, a field without internal values is not a field at all *(for these values make the field what it is), while a field that is influenced by external values has been seduced.*

This discussion should serve to throw light on a recent pronouncement by Michael Scriven, which seems to go off track because of failure to take really seriously the external/internal distinction. Scriven criticizes those

> who are essentially arguing for the position that value judgments within science are *improper* or *illegitimate*. Because this formulation is a value claim itself, one that is said to be rationally defensible in terms of the usual scientific standards of evidence and inference, it thereby becomes self-refuting. (Scriven 1991, 31n)

But *is* this a value claim, in the normal sense of the term? Consider a simple but direct analogy, where the issues become unmistakably clear: If I were to say that in tennis it is not allowable to strike one's opponent over the head with a racquet, have I made a value judgment? I think not; what I am doing is to report that, according to the (formal and informal) rules of tennis (i.e., the internal criteria, values and so on), physical abuse of one's opponent is not allowed. And, in reporting what the rules state, I am not taking a stand on whether these rules are good or bad. Furthermore, when I play tennis, and abide by the internal rules of the game by not smiting my opponent over the cranium, I have not made a value judgment either—I simply have been *playing* the game. (For, if I were to flaunt the internal rules of any game or activity, I would thereby be demonstrating that I was not pursuing that activity—to play a particular game *is* to play by the rules!) So, to return to Scriven, he is wrong when he claims that it is self-refuting to report that, according to the (internal) rules of science, it is improper to allow (external) value judgments to play a decisive (internal) role. Indeed, rather than this statement being a value judgment, as Scriven holds, it seems more like a factual report of a real state of affairs—for this *is* one of the internal rules of science.

This is not the whole story, however, for it is clear that external values do play some sort of role. Every science is pursued within a social context—and this context might be supportive, directive, or punitive. Thus, the physical sciences are these days pursued within an environment where they are heavily dependent upon governmental financing, and it is a fact of life that some projects (such as those relating to defense or those having direct industrial applications) are greatly favored. In other words, values espoused by agencies of government—extra-scientific values—may have a direct influence upon what problems certain physicists will pursue. And, of course, scientists themselves, being complex people, have complex motivations that lead them to personally favor some kinds of problems rather than others—again showing that extra-scientific values may "externally" shape the track that a science follows. But great care has to be taken not to overestimate the significance of this fact. A vital point needs to be insisted upon here: It must be recognized that the sort of evidence that is required to substantiate a claim that in any particular case external values are having an influence is quite different from the evidence required to substantiate a claim that such external values are having an internal influence. From the fact that, in a particular case, governmental values are influencing (via funding decisions) the nature of the problems that scientists are pursuing, it *cannot* be concluded that governmental values are influencing the internal criteria and values of that particular branch of science. While external influences upon science are an inevitable fact of life, external influences upon the internal workings are not.

Indeed, it can be stated that a branch of science that is externally influenced by values may not (and indeed, will often not) be internally affected. For the point is that if extra-scientific values are allowed to influence the internal dynamic, the resulting science will in all probability be *poor* science—for the rules and procedures of the science will have been over-ridden by these external values. And the point is that scientists, who wish to do *good* science, will be eager to expose and expunge such illicit values, and they will have as allies in this endeavor the Popperian mechanisms of criticism and freedom of expression of opposing viewpoints that were mentioned earlier. (For, good science is science that is judged as worthy on *internal* criteria.) Thus, a physical scientist whose research program has been externally shaped by government funding priorities, nonetheless will try, while pursuing this program, to adhere to the internal or epistemic working rules and conventions of science—and if he or she doesn't, then other scientists will be quick to expose any scientific flaws. (This is one reason why good research universities, like my own institution, refuse to undertake governmentally sponsored research that is also secret; for secret research is relatively immune from the scrutiny of the wider scientific community.)

The "Lysenko Affair," as it is commonly known, is a nice example here (Zirkle 1959; Lecourt 1977). In the USSR, when Stalin was in power, Western-style genetics fell into disfavor for ideological reasons—it was regarded as a bourgeois field that was incompatible with the principles of Marxism-Leninism. The government externally influenced this area of science, both by funding decisions and by the rather severe mechanism of purging Western-style geneticists! Academician Lysenko became influential and developed theories of inheritance that also were *internally* influenced by the government-favored ideology (he adopted a form of Lamarckian heredity, which, although long abandoned in mainstream biology, seemed to him to be easily related to the principles of Marxism). When put into practice (for example, in Soviet agricultural policy) his theories led to disaster, and in the end *he*—together with his pseudo-science—was purged, and genetics was reinstated.

E. The acknowledgment that there are internal (or epistemic) values in science, and that these must by necessity play a central role, might seem to concede the whole topic in dispute: Science is not value-free, and could never be so, because there are essential internal values; insofar as scientists value truth, objectivity, simplicity, testability, precision, consistency, unbiasedness, mathematical elegance, and so on, their work is not value-free.

The philosopher Hilary Putnam endorses the general position that there are such internal values, in his influential discussion "Fact and Value" (Putnam 1981); and he stresses that these are *genuine ethical values* (or rest upon such values). But he also acknowledges that his view is somewhat out of fashion. He supports the view that "the practices of scientific inquiry upon which we rely to decide what is and what is not a fact, presuppose values" (128). He then goes on to explain why this view is out of fashion:

> The reason this is a somewhat discredited move is that there is an obvious rejoinder to it. The rejoinder to the view that science presupposes values is a protective concession. The defenders of the fact-value dichotomy concede that science does presuppose some values, for example, science presupposes that we want *truth*, but argue that these values are not *ethical* values. (Putnam 1981, 128)

The point that Putnam's "opponents" make—and to which the present author is sympathetic—can be amplified in the following manner. As stressed earlier, most (if not all) human social activities—ranging from the doing of philosophy, the pursuit of science, the writing of poetry, the playing of tennis, the coaching of a football team, or engaging in competitive ice-skating—are "governed" by rules, norms, conventions, criteria, and theories. If they were not, of course, any untutored person could participate successfully in these activities. The term *governed* is placed in quotation marks to highlight the obvious fact that the governance is to some degree loose; the rules or conventions are sometimes broken by an expert practitioner in that field, but when they are contravened it is either done accidentally (as when an ice-skater makes a new move because she has slipped) or more usually for some definite reason—which is only to say that the rule-breaker can justify the new practice by reference to some other rules or criteria or theories within the relevant domain. Thus, a poet like e.e. cummings can decide to flaunt the normal rules of spelling and punctuation, and a football coach can decide to adopt a novel offensive formation—as when the "T" formation was first introduced into American football; but in both cases they are able to justify their new practices in terms of the theories of their field and the goals of the activities in which they are engaged.

Now, these rules and theories and so on—which clearly are what we have been calling the internal aspects of a field—are what allow the practitioners of that field to make judgments of value within the field. In other words, these are the elements that are appealed to in order to justify and to inform the intra-scientific value judgments that are made. "That was a good freestyle exhibition by Torville and Dean," an ice-skating judge may decide and award the competitors a perfect score; "this is a good poem and it will be published," a journal editor may decide; and "this scientific paper is so flawed that we should reject it outright, and it is so bad the authors ought not be invited to rework it and then re-submit it for publication," a scientific referee may write. All these judgments are value judgments, to be sure, but they are *not* ethical value judgments—they are judgments that are made within domains of activity or discourse, and they are judgments that stand or fall according to how well they can be justified in terms of the technical considerations internal to the relevant fields. (This might be the position that Richard Rudner and Michael Scriven—discussed at the beginning of this chapter—were supporting, although this was not absolutely clear; but if so, they stand vindicated.) The philosopher Harold Kincaid has stated the core issues in a way that could hardly be bettered:

> The quest for a value-free social science is not a quest for science that
> presupposes no value judgments. Science essentially involves innumer-

able judgments about what is good and what ought to be done. However, value assumptions are problematic only if they are moral or political values—as distinct from epistemic values. Reliability, objectivity, fruitfulness, scope, and so on are important values in science, but they are epistemic values. (Kincaid 1996, 44)

The moral is simple and worth stating clearly: The fact that there are internal or intra-scientific values does *not* establish that extra-scientific values do, or ought to, play a role in the internal dynamics of science.

The preceding discussion should not be read as arguing that a field's internal theories, criteria, conventions, rules, and so forth are sacrosanct. As mentioned previously, they are sometimes flaunted by experts in the field (but for a reason), and it is evident that they gradually evolve or change over time. The rules of tennis, baseball, and football have not been static; views of scientific method have undergone change over the ages; even the criteria of good music have not remained static (I recall coming across a book more than a century old that depicted composers arranged in a pyramid, with the best at the top; Mozart was somewhere down near the base, and at the very pinnacle was—Palestrina! Judgments made today would somewhat demote the latter and would no doubt slightly promote the former).

Recent developments in philosophy of science are quite relevant here. The "new historicist" work of Kuhn, Lakatos, Feyerabend, and others has led to a change in some of the internal or epistemic values or criteria of science (or, a cynic might say, has merely led philosophers to a more adequate understanding of the criteria that scientists have always used but that "ivory tower" philosophers have not appreciated); but at any rate—to cite merely one example—it is no longer the case that the use of ad hoc hypotheses to defend a scientific theory against criticism is judged to be an entirely bad thing. In short, an important value judgment has changed. And, of course, the work of feminist critics of science, such as Sandra Harding, might conceivably result in other important revisions.

There is one loose end to be dealt with here. Why did Putnam hold that the internal values of science *were* genuine ethical values of the kind that have been contentious in the dispute over the presence of values in the social sciences? His reasoning appears to have followed these lines: It is revealing to ask how these internal values are themselves justified. The answer I gave earlier was that they depend upon the corpus of theories, rules, procedures, criteria, and goals of the field (they require an *epistemic* justification). Putnam suggests that this answer does not go deep enough—

we have not reached "the bottom line" (Putnam 1981, 130). If we push, he suggests, we eventually come face-to-face with the issue of why the whole corpus of scientific rules and theories and so forth are valued. At the base we will come across our general criteria of "rational acceptability," and these in turn are part and parcel of "our idea of human cognitive flourishing" (Putnam 1981, 134). Thus,

> What I am saying is that we must have criteria of rational acceptability to even have an empirical world, that these reveal part of our notion of an optimal speculative intelligence. In short, I am saying that the "real world" depends upon our values (and again, vice versa). (Putnam 1981, 134–135)

Putnam might well have used an example of a system like voodoo (although he doesn't); here the natural realm is populated with entities quite different from those seen from the scientific point of view. And arguably, the difference results from the different standards or ideals of rationality that are accepted within the two systems of voodoo and modern science.

I do not find this argument convincing. Certainly, a person might not *pursue* a scientific career if his or her values run counter to those values that are embedded within the practice of science—a charismatic mystic or a voodoo priestess would not, presumably, choose to become an experimental physicist or a cognitive psychologist. And I may choose not to play American football because my personal values make it difficult for me to accept the violence that is part of this activity—but this is a point about my personal motivations, and it is not an argument about the foundations of the rules of football. On the other hand, it must be emphasized that the game of football *is* a game, and one can decide to play it (and thereby decide to abide by its internal rules, criteria, and values) without being committed to anything more. It is logically possible for the toughest of football tacklers to be a political pacifist. Thus, it is simply a non sequitur to argue that, because I play football, I am committed to a lifestyle of violence off the field. Similarly, I might be a person with strong religious or metaphysical leanings and yet decide that it would be interesting (or simply a panacea against boredom, much like chess) to view the world according to the principles of the "science game"—to pursue this as far as it could be pursued, without thereby committing myself in advance to accepting or believing all that this game turns up. (Clearly, most mortals would find this a hard thing to do—most people who play games end up being converts; but this is a psychological point about people and it is not a logical point. The notion of, as it were, a pragmatic acceptance of the values of science, without implying a commitment to broader views of rationality, is not incoherent; and it shows that the former commitment does not *depend upon* the latter. And, to offer some empirical evidence here, there are many cases of competent scientists who, on the weekends, abandon the values internal to science, and the broader value of rationality that Putnam says must undergird it, and who adopt quite different values and principles of rationality as found in, for example, many religions. This example shows that it is possible to practice science without having at a deeper level some sort of overriding value commitment to a particular ideal of rationality.)

F. We are now in a position to consider a final argument for the value-laden nature of the social sciences. This argument hinges upon the supposition that the distinction between facts and values is no longer viable. (This distinction is traceable back to the philosopher David Hume in the eighteenth century.) As long ago as 1962, the British philosopher J. L. Austin wrote negatively of the "fact/value fetish" (Austin, cited in Flew 1964)—although, as Antony Flew points out, Austin never lived to substantiate this judgment. Flew suggests that it is not clear when and how this distinction was ever decisively refuted, but he reports that:

> The word nevertheless seems to have gone round that the idea that there is a radical difference between *ought* and *is* is old hat, something which though still perhaps cherished by out-group backwoodsmen has long since been seen through and discarded by all with-it mainstream philosophers. (Flew 1964, 135)

Writing more recently, Brenda (Cohen) Almond also agrees that the substantial body of literature on this topic has not undermined the distinction between on one side "the world of empirical facts," and on the other "the world of moral judgement" (Cohen/Almond 1982, 62–63); she sees the arguments as focusing upon a somewhat different issue—the relationship between these two realms and in particular upon the issue of whether statements of one of these kinds can be *deduced* from statements of the other kind.

The point of all this is as follows: If those who hold that the fact/value distinction does not hold water can substantiate their position, then it would automatically follow (so, at least, the train of thought runs) that values *do* enter the sciences, for facts and values are not clearly demarcated and it is apparent that so-called facts do enter into deliberations in the sciences. And whence go facts, there also go values.

There are two simple replies. First, as Flew and Almond point out, it is far from clear that the distinction does not hold up. The onus is upon the opponents of the distinction to back up their claim with arguments of substance. (For a guide to this literature, as at least it stood some years ago, see Hudson 1969.) Second, even if the distinction is abandoned—which I do not believe it has to be—the rest of the argument does not follow through. Even if it should turn out that no clear-cut distinction can be drawn between facts and values, it does not follow that anything and everything is admissible into social science. Certain considerations—whether facts or values or whatever—can still be ruled inadmissible on the grounds of irrelevance. (After all, because it is a fact that it is a fine day outside, it does not follow that this is a matter that ought to be of influence in a particular piece of social science, say some work on the caste-like nature of ethnic groups within the United States. This meteorological fact can be dismissed from consideration on the ground that it is not relevant to the matter at hand. Similarly, because a scientist holds a particular religious or value position, it does not follow that this must be admitted as relevant to his or her work simply because the fact/value distinction has been abandoned!)

CONCLUSION

We have now reached the exciting *piece de resistance* more or less promised at the outset: It is the revelation that in complex topics, such as the present one concerning the role played by values in the social sciences, there *are* no simple and exciting conclusions to be reached! Truth is often more complex, and less exciting, than fiction.

The substantive conclusion that has been reached is many-pronged. (1) Those who are pursuing a science have a commitment to abide by the internal (epistemic) rules, theories, goals, and so on, of their field. This, in essence, is no different from the commitment undertaken by auditors, mathematicians, or football players. As scientists they can depart from these disciplinary principles, but only for reasons that can be publicly justified to their colleagues in a context of open communication. The commitment to the internal rules and principles does not have to be justified in terms of some further allegiance to deeper metaphysical or ethical principles or values; it just may come from these scientists regarding their work as an interesting enterprise with rules and conventions that seem well-adjusted to achieve the goals that have evolved for it. (2) These disciplinary rules, conventions, and the like provide the framework within which the scientists can make intra-scientific value judgments; but the framework also enables them to detect the improper intrusion of extra-scientific values. (3) Science in which extra-scientific values are internally (epistemically) influential is generally (if not always) poor science; this means that it can be criticized on some technical internal basis. (4) Value-neutrality of science, in the sense of freedom from internal interference by extra-scientific values, is widely prized; and it is presupposed as a regulative ideal even by those who argue that examples of bias and lack of value-neutrality can rather easily be found. (5) The fact that some scientists do succumb and allow extra-scientific values or biases to intrude into their work is not an argument either that the ideal of internal freedom from extra-scientific values is flawed or that it is widely challenged (for those who do succumb almost always are embarrassed when they are caught). (6) The social sciences, like the physical, are influenced externally by values, as when research programs are started or terminated because of governmental funding decisions. (7) Neither physical scientists nor social scientists have to engage in some superhuman (and misguided) effort to lose the values and interests that, as human beings, they necessarily possess. As Popper argues, the objectivity of science does not come from scientists shedding their values, but rather it flows from the freedom of their colleagues to issue a challenge when it is judged that these values are intruding improperly (improperly, that is, according to the internal values and criteria and theories of the particular branch of science).

REFERENCES

Aiken, Henry D. *The Age of Ideology.* New York: Mentor, 1956.

Alcoff, Linda, and Elizabeth Potter, eds. *Feminist Epistemologies.* New York: Routledge, 1993.

Angyal, Andras. "Logic of Systems." In Fred Emery, ed., *Systems Thinking.* Harmondsworth: Penguin, 1969.

———. *Foundations for a Science of Personality.* New York: The Commonwealth Fund, 1941.

Apel, Karl-Otto. "The A Priori of Communication and the Foundation of the Humanities." In F. Dallmayr and T. McCarthy, eds., *Understanding and Social Inquiry.* Notre Dame, Ind.: Notre Dame Press, 1977.

Ashby, R. W. "Logical Positivism." In D. J. O'Connor, ed., *A Critical History of Western Philosophy.* New York: The Free Press, 1964.

Ayer, A. J. *Language, Truth, and Logic.* London: Gollancz, 1960.

Bandura, Albert. "The Self System in Reciprocal Determinism." *American Psychologist* 33 (1978): 344–358.

Barnes, Barry. "How Not to Do the Sociology of Knowledge." In Allen Megill, ed., *Rethinking Objectivity.* Durham, N.C.: Duke University Press, 1994.

———. *Scientific Knowledge and Sociological Theory.* London: Routledge, 1974.

Barnes, Barry, and David Bloor. "Relativism, Rationalism and the Sociology of Knowledge." In M. Hollis and S. Lukes, eds., *Rationality and Relativism.* Cambridge, Mass.: MIT Press, 1982.

Barone, Thomas. "A Narrative of Enhanced Professionalism: Educational Researchers and Popular Storybooks about Schoolpeople." *Educational Researcher* 21 (8) (1992): 15–24.

Bauman, Zygmunt. *Hermeneutics and Social Science.* New York: Columbia University Press, 1978.

Bereiter, Carl. "Constructivism, Socioculturalism, and Popper's World 3." *Educational Researcher* 23 (7) (October 1994): 21–23.

Berkson, William, and John Wettersten. *Learning from Error: Karl Popper's Psychology of Learning.* La Salle, Ill.: Open Court, 1984.

Bertalanffy, Ludwig von. *General System Theory.* New York: Brazilier, 1969.

Betti, Emilio. "Hermeneutics as the General Methodology of *Geisteswissenschaften.*" In J. Bleicher, ed., *Contemporary Hermeneutics.* London: Routledge, 1980.

Blalock, Hubert M. *Theory Construction.* Englewood Cliffs, N.J.: Prentice-Hall, 1969.

Bloor, David. *Knowledge and Social Imagery.* London: Routledge, 1976.

———. "The Strengths of the Strong Programme." *Philosophy of the Social Sciences* 11 (2) (1981): 199–213.

Boudon, Raymond. *The Uses of Structuralism.* London: Heinemann, 1971.

Braithwaite, R. B. "The Nature of Theoretical Concepts and the Role of Models in an Advanced Science." In Richard Grandy, ed., *Theories and Observation in Science.* Englewood Cliffs, N.J.: Prentice-Hall, 1973.

Bridgman, P. W. *The Logic of Modern Physics.* New York: Macmillan, 1927.

Brown, James Robert, ed. *The Rationality Debates: The Sociological Turn.* Dordrecht, Netherlands: Reidel, 1984.

Bruner, Jerome. *Acts of Meaning.* Cambridge, Mass.: Harvard University Press, 1990.

———. *Actual Minds, Possible Worlds.* Cambridge, Mass.: Harvard University Press, 1986.

Bryman, Alan. "The Debate about Quantitative and Qualitative Research: A Question of Method or Epistemology?" *British Journal of Sociology* 35 (1) (1984): 75–92.

Bunge, Mario. "A Critical Examination of the New Sociology of Science: Part 2." *Philosophy of the Social Sciences* 22 (1) (1992): 46–76.

Butterfield, Herbert. *The Origins of Modern Science,* new ed. London: G. Bell and Sons, 1957.

Campbell, Norman. "Definition of a Theory." In Richard Grandy, ed., *Theories and Observation in Science.* Englewood Cliffs, N.J.: Prentice-Hall, 1973.

Campbell, Patricia. *The Hidden Discriminator: Sex and Race Bias in Educational Research.* Newton, Mass.: WEEA Publishing Center, 1989.

Caplan, Arthur. "Seek and Ye Might Find." In C. Wade Savage, ed., *Scientific Theories. Minnesota Studies in the Philosophy of Science,* vol. 14. Minneapolis: University of Minnesota Press, 1990.

Carnap, Rudolf. "The Methodological Character of Theoretical Concepts." In Herbert Feigl and Michael Scriven, eds., *Minnesota Studies in the Philosophy of Science,* vol. 1. Minneapolis: University of Minnesota Press, 1956.

Carnap, Rudolf. *The Logical Structure of the World and Pseudoproblems in Philosophy.* Berkeley: University of California Press, 1969.

Carter, Kathy. "The Place of Story in the Study of Teaching and Teacher Education." *Educational Researcher* 22 (1) (1993): 5–12, 18.

Cartwright, Nancy. *How the Laws of Physics Lie.* Oxford: Clarendon Press, 1983.

Cherryholmes, Cleo. *Power and Criticism.* New York: Teachers College Press, 1988.

Chomsky, Noam. *Language and Responsibility.* New York: Pantheon, 1979.

Cleverley, John, and D. C. Phillips. *Visions of Childhood.* New York: Teachers College Press, 1986.

Cohen, Brenda. "Return to the Cave." Reprinted in Brenda Almond, *Moral Concerns.* Atlantic Highlands, N.J.: Humanities Press International, 1987 (1982).

Cole, Stephen. *Making Science.* Cambridge, Mass.: Harvard University Press, 1992.

Collins, Harry. "Stages in the Empirical Program of Relativism." *Social Studies of Science* 11 (1981): 3–10.

———. *Changing Order.* Chicago: University of Chicago Press, 1992, and London: Sage, 1985.

Comte, Auguste. *Introduction to Positive Philosophy,* translated by Frederick Ferre. Indianapolis and New York: Bobbs-Merrill, 1970.

Confrey, Jere. "What Constructivism Implies for Teaching." *Constructivist Views on the Teaching and Learning of Mathematics. Journal for Research in Mathematics Education,* Monograph Number 4, 1990.

Connelly, F. Michael, and D. Jean Clandinin. "Stories of Experience and Narrative Inquiry." *Educational Researcher* 19 (5) (1990): 2–14.

Connolly, J., and T. Keutner, eds. *Hermeneutics versus Science?* Notre Dame, Ind.: University of Notre Dame Press, 1988.

Cook, Thomas, and Donald Campbell. *Quasi-Experimentation.* Chicago: Rand McNally, 1979.

Dancy, Jonathan, and Ernest Sosa, eds. *A Companion to Epistemology.* Oxford: Blackwell, 1992.

Dennis, Wayne. *Readings in the History of Psychology.* New York: Appleton-Century-Crofts, 1948.

Descartes, Rene. *Philosophical Writings,* ed. Elizabeth Anscombe and Peter Geach. Edinburgh: Thomas Nelson and Sons, 1963.

Dewey, John. *Democracy and Education.* New York: Free Press, 1966.

———. *How We Think.* Chicago: Henry Regnery, 1971.

———. *Logic: The Theory of Inquiry.* New York: Holt, Rinehart & Winston, 1966.

———. "The Need for a Recovery of Philosophy." In *Creative Intelligence.* New York: Holt, 1917.

———. "The Objectivism-Subjectivism of Modern Philosophy." *Journal of Philosophy* 38 (20) (September 25, 1941).

———. *The Quest for Certainty.* New York: Capricorn, 1960.

———. *The School and Society* (reprinted as a joint edition with *The Child and the Curriculum*). Chicago: University of Chicago Press, 1969.

Dewey, John, and Arthur Bentley. "Transactions as Known and Named." *Journal of Philosophy* 43 (1946): 533–551.

Dijksterhuis, E. J. *The Mechanization of the World Picture,* translated by C. Dikshoorn. Oxford: Clarendon Press, 1961.

Dilthey, Wilhelm. *Dilthey: Selected Writings.* Cambridge: Cambridge University Press, 1976.

Dornbush, Sandford, and Richard Scott. *Evaluation and the Exercise of Authority.* San Francisco, Calif.: Jossey-Bass, 1975.

Duit, Reinders. "The Constructivist View: A Fashionable and Fruitful Paradigm for Science Education Research and Practice." In Leslie Steffe, ed., *Epistemological Foundations of Mathematical Experience.* New York: Springer-Verlag, 1993.

Dupre, John. "The Disunity of Science." *Mind* 92 (1983): 321–346.

——. *The Disorder of Things.* Cambridge, Mass.: Harvard University Press, 1993.

Eisner, Elliot. "Anastasia Might Still Be Alive, but the Monarchy Is Dead." *Educational Researcher* 12 (5) (May 1983).

——. *The Educational Imagination.* New York: Macmillan, 1979.

——. "The Primacy of Experience and the Politics of Method." Lecture delivered at the University of Oslo, Norway, September 1986.

Eisner, Elliot, and Alan Peshkin, eds. *Qualitative Inquiry in Education.* New York: Teachers College Press, 1990.

Elgin, Catherine. *Between the Absolute and the Arbitrary.* Ithaca, N.Y.: Cornell University Press, 1997.

Fay, Brian. *Contemporary Philosophy of Social Science.* Oxford: Blackwell, 1996.

Feyerabend, Paul. "Against Method." In M. Radner and S. Winokur, eds., *Analyses of Theories and Methods of Physics and Psychology.* Minneapolis: University of Minnesota Press, 1970.

Feyerabend, Paul. *Against Method.* London: Verso, 1978.

Filstead, W. "Qualitative Method: A Needed Perspective in Evaluation Research." In T. Cook and C. Reichardt, eds., *Qualitative and Quantitative Methods in Evaluation Research.* Beverly Hills: Sage, 1979.

Fine, Arthur. "And Not Antirealism Either." In J. Kourany, ed., *Scientific Knowledge.* Belmont, Calif.: Wadsworth, 1987.

Fish, Stanley. *Is There a Text in This Class?* Cambridge, Mass.: Harvard University Press, 1980.

Flew, Antony. "On Not Deriving 'Ought' from 'Is.'" Reprinted in W. D. Hudson, ed., *The Is/Ought Question.* London: Macmillan, 1964.

Fodor, Jerry. "Observation Reconsidered." *Philosophy of Science* 51 (1) (1984): 23–44.

Fodor, Jerry, and Lepore, Ernest. *Holism: A Shopper's Guide.* Oxford: Blackwell, 1992.

Follesdal, Dagfinn. "Hermeneutics and the Hypothetico-Deductive Method." *Dialectica* 33 (1979): 319–336.

Ford, Martin, and Donald Ford, eds., *Humans as Self-Constructing Living Systems.* Hillsdale, N.J.: Erlbaum, 1987.

Forman, Paul, "Truth and Objectivity, Part 1." *Science* 269 (July 28, 1995): 565–567.

Forrest, D. W. *Francis Galton: The Life and Work of a Victorian Genius.* New York: Taplinger, 1974.

Freud, Sigmund. *Five Lectures on Psychoanalysis.* New York: Norton, 1989.

Fuller, Steve. *Philosophy of Science and Its Discontents.* New York: Guilford Press, 1993.

———. *Social Epistemology.* Bloomington and Indianapolis: Indiana University Press, 1988.

Gadamer, Hans-Georg. *Philosophical Hermeneutics,* translated by D. Linge. Berkeley: University of California Press, 1977.

Gage, N. L. "Confronting Counsels of Despair for the Behavioral Sciences." *Educational Researcher* 25 (3) (1996): 5–15, 22.

Galton, Francis. "Statistical Inquiries into the Efficacy of Prayer." *Fortnightly Review* 68 (1872): 125–135.

Gasper, Philip. "The Philosophy of Biology." In Richard Boyd et al., eds., *The Philosophy of Science.* Cambridge, Mass.: Bradford, 1991.

Geertz, Clifford. *The Interpretation of Cultures.* New York: Basic Books, 1973.

Gellner, Ernest. *Spectacles and Predicaments: Essays in Social Theory.* Cambridge: Cambridge University Press, 1979.

Glaser, Barney, and Anselm Strauss. *The Discovery of Grounded Theory.* New York: Aldine, 1967.

Glasersfeld, Ernst von. "An Exposition of Constructivism: Why Some Like It Radical." In *Constructivist Views on the Teaching and Learning of Mathematics. Journal for Research in Mathematics Education,* Monograph Number 4, 1990.

———. "An Introduction to Radical Constructivism." In Paul Watzlawick, ed., *The Invented Reality.* New York: W. W. Norton, 1984.

———. "Cognition, Construction of Knowledge, and Teaching." Reprinted in Michael R. Matthews, ed., *History, Philosophy, and Science Teaching.* New York: Teachers College Press, 1991 (a).

———. "Introduction." In Ernst von Glasersfeld, ed., *Radical Constructivism in Mathematics Education.* Dordrecht, Netherlands: Kluwer, 1991 (b).

Goldman, Alvin. *Liaisons.* Cambridge, Mass.: MIT Press/Bradford, 1992.

Goldstein, Kurt. *The Organism.* Boston: Beacon, 1963.

Goodman, Nelson, and Catherine Elgin. *Reconceptions in Philosophy.* Indianapolis: Hackett, 1988.

Goodman, Nelson. *Fact, Fiction and Forecast.* Indianapolis: Bobbs-Merrill, 1973.

Gould, Stephen J. *The Mismeasure of Man.* New York: Norton, 1981.

Gross, Paul, and Norman Levitt. *Higher Superstition.* Baltimore, Md.: Johns Hopkins University Press, 1994.

Grunbaum, Adolf. "The Pseudo-Problem of Creation in Physical Cosmology." *Philosophy of Science* 56 (3) (1989): 373–394.

Guba, Egon. "Subjectivity and Objectivity." In E. Eisner and A. Peshkin, eds., *Qualitative Inquiry in Education.* New York: Teachers College Press, 1990.

Guba, Egon, and Yvonna Lincoln. *Effective Evaluation.* San Francisco: Jossey-Bass, 1982.

Habermas, Jürgen. *Knowledge and Human Interests.* Boston: Beacon Press, 1971.

Hacking, Ian. *The Social Construction of What?* Cambridge, Mass.: Harvard University Press, 1999.

———. *The Taming of Chance.* Cambridge: Cambridge University Press, 1990.

Hammersley, Martin. *The Dilemma of Qualitative Method: Herbert Blumer and the Chicago Tradition.* London and New York: Routledge, 1989.

Hanson, N. R. *Patterns of Discovery.* Cambridge: Cambridge University Press, 1965 and 1958.

Harding, Sandra. "Rethinking Standpoint Epistemology: What Is 'Strong Objectivity'?" In Evelyn Fox Keller and Helen Longino, eds., *Feminism and Science.* Oxford: Oxford University Press, 1996.

———. "Rethinking Standpoint Epistemology: What is 'Strong Objectivity'?" In L. Alcoff and E. Potter, eds., *Feminist Epistemologies.* New York: Routledge, 1993.

———. "The Instability of the Analytical Categories of Feminist Theory." In Sandra Harding and Jean O'Barr, eds., *Sex and Scientific Inquiry.* Chicago: University of Chicago Press, 1987.

Hawkesworth, Mary. "Knowers, Knowing, Known: Feminist Theory and Claims of Truth." *Signs* 14 (3) (1989): 533–557.

Hawking, Stephen. *A Brief History of Time.* New York: Bantam, 1988.

Hearnshaw, L. S. *Cyril Burt: Psychologist.* Ithaca, N.Y.: Cornell University Press, 1979.

Hempel, Carl. *Philosophy of Natural Science.* Englewood Cliffs, N.J.: Prentice Hall, 1966.

Hirsch, E. D., Jr. *The Aims of Interpretation.* Chicago: University of Chicago Press, 1978.

———. *Validity in Interpretation.* New Haven, Conn.: Yale University Press, 1967.

Hofstadter, Richard. *Social Darwinism in American Thought.* Boston: Beacon Press, 1955.

Hollis, Martin. "The Social Destruction of Reality." In M. Hollis and S. Lukes, eds., *Rationality and Relativism.* Cambridge, Mass.: MIT Press, 1982.

House, Ernest. "Methodology and Justice." In K. Sirotnik, ed., *Evaluation and Social Justice.* New Directions in Program Evaluation, 45. San Francisco, Calif.: Jossey-Bass, 1990.

House, Ernest. *Evaluating with Validity.* Beverly Hills: Sage, 1980.

Hudson, W. D. *The Is/Ought Question.* London: Macmillan, 1969.

Husserl, Edmund. *The Crisis of European Sciences and Transcendental Phenomenology.* Evanston, Ill.: Northwestern University Press, 1970.

James, William. "Absolutism and Empiricism." *Mind* 9 (1884).

———. "Remarks on Spencer's Definition of Mind as Correspondence." In W. James, *Collected Essays and Reviews.* London: Longman, 1920.

Jardine, David. "The Fecundity of the Individual Case: Considerations of the Pedagogic Heart of Interpretive Work." *Journal of the Philosophy of Education* 26 (1) (1992): 51–61.

Kant, Immanuel. *Critique of Pure Reason*. London: Dent/Everyman, 1959.

Keat, Russell, and John Urry. *Social Theory as Science*. 2d ed. London: Routledge, 1982.

Keller, Evelyn Fox. "Science and Its Critics." *Academe* 81 (5) (1995): 10–15.

Kennedy, J. G. *Herbert Spencer*. Boston: Twayne, 1978.

Kerlinger, Fred. *Foundations of Behavioral Research*. 2d ed. New York: Holt, Rinehart & Winston, 1973.

Kincaid, Harold. *Philosophical Foundations of the Social Sciences*. Cambridge: Cambridge University Press, 1996.

Kitcher, Philip. *The Advancement of Science*. New York: Oxford University Press, 1993.

Koestler, Arthur. *Janus*. New York: Vintage, 1979.

Konvitz, Milton, and Gail Kennedy, eds., *The American Pragmatists*. New York: Meridian, 1960.

Kornblith, Hilary. "A Conservative Approach to Social Epistemology." In F. Schmitt, ed., *Socializing Epistemology: The Social Dimensions of Knowledge*. Lanham, Md.: Rowman & Littlefield, 1994.

Kuhn, Thomas S. *The Structure of Scientific Revolutions*. Chicago: University of Chicago Press, 1962.

Kuhn, Thomas S. *The Trouble with the Historical Philosophy of Science*. The Robert and Maureen Rothschild Distinguished Lecture, Harvard Department of the History of Science, Cambridge, Mass., 1992.

Kulp, Christopher B. *The End of Epistemology*. Westport, Conn.: Greenwood Press, 1992.

Lakatos, Imre. "Falsification and the Methodology of Scientific Research Programs." In I. Lakatos and A. Musgrave, eds., *Criticism and the Growth of Knowledge*. Cambridge: Cambridge University Press, 1970.

———. "History of Science and Its Rational Reconstructions." In I. Lakatos, *The Methodology of Scientific Research Programs*. Cambridge: Cambridge University Press, 1978.

Lambert, Karel, and Gordon Brittan. *An Introduction to the Philosophy of Science*. Englewood Cliffs, N.J.: Prentice-Hall, 1970.

Latour, Bruno. "One More Turn after the Social Turn." In E. McMullin, ed., *The Social Dimensions of Science*. Notre Dame, Ind.: University of Notre Dame Press, 1992.

Latour, Bruno, and Steve Woolgar. *Laboratory Life: The Construction of Scientific Facts*. Princeton, N.J.: Princeton University Press, 1986.

Laudan, Larry. "Demystifying Underdetermination." In C. Wade Savage, ed., *Scientific Theories*. Minnesota Studies in Philosophy of Science, 14. Minneapolis: University of Minnesota Press, 1990.

———. *Progress and Its Problems*. Berkeley: University of California Press, 1977.

———. *Science and Relativism*. Chicago: University of Chicago Press, 1990.

————. "The Pseudo-Science of Science?" *Philosophy of the Social Sciences* 11 (1981): 173–198.

Lecourt, Dominique. *Proletarian Science? The Case of Lysenko*. London: NLB, 1977.

Leplin, Jarrett, ed. *Scientific Realism*. Berkeley: University of California Press, 1984.

Lincoln, Yvonna, and Egon Guba. *Naturalistic Inquiry*. Beverley Hills, Calif.: Russell Sage, 1985.

Locke, John. *An Essay Concerning Human Understanding*. London: Dent/Everyman, 1947.

Longino, Helen. *Science as Social Knowledge*. Princeton, N.J.: Princeton University Press, 1990.

————. "Subjects, Power and Knowledge: Description and Prescription in Feminist Philosophies of Science." In L. Alcoff and E. Potter, eds., *Feminist Epistemologies*. New York: Routledge, 1993.

Lovie, Sandy. "Review Note: Stephen Cole, Making Science." *Theory and Psychology* 5 (4) (1995): 611–612.

Lyotard, Jean-François. *The Postmodern Condition: A Report on Knowledge*. Manchester: Manchester University Press, 1984.

Lytle, Susan, and Marilyn Cochran-Smith. "Learning from Teacher Research: A Working Typology." *Teachers College Record* 92 (1) (1990): 83–102.

Macdonald, G., and P. Pettit. *Semantics and Social Science*. London: Routledge, 1981.

Madden, Edward H. *Philosophical Problems of Psychology*. New York: Odyssey, 1962.

Magee, Bryan. *Philosophy and the Real World*. La Salle, Ill.: Open Court, 1985.

Matthew, J. A. D. "Cartoons in Science." *Physics Education* 26 (1991): 110–113.

Matthews, Michael R. "Old Wine in New Bottles: A Problem with Constructivist Epistemology." In H. Alexander, ed., *Philosophy of Education 1992*. Proceedings of the Forty-Eighth Annual Meeting of the Philosophy of Education Society, 1992.

————. *Science Teaching: The Role of History and Philosophy of Science*. New York: Routledge, 1994.

Maxwell, Grover. "The Ontological Status of Theoretical Entities." In H. Feigl and G. Maxwell, eds., *Minnesota Studies in the Philosophy of Science* 3. Minneapolis: University of Minnesota Press, 1962.

McCarty, Luise P., and Thomas A. Schwandt. "Seductive Illusions: Von Glasersfeld and Gergen on Epistemology and Education." In D. C. Phillips, ed., *Constructivism in Education: Opinions and Second Opinions on Controversial Issues*. 99th Yearbook of the National Society for the Study of Education. Chicago: NSSE/University of Chicago Press, 2000.

McGonagall, W. T. *Yet Further Poetic Gems*. London: Duckworth, 1980.

Meehl, Paul. *Selected Philosophical and Methodological Papers*, ed. C. A. Anderson and K. Gunderson. Minneapolis: University of Minnesota Press, 1991.

Megill, Allen, ed. *Rethinking Objectivity*. Durham, N.C.: Duke University Press, 1994.

Merton, Robert. *On Theoretical Sociology*. New York: Free Press, 1967.

Midgley, Mary. *Evolution as a Religion*. London: Methuen, 1985.

Miles, Matthew, and A. Michael Huberman. "Drawing Valid Meaning from Qualitative Data." *Educational Researcher* 13 (5) (May 1984).

———. *Qualitative Data Analysis*. Beverly Hills: Sage, 1985.

Mill, John Stuart. In E. Nagel, ed., *Philosophy of Scientific Method*. New York: Hafner, 1950.

———. *The Logic of the Moral Sciences*. La Salle, Ill.: Open Court, 1988.

Miller, David. *Critical Rationalism*. La Salle, Ill.: Open Court, 1994.

Miller, Richard W. *Fact and Method*. Princeton, N.J.: Princeton University Press, 1987.

Mills, C. Wright. *The Sociological Imagination*. New York: Oxford University Press, 1959.

Morrison, D., and R. Henkel, eds. *The Significance Test Controversy*. Chicago: Aldine, 1970.

Moten, A. Rashid. "Islamization of Knowledge: Methodology of Research in Political Science." *American Journal of Islamic Social Science* 7 (1990): 106–113.

Myrdal, Gunnar. *Objectivity in Social Research*. New York: Pantheon Books, 1969.

Nagel, Ernest. *Teleology Revised*. New York: Columbia University Press, 1979.

———. *The Structure of Science*. London: Routledge, 1961.

Nelson, Lynn Hankinson. "Epistemological Communities." In L. Alcoff and E. Potter, eds., *Feminist Epistemologies*. New York: Routledge, 1993.

New York Review of Books. "Feminism and Philosophy: An Exchange," 42 (6) (1995): 48–49.

Newton-Smith, William H. *The Rationality of Science*. Boston and London: Routledge, 1981.

Nisbet, Robert. "Subjective Si! Objective No!" In G. Riley, ed., *Values, Objectivity, and the Social Sciences*. Reading, Mass.: Addison-Wesley, 1974.

Noddings, Nel. "Constructivism in Mathematics Education." In *Constructivist Views on the Teaching and Learning of Mathematics. Journal for Research in Mathematics Education*, Monograph Number 4, 1990.

Norman, Donald. "What Goes On in the Mind of the Learner." In W. McKeachie, ed., *Learning, Cognition, and College Teaching*. San Francisco: Jossey-Bass, 1980.

Nussbaum, Martha. "Feminists and Philosophy." *New York Review of Books* 41 (17) (October 20, 1994): 59–63.

Palmer, R. *Hermeneutics*. Evanston, Ill.: Northwestern University Press, 1969.

Phillips, D. C., ed. *Constructivism in Education: Opinions and Second Opinions on Controversial Issues*. 99th Yearbook of the National Society for the Study of Education. Chicago: NSSE/University of Chicago Press, 2000.

———. *Holistic Thought in Social Science*. Stanford: Stanford University Press, 1976.

———. "How, Why, What, When, and Where: Perspectives on Constructivism in Psychology and Education." *Issues in Education* 3 (2) (1997): 151–194.

———. "John Dewey and the Organismic Archetype." In R. J. W. Selleck, ed.,

Melbourne Studies in Education 1971. Melbourne: Melbourne University Press, 1971.

———. "On Castigating Constructivists." In H. Alexander, ed., *Philosophy of Education 1992*. Proceedings of the Forty-Eighth Annual Meeting of the Philosophy of Education Society, 1992.

———. "Organicism in the Late Nineteenth and Early Twentieth Centuries." *Journal of the History of Ideas* 31 (1970): 413–432.

———. "Perspectives on Piaget as Philosopher." In S. and C. Modgil, eds., *Jean Piaget: Consensus and Controversy*. London: Holt, 1982.

———. *Philosophy, Science, and Social Inquiry*. Oxford and New York: Pergamon Press, 1987.

———. "Was William James Telling the Truth after All?" *The Monist* 67 (3) (July 1984).

Phillips, D. C., and Nicholas Burbules. *Postpositivism and Educational Research*. Boulder, Colo.: Rowman & Littlefield, 2000.

Piaget, Jean. "The Psychogenesis of Knowledge and Its Epistemological Significance." In M. Piattelli-Palmarini, ed., *Language and Learning*. Cambridge, Mass.: Harvard University Press, 1980.

Pile, Stephen. *The Book of Heroic Failures*. London: Futura Publications, 1980.

Polkinghorne, Donald. "Narrative Configuration in Qualitative Analysis." *International Journal of Qualitative Studies in Education* 8 (1) (1995): 5–23.

———. *Narrative Knowing and the Human Sciences*. Albany: State University of New York Press, 1988.

Popper, Karl. "Autobiography." In P. A. Schilpp, ed., *The Philosophy of Karl Popper*. La Salle, Ill.: Open Court, 1974.

———. *Conjectures and Refutations*. 2d ed. New York: Basic Books, 1965, and New York: Harper Torchbooks, 1968.

———. *Objective Knowledge*. London: Oxford University Press, 1972, and Oxford: Clarendon Press, 1972.

———. "The Logic of the Social Sciences." In T. Adorno et al., eds., *The Positivist Dispute in German Sociology*. London: Heinemann, 1976, and New York: Harper & Row, 1976.

———. *The Logic of Scientific Discovery*. London: Hutchinson, 1959.

———. *The Poverty of Historicism*. London: Routledge, 1961.

———. "Reason or Revolution?" In T. Adorno et al., *The Positivist Dispute in German Sociology*. New York: Harper and Row, 1976.

———. In David Miller, ed., *Popper Selections*. Princeton, N.J.: Princeton University Press, 1985.

Putnam, Hilary. *The Many Faces of Realism*. La Salle, Ill.: Open Court, 1987.

———. *Reason, Truth and History*. Cambridge: Cambridge University Press, 1981.

Quetelet, M. A. *A Treatise on Man*. New York: Franklin, 1968.

Rabinow, P., and W. Sullivan, eds., *Interpretive Social Science: A Reader*. Berkeley: University of California Press, 1979.

Randall, John Herman, Jr. *The Making of the Modern Mind.* New York: Columbia University Press, 1976.

Ratcliffe, John W. "Notions of Validity in Qualitative Research Methodology" *Knowledge Creation, Diffusion, Utilization* 5 (2) (December 1983).

Ricoeur, Paul. "The Model of the Text." In F. Dallmayr and T. McCarthy, eds., *Understanding and Social Inquiry.* Notre Dame, Ind.: University of Notre Dame Press, 1977.

Rogers, Eric. *Physics for the Inquiring Mind.* Princeton, N.J.: Princeton University Press, 1960.

Rogers, Michael, ed. *Contradictory Quotations.* Harlow, Essex: Longman, 1983.

Rorty, Richard. *Philosophy and the Mirror of Nature.* Princeton, N.J.: Princeton University Press, 1979.

Rosaldo, Renato. "Where Objectivity Lies: The Rhetoric of Anthropology." In J. Nelson, A. Megill, and D. McCloskey, eds., *The Rhetoric of the Human Sciences.* Madison: University of Wisconsin Press, 1987.

Rousseau, J. J. *The Confessions,* translated by J. M. Cohen. Harmondsworth, Middlesex: Penguin Books, 1953.

Ruben, David-Hillel. *The Metaphysics of the Social World.* London: Routledge, 1985.

Rudner, Richard. "The Scientist *Qua* Scientist Makes Value Judgments" (1953). Reprinted in E. D. Klemke, Robert Hollinger, and A. David Kline, eds., *Introductory Readings in the Philosophy of Science.* Buffalo, N.Y.: Prometheus Books, 1980.

Russell, Bertrand. *An Outline of Philosophy.* London: Allen and Unwin, 1948.

Sadler, D. Royce. "Intuitive Data Processing as a Potential Source of Bias in Naturalistic Evaluations." In E. House et al., eds., *Evaluation Studies Review Annual* 7 (1982).

Salomon, Gavriel. "Transcending the Qualitative-Quantitative Debate: The Analytic and Systemic Approaches to Educational Research." *Educational Researcher* 20 (1991): 10–18.

Scheffler, Israel. *Science and Subjectivity.* New York: Bobbs-Merrill, 1967.

Schelling, Thomas. *Micromotives and Macrobehavior.* New York: Norton, 1978.

Scheurich, James. *Research Method in the Postmodern.* London: Falmer Press, 1997.

Schrag, Francis. "Values in Educational Inquiry." *American Journal of Education* 97 (2) (1989): 171–183.

Schutz, Alfred. *The Problem of Social Reality: Collected Papers 1.* The Hague: Martinus Nijhoff, 1962.

Scriven, Michael. *Evaluation Thesaurus.* Beverley Hills, Calif.: Sage, 1991.

———. "Objectivity and Subjectivity in Educational Research." In Lawrence Thomas, ed., *Philosophical Redirection of Educational Research.* Part 1 of 71st Yearbook of the NSSE. Chicago: NSSE/University of Chicago Press, 1972.

———. "The Exact Role of Value Judgments in Science." In E. D. Klemke, Robert Hollinger, and A. David Kline, eds., *Introductory Readings in the Philosophy of Science.* Buffalo, N.Y.: Prometheus Books, 1980 (1974).

———. "Logical Positivism." In P. Achinstein and F. Barker, eds. *The Legacy of Logical Positivism*. Baltimore: Johns Hopkins Press, 1969.

Searle, John. "Intentionalistic Explanations in the Social Sciences." *Philosophy of the Social Sciences* 21 (3) (1991): 332–344.

———. *The Rediscovery of Mind*. Cambridge, Mass.: Bradford/MIT, 1992.

Shapin, Steve. "History of Science and Its Sociological Reconstructions." *History of Science* 20 (1982): 157–211.

Siegel, Harvey. *Relativism Refuted*. Dordrecht, Netherlands: Reidel, 1987.

Simon, M. A. *Understanding Human Action*. Albany: State University of New York Press, 1982.

Sismondo, Sergio. *Science without Myth*. Albany: State University of New York, 1996.

Skinner, B. F. *Science and Human Behavior*. New York: Free Press, 1953.

Slezak, Peter. "A Critique of Radical Social Constructivism." In D. C. Phillips, ed., *Constructivism in Education: Opinions and Second Opinions on Controversial Issues*. 99th Yearbook of the NSSE. Chicago: NSSE/University of Chicago Press, 2000.

———. "Sociology of Scientific Knowledge and Scientific Education, Part 1." *Science & Education* 3 (1994): 265–294.

———. "Sociology of Scientific Knowledge and Science Education, Part 2: Laboratory Life under the Microscope." *Science & Education* 3 (1994): 329–355.

"Sociology Row Erupts at BA." *Times Higher Education Supplement*. September 16, 1994, 44.

Sokal, Alan. "Transgressing the Boundaries: Towards a Transformative Hermeneutics of Quantum Gravity." *Social Text* 14 (1996): 217–252.

Spencer, Herbert. *Essays on Education, etc.* London: Dent/Everyman, 1949.

———. "On the Genesis of Science." In *Essays on Education*. London: Dent/Everyman, 1949.

Starling, S. G., and A. J. Woodall. *Physics*. London: Longmans, Green & Co, 1955.

Stegmuller, Wolfgang. "Walther von der Vogelweide's Lyric of Dream Love and Quasar 3C 273." In J. Connolly and T. Keutner, eds., *Hermeneutics versus Science?* Notre Dame, Ind.: University of Notre Dame Press, 1988.

Stich, Stephen. *From Folk Psychology to Cognitive Science*. Cambridge, Mass.: Bradford/MIT Press, 1985.

Stinchcombe, Arthur. "The Conditions of Fruitfulness of Theorizing about Mechanisms in Social Science." *Philosophy of the Social Sciences* 21 (3) (1991): 367–388.

Stokes, Geoffrey. *Popper: Philosophy, Politics, and Scientific Method*. Cambridge: Polity Press, 1998.

Stokols, Daniel, and Irwin Altman, eds. *Handbook of Environmental Psychology*. New York: John Wiley, 1987.

Stove, David. *Popper and After*. Oxford: Pergamon, 1982.

Suppe, Frederick, ed. *The Structure of Scientific Theories*. Urbana: University of Illinois Press, 1974.

Taylor, Charles. "Interpretation and the Sciences of Man." Reprinted in F. Dallmayr and T. McCarthy, eds. *Understanding and Social Inquiry*. Notre Dame, Ind.: University of Notre Dame Press, 1977.

Thomas, David. *Naturalism and Social Science*. Cambridge: Cambridge University Press, 1979.

Thompson, Paul. *The Structure of Biological Theories*. Albany: State University of New York Press, 1989.

van Fraassen, Bas. *The Scientific Image*. Oxford: Oxford University Press, 1980.

van Manen, Max. *Researching Lived Experience*. Albany: State University of New York Press, 1990.

Vico, Giambattista. *Vico: Selected Writings*, edited and translated by Leon Pompa. Cambridge: Cambridge University Press, 1982.

Watson, J. B. "Psychology as the Behaviorist Views It." In Wayne Dennis, ed., *Readings in the History of Psychology*. New York: Appleton-Century-Crofts, 1948.

Weber, Max. *Weber Selections*, ed. W. G. Runciman. Cambridge: Cambridge University Press, 1978.

Weimer, Walter. *Notes on The Methodology of Scientific Research*. Hillsdale, N.J.: Lawrence Erlbaum, 1979.

Weisskopf, Victor. "The Origin of the Universe." *Bulletin of the American Academy of Arts and Sciences* 42 (4) (1989): 22–39.

Winch, Peter. "Comment." In R. Borger and F. Cioffi, eds., *Explanation in the Behavioral Sciences*. Cambridge: Cambridge University Press, 1970.

Winch, Peter. *The Idea of a Social Science*. London: Routledge and Kegan Paul, 1967, and London: Routledge, 1958.

Woolgar, Steve. *Science: The Very Idea*. New York: Routledge, 1993.

Zirkle, Conway. (1959). *Evolution, Marxian Biology, and the Social Scene*. Philadelphia: University of Pennsylvania Press.

INDEX

Note: Page numbers in italics indicate that the term will be found in a diagram.

265

James, William: Comtean positivism and, 161; on constructivism, 12; on holism, 42; on knowledge, 5; on logic, 49; on scientific psychology, 89
Jardine, David, 65
Jarvie, Ian, 37
judgments, 238–39
justifications, 74, 134–35

Kant, Immanuel, 3, 239
Keller, Evelyn Fox, 190
Kerlinger, Fred, 129
Keutner, T., 25–26
Kincaid, Harold: on internal/external distinctions, 206; on reductionism, 54; on scientific method and naturalism, 97–98
Kinetic Theory of Gases, 211–22, *213*; as model in social sciences, 225–26; theories, logical structure of, 95, 96; theory of psychoanalysis and, 225
knowledge: discovery of, 8; feminist epistemology and, 4; humanity and, 5–6; natural sciences and, 192; origin of sciences and, 10; problems of, 5; scientific communities and, 4–5; social constructivism and, 187–207; social values and, 4; sources of, 102. *See also* knowledge construction; scientific knowledge; spectator theory of knowledge
Knowledge and Human Interests (Habermas), 5
knowledge construction, 7, 8–13, 199–200; epistemology and, 206, 207; hermeneutics and, 207; internal/external distinctions and, 204–7; sociology of, 200–201; truth and, 203, 204–6. *See also* knowledge; scientific knowledge; spectator theory of knowledge

Koestler, Arthur, 55
Kornblith, Hilary, 206
Kuhn, Thomas S.: and dynamics of sciences, 107; on objectivity and paradigms, 3, 4–5; on paradigms and truth, 172; on relativism and epistemology, 111; and role of observations, 103; and semantic holism, 58; social constructivism debates and, 189
Kuhnism, 131–34

Laboratory Life (Latour and Woolgar), 201
Lakatos, Imre: on counter-evidence and scientific theory, 107; on internal/external distinctions, 204–6; on natural science's deeper presuppositions, 94–95; on role of observations, 103
Latour, Bruno: on knowledge construction, 201, 204; on scientific research, 189–90
Laudan, Larry, 106, 205–6
laws: accidental generalizations and, 217–18, 229; definition of, 218; of natural sciences, 92–93; of nature vs. human behavior, 228; and theories, 221–22; vs. theories, 215–16
Lincoln, Yvonna, 42, 173–74, 181–82
Linge, David, 23
Locke, John, 8–9, 11
Logic: The Theory of Inquiry (Dewey), 171
logical positivism: antirealism and, 110; definition of, 107, 162–66; holism and, 58; and interpretivist case, 20; realism and, 110; scientific method and, 167–68; semantic holism and, 56–57, 58; social sciences and, 34. *See also* positivism; postpositivism

ABOUT THE AUTHOR

D. C. Phillips was born and educated in Australia and moved to the United States in 1974; currently he is Professor of Education, and (by courtesy) Professor of Philosphy, at Stanford University (where he is also Associate Dean for Academic Affairs in the School of Education). In the early 70s he spent six months as Academic Visitor in the Department of Philosophy, Logic, and Scientific Method at the London School of Economics; and in 1993 he was Christensen Visiting Fellow at St. Catherine's College, Oxford. He was President of the Philosophy of Education Society during its golden jubilee year in 1990–1991; he is a Fellow of the International Academy of Education; and he is a Fellow-elect of the Center of Advanced Study in the Behavioral Sciences. He has authored, coauthored, or edited ten books and written more than one hundred journal articles and book chapters, which span educational research and evaluation methodology, philosophy of social science, philosophy of education, and history of nineteenth- and twentieth-century thought. He has given workshops on many of the topics discussed in this volume to graduate students and university faculty members in the United States, Australia, Israel, New Zealand, Norway, Sweden, and Switzerland.